D0875322

Russian Banking

NEW HORIZONS IN MONEY AND FINANCE

Series Editor: Mervyn K. Lewis, *University of South Australia*

This important series is designed to make a significant contribution to the shaping and development of thinking in finance. The series will provide an invaluable forum for the publication of high quality works of scholarship on a breadth of topics ranging from financial markets and financial systems to monetary policy and banking reform, and will show the diversity of theory, issues and practices.

The focus of the series is on the development and application of new original ideas in finance. Rigorous and often path-breaking in its approach, it will pay particular attention to the international and comparative dimension of finance and will include innovative theoretical and empirical work from both well-established authors and the new generation of scholars.

Titles in the series include:

Banking Reforms in South-East Europe
Edited by Zeljko Sevic

Russian Banking
Evolution, Problems and Prospects
Edited by David Lane

Russian Banking

Evolution, Problems and Prospects

Edited by

David Lane

Senior Research Associate, University of Cambridge, UK

NEW HORIZONS IN MONEY AND FINANCE

Edward Elgar

Cheltenham, UK • Northampton, MA, USA

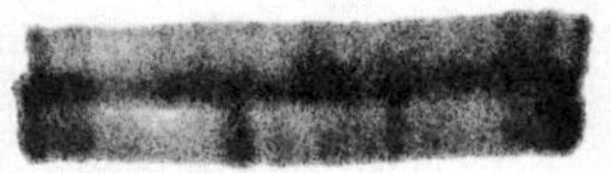

Published by
Edward Elgar Publishing Limited
Glensanda House
Montpellier Parade
Cheltenham
Glos GL50 1UA
UK

Edward Elgar Publishing, Inc.
136 West Street
Suite 202
Northampton
Massachusetts 01060
USA

A catalogue record for this book
is available from the British Library

Library of Congress Cataloguing in Publication Data

Russian banking: evolution, problems and prospects/edited by
David Lane.
p. cm. (New Horizons in Money and Finance series)
Includes index.
1. Banks and banking—Russia (Federation). 2. Finance—
Russia (Federation). I. Lane, David Stuart. II. Series.
HG3130.2.A6 R865 2003
332.1'0947—dc21

2002072167

ISBN 1 84064 941 0

Printed and bound in Great Britain by MPG Books Ltd, Bodmin, Cornwall

Contents

PART III ECONOMIC AND GLOBAL ASPECTS

Figures and tables

FIGURES

TABLES

Contributors

Duncan Allan is a Principal Research Officer, Eastern Research Group, Foreign and Commonwealth Office, specializing in Russian economic and political issues; and Honorary Research Fellow, Centre for Russian and East European Studies, University of Birmingham. He worked at the British Embassy, Moscow, between 1992 and 1996.

Claudia M. Buch graduated from the University of Bonn, Germany, with a Master of Economics degree and from the University of Wisconsin with a Master of Business Administration. She holds a PhD in Economics from the University of Kiel. Dr Buch has been a visiting scholar at the Salomon Center for the Study of Financial Institutions (New York University), the University of Michigan (Ann Arbor), and the National Bureau of Economic Research (Cambridge, MA). She has been a research associate with the Kiel Institute of World Economics since 1992 and has published widely on financial markets in central and eastern Europe and on European financial integration, with a special focus on the role of banks.

Sheila A. Chapman graduated in Economics at the University of Rome 'La Sapienza'. She then studied at CREES, Birmingham, and at the European University Institute, Florence. She became a lecturer in Economics in 1991 at the University of Molise, Campobasso. Currently she is at LUMSA University, Rome, where she teaches Economics and Monetary Economics. Her current fields of research include monetary and international economics, the theory of financial crises and transition economies.

Brigitte Granville is Head of the Economics Programme at the Royal Institute of International Affairs. She is the author of many articles and books on inflation and exchange rates in transition economies, most recently 'The Problem of Monetary Stabilisation', in *Russia's Post-Communist Economy*, edited by B. Granville and P. Oppenheimer, published by Oxford University Press.

Ralph P. Heinrich has been a research associate at the Kiel Institute of World Economics since 1991. He holds a PhD from the University of Kiel and has been a visiting scholar at the Massachusetts Institute of Technology (MIT).

He has published extensively on corporate governance systems, on the interaction between capital structure and corporate governance, on the integration of transition economies into international capital markets and on the role of banks in cross-border capital flows.

David Lane is Senior Research Associate at the Faculty of Social and Political Sciences at the University of Cambridge. The current work was completed with a grant from the British Economic and Social Research Council. His recent works include: *The Legacy of State Socialism and the Future of Transformation* (editor and contributor) Maryland and Oxford: Rowman and Littlefield, 2002; *The Transition from Communism to Capitalism: Ruling Elites from Gorbachev to Yeltsin* (with Cameron Ross), New York: St Martin's and London: Macmillan, 1998; *The Political Economy of Russian Oil* (editor and contributor), Maryland and Oxford: Rowman and Littlefield, 1999.

Irene Lavrentieva is currently Senior Researcher at the econometric company VEDI, Moscow.

Lusine Lusinyan is a PhD student in Economics at the European University Institute, Florence. She graduated from the Yerevan State University, Armenia, and continued her postgraduate study at Kiel University and the Kiel Institute of World Economics, Germany. Her current research focuses on international capital flows to developing countries and their external debt.

Satoshi Mizobata is currently Professor of Comparative Economic Systems at the University of Kyoto, Kyoto Institute of Economic Research. He gained his PhD in Economics at the University of Kyoto. He has been an honorary research fellow at the universities of Birmingham, Seoul and Moscow. His books include *Economic and Management System in Russia* (Houritsubunka, 1996), *Transformation of the Economic System* (Sekaishisousha, 1993), *System Transformation in Russia and East Europe* (Sekaishisousha, 1994, 1998), and *The Economics of Transition* (Sekaishisousha, 2002). He has served as a director of the Japanese Association for Comparative Economic Studies. He also is editor of the journal *Comparative Economic Studies*.

Marcella Mulino graduated in Economics at the University of Rome 'La Sapienza', where she became a lecturer in Economics in 1981 specializing in Macroeconomics and Monetary Economics. Presently she is Associate Professor at the University of L'Aquila, where she teaches Economic Policy and Applied Economics. Her main fields of research include international monetary policy, transformation processes in Eastern Europe and Russia, wage bargaining models and investment decision criteria.

Martin Myant is a Professor at the Paisley Business School and Centre for Contemporary European Studies, University of Paisley. He has written widely on the economic and political transformation of east-central Europe, particularly the Czech Republic. His recent works include an edited volume *Industrial Competitiveness in East-Central Europe* (Edward Elgar, 1999). He is currently working on a study of the transformation of the Czech economy since 1989.

Heiko Pleines is a researcher at the Research Centre for East European Studies (Forschungsstelle Osteuropa) in Bremen, Germany. Corruption and crime in Russia are his main research interests. His publications include: 'Large-scale corruption and rent-seeking in the Russian banking sector', in A. Ledeneva and M. Kurkchiyan (eds), *Economic crime in Russia* (The Hague, 2000); 'Corruption networks in the Russian economy', in *Slovo* (2000) (special issue); 'Corruption and crime in the Russian oil industry', in David Lane (ed.), *The Russian oil industry* (Lanham/Oxford, 1999).

Mechthild Schrooten has been a research associate at the German Institute for Economic Research (DIW Berlin) since 1992. She holds a PhD from the Free University Berlin. Her main research interests are financial markets and growth, regulation and international financial integration, and the relationship between institutional and financial development in Central-Eastern Europe and Asia.

Julia A. Solovieva (BA, MSc) is an Associate with Dresdner Kleinwort Wasserstein, the London-based investment banking arm of Dresdner Bank AG. She works in the Fixed Income Emerging Markets Illiquids Group, that trades distressed and defaulted assets. Her main academic interests are the Russian financial markets, in particular the GKO market before August 1998, and the privatization process of the mid-1990s.

William Tompson is Reader in Politics at Birkbeck College, University of London, and an Associate Fellow of the Royal Institute of International Affairs. He is the author of *Khrushchev: A Political Life* (1995) and of numerous articles and chapters on Soviet/Russian high politics and the political economy of post-Soviet Russia.

Acknowledgements

Acknowledgement is made to the British Economic and Social Research Council, which supported the research of David Lane (Grant R 222954) and a conference organized to discuss the papers commissioned for this book. In addition to the authors included in this collection, the following are thanked for their participation and contributions to discussion of the papers: Sir Rodric Braithwaite, Deutsche Bank; Vladimir Chorniy, Barclays Bank; Peter Constable, ex-Chief Executive, Barclaycard; Nigel Gould-Davies, Foreign Commonwealth Office; Juliet Johnson, Loyola University, Chicago; Janet Ilieva, Manchester Metropolitan University; Geoffrey Ingham, Cambridge University; Alena Ledeneva, School of Slavonic and East European Studies, University of London; Mario Nuti, London Business School; Akihiro Tokuno, Nomura Bank, Japan; Marcin Piatkowski, Institute of Entrepreneurship and Management, Warsaw.

Glossary

Term	Transcription	Explanation
Agroprombank		Agro-Industry Bank.
AKB	Aktsionerny Kommercheski Bank	Joint stock commercial bank.
AO	Aktsionernoe Obschestvo	Joint stock company.
ARCO	Agency for the Reconstruction of Credit Institutions	Russian Agency for Bank Restructuring.
ARKO	Agentstvo po Restrukturizatsii Kreditnikh Organizatsiy	See above.
BIS	Bank for International Settlements	Multilateral institution which fosters international monetary and financial cooperation and serves as a bank for central banks.
C&S	Codes and standards	The adoption of internationally recognized standards, or codes of good practices, are designed to improve economic policy making and strengthen the international financial system. The international community has called upon the IMF and other standard setting agencies to develop standards/ codes covering a number of economic and financial areas.
CBR	Central Bank of Russia	
CIS	Commonwealth of Independent States (Sodruzhestvo nezavisimykh gosudarstv)	CIS included Armenia, Azerbaijan, Belarus, Estonia, Georgia, Kazakhstan, Kyrgyz Republic, Latvia, Lithuania, Moldova, Russia, Tajikistan, Turkmenistan, Ukraine, Uzbekistan.

Term	Transcription	Explanation
CPI	Consumer price index	
ČS	Česká spořitelna	Czech Savings Bank.
ČSOB	Československá obchodní banka	Czechoslovak (Foreign-)Trade Bank.
EBRD	European Bank for Reconstruction and Development	
FATF	Financial Action Task Force	
FDI	Foreign Direct Investments	
FIG	Financial Industrial Group	
G7		The group of the seven most industrialized countries. Includes Canada, France, Germany, Italy, Japan, the United Kingdom and the United States.
GDP	Gross Domestic Product	
GKI	Gosudarstvennyi komitet po upravleniyu imushchestva (State Committee for the Management of Property)	The organ of the Russian Government responsible for the management and privatization of state-owned property.
GKO	Gosudarstvennaya kratkosrochnaya obligatsiya (State Treasury Obligation)	Short-term government securities issued by Russia's Ministry of Finance to finance Russia's budget deficit. The Russian equivalent of short-term treasury bonds. The first GKO auction was held in May 1993. On 17 August 1998, the Russian government defaulted on GKOs.
Gosbank USSR		State Bank USSR.
GP	Gosudarstvennoe Predpriyatie	State enterprise.
GUVD of Moscow		Main Department of Internal Affairs of the City of Moscow.
IANs	Interest Arrear Notes	Debentures issued by Russia to replace overdue interest on old debt.

Term	Transcription	Explanation
IAS	International Accounting Standards	
IFA	International Financial Architecture	
IMF	International Monetary Fund	
IPB	Investiční a poštovní banka	Investment and Postal Bank.
KB	Komerční banka	Commercial Bank (Czech).
LIBOR	London Interbank Offer Rate	The interest rate banks charge each other on short-term money.
M2		Notes and coins in circulation plus residents' current account and settlement account bank deposits in national currency.
MFK	Mezhdunarodnaya finansovaya kompaniya	International Finance Company. A member of the banking consortium which tabled the loans-for-shares proposal.
MinFins		Debentures issued by the Russian Ministry of Finance.
MKS		Inter-Bank Credit Alliance. The banking consortium which made the loans-for-shares proposal to the Russian Government in March 1995.
NMP	Net Material Product	
OAO	Otkrytoe Aktsionernoe Obschestvo	Open joint stock company.
OECD	Organisation for Economic Cooperation and Development	
OFZ	Obligatsii Federalnogo Zaima	Federal government bonds issued by Russia's Ministry of Finance to finance Russia's budget deficit. The Russian government defaulted on OFZs on 17 August 1998.
Oneksimbank	Obedinennyi Eksportno-importnyi Bank	The Russian title, often written ONEKSIMbank. English title: Uneximbank.

Term	Transcription	Explanation
OVVZ	Obligatsiya vnutrennogo valyutnogo zaima	Domestic hard-currency denominated bonds into which Vneshtorgbank's debt to companies involved in foreign trade during the Soviet era was converted.
PRINs	Principal notes	Debentures issued by Russia to replace the principal of overdue debts.
Promstroibank		Industry and Building Bank.
RAO	Rossiyskoye Aktsionernoe Obschestvo	Russian joint stock company.
RAS	Russian Accounting Standards	
ROSCs	Reports on Standards and Codes	
RSFSR	Rossiyskaya Sovetskaya Federativnaya Sotsialisticheskaya Respublika	The former main republic of the USSR, transformed to Russian Republic after collapse of the USSR.
SBA	Stand-By Arrangement	The three-year financial assistance programme agreed by the Russian Government and the IMF in 1995.
Sberegatel'ny Bank		Savings Bank.
SDDS	Special Data Dissemination Standard	
Sovet Direktorov		Board of Directors (Supervisory Board) of a company.
SP	Sovmestnoe Predpriyatie	(Joint Venture).
Svyazinvest		Russia's largest telecommunications holding, which owns controlling stakes in all Russian regional telecommunications companies and Rostelekom, Russia's international telephone operator. The controlling stake in Svyazinvest is in the hands of the Russian government.

Term	Transcription	Explanation
UCS	Kompaniya Ob'edinennikh Kreditnikh Kartochek	Processing company, which also held exclusive rights for servicing Diners Club card holders through its network until 1 October 1999.
Uneximbank	United Export-Import Bank	The English title used by the bank. Often written UNEXIM Bank. Russian title: Oneximbank.
VAT	Value-added tax	
Vneshtorgbank	Foreign Trade Bank	
WTO	World Trade Organization	

Introduction

David Lane

In the post-communist societies, the paths of transition to a market and privatized economy are embedded in the legacy of the structure of state socialism. The hegemonic role of the state, as regulator, provider of welfare and owner of economic wealth made state socialism qualitatively different from the capitalist systems of the West. The countries of the former USSR (and particularly the Russian Federation) have not, on a comparative basis, made a successful transition to a market economic system or to a pluralist political order. The research in this volume considers just one element in the transition process: the rise of commercial market-oriented banks, their links with government and non-financial companies and their role as intermediaries in the provision of finance for investment. The contributors also consider the international aspects of Russian banking and particularly the impact and consequences of the financial crisis of 1998.

Discussion of economic transformation/transition in the post-communist countries has revolved around the focal points of the introduction of markets and the privatization of assets. The banking system, the role of money and their implications for economic development have been considerations of a secondary order brought into focus as a consequence of the hyperinflation of the early 1990s and the financial collapse of 1998. The essays in this collection are arranged in three parts, the first covering the evolution of the post-communist system of banks and their functioning, the second focusing on governance and the third considering global aspects of Russia's financial crises, reform and the implications for foreign debt. It is hoped that the collection will provide an outline of Russian banking in the post-communist period.

The legacy of state socialism to the evolving banking system in Russia is addressed in the chapter by David Lane, who argues that the processes of Soviet banks were not conducive to the formation of a capitalist type of banking system. Soviet banks had no role in the appraisal of risk, either in the production of commodities or with respect to enterprises which produced them. The absence of money as an independent regulator of economic activity has led to the 'remonetarization' of the economies of post-communist countries. In the case of Russia, however, the ways such remonetarization has taken place have been one of the fundamental faults in the process of transformation. Under conditions of modern capitalism, banks have the function of managing a monetary payments system; to further accumulation, they allocate savings to investment; they perform entrepreneurial functions with respect to business; they also utilize money to make money, often by depositing abroad. Many chapters in the book acknowledge that Russian banks have played a very minor role in the provision of capital for Russian industry and have been more concerned with financial speculation. Martin Myant makes the case that Eastern European banks have been somewhat more successful. They were part of a better ordered system of transition from state socialism and there was a greater concern with stability in countries such as Czechoslovakia. Also, even under the communist system banks were more effective. The financial and economic environment was also more conducive to an effective banking system. Proximity to Western Europe and the greater affinity with a market culture have led to a more positive role being played by foreign banks, which have been able to penetrate the market and also buy shares in local banks. However, he points out that, as in the Russian Federation, banks pursuing profit and self-interest would not rationally support the high-risk domestic industries and so the economic transformation of industry, without government pressure, would have been thwarted.

It is recognized that the movement to a market economy has taken place in the context of a high level of dependency on the state: a large part of the economy is still controlled by it and government institutions have large stakes in different types of bank. A path-dependent approach is taken in many of the chapters and this explains why non-financial companies, which themselves may be partially owned by the state in various forms, have large stakes in many banks. The chapter by Satoshi Mizobata demonstrates that the government provides large subsidies to non-financial corporations. In this context, he shows how different political interests seek either greater state control of banks or the large-scale privatization of state assets in banks. Both his chapter and that by William Tompson emphasize the very small contribution that the banks in the post-Soviet period made to investment in the real sector and their very low commitment to granting long-term loans. In this respect Tompson points out that they are constrained by a high-risk environment with a dearth of borrowers with good prospects of repaying debts. A theme which runs through many of the chapters is the way in which banks sought profits through the purchase of government loans.

Popular literature defines control of Russian companies in terms of 'oligarchs' many of whom derived their power from bank capital. Tompson's chapter modifies this view somewhat by arguing that the power wielded by banks as autonomous units has been exaggerated. Banks were unable to survive without support from the state which controls one-third of the banking sector's assets. The focus of control, he contends, has moved to parent holding companies which are in the non-financial sector. It is here, particularly in export-oriented industries such as gas and oil, that profits and economic power are concentrated.

The role of banks in the purchase of assets in the 'loans for shares' process is taken up by Duncan Allan. The point again is made concerning the dependence of the emergent banks on the state, which had the authority to privatize public assets and which gave the banks the possibility of self-enrichment. This chapter sets the banks' role in purchasing shares on the basis of loans in the context of privatization policy and of political pressures. Here insider dealing undoubtedly led to some banks securing undervalued assets. However, the branch ministries and managerial interests as well as existing non-financial companies were able to bring their own interests to bear and significantly reduced the scope of the proposals. Once more, Allan points out that 'state patronage remained the key to business success', echoing voices in other chapters, and he concludes that banks were lobbyists rather than oligarchs.

An inadequate legal framework and possibilities for corruption are also characteristics of the business environment of post-communist banks. Heiko Pleines considers the role of Russian banks in illegal capital flight, tax evasion and money laundering. He contends that while the banks are implicated to some extent in these forms of crime they are not major players, accounting for no more than 20 per cent of illegal capital flight and 10 per cent of tax evasion. He also concludes that there is no evidence to substantiate the view that organized crime controls a large part of the banking sector, though it applies to some small banks.

Mizobata and Lane suggest that the reciprocal ownership of assets by banks, non-financial companies and state institutions has led to the evolution of a depersonalized and corporate form of capitalism in Russia. The privatization of companies, both financial and non-financial, led to a dominant pattern of corporate control in which clients of banks are significant shareholders. This is detailed in a study of three Russian banks in Chapter 4.

The move to a market and the initial monetarization of the economy led to high profitability of financial operations consequent on the level of inflation (2 317 per cent in 1992 and 842 per cent in 1993) and the fall of the value of the ruble against the dollar. As shown in the chapter by Brigitte Granville, between 1992 and 1995 large budget deficits were financed by monetary issue. Government bonds (GKOs) were issued with rates of interest rising from 42 per cent in February 1998 to 150 per cent in May of that year. By 1998, external government debt had reached $150 billion and internal debt $44 billion, of which one-third was owed to non-residents. The government defaulted on this debt in August 1998. Granville also deals with the way in which the Russian government is dealing with the problems of the banking sector. She points out that bank restructuring has been disappointing and that many insolvent banks remain. Bank lending is still very low: only 18 per cent of GDP compared to 57 per cent in the Czech Republic. Opening up the sector to foreign banks is suggested as a way forward. Improved corporate governance and restructuring of the banking sector are necessary to achieve better microeconomic management.

The chapter by Sheila A. Chapman and Marcella Mulino attempts to explain the currency crisis in terms of a multiple set of factors. Though it is impossible in this brief introduction to do justice to their argument, they suggest that there were intertwined factors: an inconsistency between domestic policies and a fixed exchange rate, speculation against the currency and also the consequences of broader financial crises. They consider that the IMF's liberalization policies were incompatible with the structural weaknesses of the Russian economy during the transformation process. Thus the policy of defence of the ruble (advocated by the IMF) was not sustainable. Devaluation, they contend, could have happened sooner with overall positive results.

After the crisis of 1998, Russia's foreign debt stood at more than 100 per cent of GDP: much above the average of 33–35 per cent of developing countries. The ratio of currency reserves to debt was only 6.6 per cent, compared to the average of developing countries of 28 per cent. Claudia M. Buch, Ralph P. Heinrich, Lusine Lusinyan and Mechthild Schrooten discuss the political economy of banking reform in the context of ongoing negotiations on foreign debt restructuring. They argue that banking reform is important for post-crisis recovery because of the important role sound banks could play both in the financing of domestic investment and in the intermediation of foreign capital inflows. Because economic recovery improves Russia's ability to service its foreign debt, banking reform is in the interest not just of the government, but also of its foreign creditors. This creates room for negotiations between the government and its foreign creditors about restructuring the debt as a way to share the costs of reform.

Julia Solovieva deals in her chapter in more detail with the ways in which foreign investors put money into Russian banks and the ways in which the default has affected their investments. She distinguishes between equity and fixed income investments and gives examples of the difficulties faced by investors during the restructuring period that followed the crisis. She contends that the 'safest' pre-crisis investments were not necessarily the ones where the recovery rates were the highest, and protracted delays further eroded the value of investments.

The general conclusions of the book are that the Russian banking system is unique in comparison to the major paradigms of Anglo/American and German/Japanese systems. It has been and is highly dependent on the state. Russian banks have not played an important part in support of the non-financial sector; their lending has been very short-term. Banks lack a legal framework and have participated in corrupt practices. However, most if not all the contributors to this volume would see the institutional framework and the legacy of the state socialist system as important determinants of the economic and political activity of the banking system. The formation of a commercial banking system in the context of a spontaneous movement to capitalism and a weak state have been contributory factors in its weaknesses. Finally, many of the contributors are positive about current developments. Broader structural reform of the economy and the strengthening of the legal system advocated by the Putin administration are considered to be necessary conditions for the banking system to develop and play a positive role in economic development.

PART I

Issues in Banking

1. The evolution of post-communist banking[1]

David Lane

The discussion of economic transition/transformation in the post-communist countries has revolved around the focal points of the introduction of markets and the privatization of assets. The banking system, the role of money and their implications for economic development have been considerations of a secondary order initiated as a consequence of the hyperinflation of the early 1990s and the financial collapse of 1998. The role of banks, however, has been crucial in the development of capitalism.

As part of a market system of autonomous profit-motivated units, banks have become a crucial part of the capitalist system. As Ingham has contended, the creation of credit-money by banks and states is 'constitutive of capitalism'. What fuelled the development of capitalism, he has argued, was the 'capacity to create "mobile" money in a form that integrated the new "private" bill and note credit-money of the banker-traders with the existing forms of "public" coinage currencies' (Ingham, 1999, p. 79). Essentially, banks are institutions which through the provision of a supply of money (bank credit) promote, or at least facilitate, the growth of wealth. As well as being a major source of wealth creation for the bankers themselves, the power to issue money gave banks considerable control over the allocation and division of economic resources. By the withdrawal of credit clients would be bankrupt, and by allocating capital between different end uses banks influence the ways economies develop.

However, banks have not always been positive for economic development. There may be disparities between the needs of national economies and governments and the economic preferences of banks. Banks may use their resources quite rationally to invest outside the home economy, to export capital to secure returns on deposits and thereby sacrifice the development of the domestic industrial base. They may not be able to make the correct predictions of risk and potential entrepreneurial return, and their financial conservatism – particularly in the case of large and long-term investments – may deny credit to industrial development. Banks may, through corruption and/or incompetence, create deposits which may be used for profligate consumption, leading to the issue of paper money and hyperinflation.

The institution of bank credit may also be dependent on other facilitating conditions. These include psychological factors, such as a propensity to invest for future wealth creation, the extent and character of individual entrepreneurship or the capacity of the state to provide an institutional framework. In their absence, banks may not develop as major instruments of capitalist development. In these conditions, '[r]ecent experience strongly suggests that banking systems as intermediaries are not highly essential to the growth process' (Gurley, 1967: 953, cited by Cameron, 1972, p. 6).[2] Banks may quite rationally act as intermediaries in the export of capital.

Governments and entrepreneurs have a stake in such outcomes and have to be considered as major interests in any financial system. The state provides a legal framework for the issue of currency and attempts to regulate the financial sector. Governments need to raise taxes and loans from the banking system, and their (usual) monopoly over the issue of legal tender impacts on the value of money and its rates of exchange.

Banks also played a minor role in the development of the USSR and other state socialist countries but figured only marginally in the discussions of economic reform under state socialism.

BANKS IN THE SOVIET PERIOD

Even more important as a legacy to the contemporary scene in Russia is the structure and process of banking in the Soviet period. Socialist countries utilized money and banks – though not in the ways of modern capitalist states. They abolished an autonomous banking system able to create money.

> Centrally planned economies [were] money-using, but quantity-maximizing economies. They require money to avoid the cumbersomeness of barter, but not a financial system beyond an elementary transfer mechanism for investment funds. Holding of money makes sense only in a world of uncertainty; an adequately functioning planned economy needs no money balances, except as required by the specific payments mechanism in use. (Garvy, 1968, p. 164)

Money continued as a standard of value and medium of exchange, but not as an economic regulator or 'economic lever'.

Banks had no role in the appraisal of risk, either in the production of commodities or with respect to enterprises which produced them. All risk-related decisions were taken by those responsible for the economic plans. In this context, a system of banks existed to exercise financial control over enterprises. Credit was allocated to enterprises and channelled through the banks, which were responsible for the expenditure of money in accordance with the plan allocated to enterprises. An important consequence of the state system of economic direction was that neither entrepreneurship (on the part of potential investors) nor risk appraisal, on the part of banks, was part of the system of planning. Transfer of the power of investment to an autonomous banking system would have undermined the objectives of planning and would have created the use or accumulation of capital outside the norms and framework of central planning. Banks had no rights independently to withdraw credit from enterprises; they were required to provide money for them as determined in the state economic plans. A major distinction may be made between industrialization under capitalism and in the state socialist societies: in the former, monetarization of economies was part of the movement from feudalism to capitalism, whereas in the latter, demonetarization took place. Hence 'remonetarization' of the economies of post-communist countries has been one of the major tasks of the transition process. In the case of Russia, however, the ways such remonetarization has taken place have been one of the fundamental faults in the process of transformation.

Before the changes instituted by Gorbachev, there were four major banks implementing government financial policy: USSR Gosbank, which had offices in the republics and regions, USSR Stroibank (Construction), USSR Vneshtorgbank (Foreign Trade) and USSR Gostrudsberkassa (Savings Bank) (also with branches in republics). Banks collected savings from the population, they were financial conduits for the allocation of credit and money to enterprises and they distributed money payments from economic enterprises and state authorities to the public. They also performed exchange functions between different currencies, particularly in international trade. The amount of money (coins and credit) in circulation was determined by the state bank (Gosbank USSR) acting on decrees issued by the economic planning bodies.

This stark picture of a centrally controlled economy was changing even before the 1980s in the USSR and, particularly, in the other state socialist economies of Eastern Europe. One of the most important ideological developments under Khrushchev was that with the movement to communism there would be a development of 'commodity–money' relations (rather than, as hitherto, of those of 'product-exchange'). Payments of interest for company assets were made in all the state socialist economies, though this was not analogous to interest rates in market societies. In Czechoslovakia and Hungary, money balances became available for use in the enterprises themselves and consequently there was a relaxation of the 'control' function of the banks. It is not appropriate to discuss in detail here the possible reforms which could have taken place in the economic organization of state socialism. It is possible that greater monetarization could have occurred, with banks being given a greater role in risk management in the context of a more decentralized economy of 'finance socialism' (Grossman, 1968, pp. 15–16). The changes which took place in Russia did not raise significantly the role of the banks in the hierarchy of economic control. In the mid-1980s, a system of credit investment was instituted through the banks (by USSR Gosbank and USSR Stroibank). Most of the credit was issued to agricultural enterprises. Probably due to the lack of commercial and monetary experience of debt management at the time, reforms did not lead to a decentralization of investment decision-making on the basis of the profitability and viability of enterprises mediated by the banking system, rather local banks (operating on what has become known as a weak budget constraint) advanced credit in order to maintain money payments of borrowers.

Under Gorbachev, proposals were made to reform the banking system (Zotov, 1998, p. 32). After study of banks in market transitional societies,[3] in July 1987 a reform of the banking system was made.[4] Consequently, in 1988 and 1989 the state banks were reorganized into a central bank (Gosbank USSR) which controlled the management of money and credit and oversaw a system of unified monetary policy; it supervised and determined the level of credit operating in the other banks. There were five specialist banks: Vneshekonbank (Foreign Trade), Promstroibank (Industry and Building), Agroprombank (Agro-industry), Zhilsotsbank (Communal Services) and Sberbank (Savings Bank). Also, and this is very important, the formation of non-state banks was now permitted.

The formation of 'new' banks was part of the establishment of 'cooperative' businesses (as well as other forms of individual private enterprise). These concerns, which were outside the economic plan, needed credit and gave an impetus to the formation of private banks, which initially operated with no legal basis. The Law on Cooperatives (26 May 1988) gave 'associations' of cooperatives the right to set up cost accounting branches or territorial cooperative banks.

The thrust of Gorbachev's *perestroika* policy was not to develop banks as mediators between savings and investment (or determinants of investments), but to move to a market system in which the major state enterprises were able to divert their surpluses into investment if they wished. No steps were taken which would have led to the formation of an autonomous banking sector.

The 'new' banks evolved in a spontaneous manner. One head of a now prosperous provincial bank explained to the author that as a communist functionary he saw that the old system was on its way out; he looked for an alternative and thought of going into financial services. He phoned some of his colleagues and, working out of his office, began trading in foreign exchange. The first non-state banks emerged in the summer of 1988,[5] and by the end of 1989, 150 non-state banks had been founded (Matovnikov, 1998, p. 5). (See list of first 25 in section 1.1.) Policy encouraged the formation of business outside the state sector and, to further new business, the government allowed the printing of money and an increase in bank credit. The interaction of new business and finance is illustrated by Vladimir Gusinsky, who later was to lead Mostbank. He founded the companies Metall and Infeks in 1986 and 1987 respectively, and in 1989 (with Arnold and Porter) he formed a joint venture, Most, of which he was General Director.

Private banks' credit at this time was relatively small (approximately 2 per cent of the total of the banking system) and, as noted above, most of the deposits were created by the state banks. The liabilities of banks were distributed as follows: of total deposits, only 0.4 per cent originated from individuals, from other banks 34 per cent, and 'legal persons' (local authorities and companies) accounted for 35 per cent (Barkovski, 1998). The state banks still played a major role in the allocation of capital.

THE RISE OF POST-COMMUNIST BANKING

The evolution of an independent banking sector has to be considered as part of two different but related strategies of transformation: the formation of governments in the Republics which broke away from the USSR, and the concurrent economic transformation leading to the privatization of state assets and the move to the market.

In December 1990, the Law on the State Bank of the USSR took Gosbank out of the control of the Council of Ministers (USSR) and made it accountable to Parliament. Gosbank USSR had the functions of maintaining a unified currency in the Soviet Republics, the regulation of money supply and control over the exchange rate. However, developments in the Republics seriously weakened it. In July 1990, Yeltsin had declared that all branches of All-Union (that is, USSR) banks located on the territory of Russia were independent of Gosbank USSR.[6] Branches or departments of specialized state banks were registered as independent banks. For example, in Tula in 1990 Priupskbank was formed out of the regional branch of Promstroibank USSR, KSERT Bank from Zhilsotsbank USSR, Tulaagroprombank from Agroprombank USSR and Baltika from Promstroi bank.[7]

Also in December, a law on the Central Bank of the RSFSR (The Bank of Russia) made it the main bank of the Russian Republic, subordinate to the Supreme Soviet of the RSFSR. After the collapse of the USSR, the Central Bank took over all the functions of Gosbank: control over the supply of money, the level of credit, the printing of money and the exchange rate of the ruble. It regulated the financial aspects of the economy of the Russian Republic and took charge of the network of Gosbank USSR's institutions.

An effect of the breakup of the USSR and the formation of banks under the early post-communist governments was that the power of the central government over the monetary system was considerably weakened. Republics of the former USSR (later sovereign states) took over control of the supply of money. Unlike under successful Western capitalist states, where often, even before advanced capitalism had been established, robust government had been secured and provided an institutional framework for a (usually unitary) monetary system, governments in the Republics were weak. In Russia, Yeltsin's economic policy destroyed the previous bank system because of its pivotal political and economic position as an agent of the USSR. Initially, the Central Bank was subordinate to the Supreme Soviet of the RSFSR (not the executive arm of government) subjecting it to popular pressures.

The 'reform' of the previous Soviet banks led to the creation in 1990 of some 800 independent banks taking the capital of the previous state banks (Matovnikov, 1998, p. 5). (These destatized and now private banks which originated from the Soviet banks are called 'old banks' to distinguish them from 'new' banks which sprang up independently.) The Savings (Sberegatelny) Bank of Russia was privatized and became a joint-stock bank, the Russian Central Bank taking a majority holding, and 8 000 organizations and 200000 persons held shares. Among the major share holders were, in addition to the Central Bank, Vneshtorgbank, Inkombank, Mezhdunarodny Bank Ekonomicheskogo Sotrudnichestva, 'Izhmash', AvtoVAZbank, Pavlovski instrumentalny zavod and Srednevolzhski kommerchesky bank.[8] A characteristic of these 'old banks' was that many had strong links with the regional administrations and also they continued their previous relationships with production enterprises, often, as we shall consider below, in an institutional form.

From December 1992, the Central Bank of Russia began to take over the functions of control and inspection of the commercial banks. As the agent of the Ministry of Finance, it organized the sale of government stock (GKOs) and became a major source of lending to the commercial banks.

Demand for the services of the banking sector came from the newly founded and privatized companies which not only sought banking services but also credit. The Central Bank printed money to finance the government budget and the commercial banks which, in turn, lent to companies. In

1990–92, commercial banks received credit from the Central Bank at annual interest rates ranging from 2 to 9 per cent, whereas their own borrowers had to pay them interest of up to 25 per cent. There were many shortcomings in the performance of the commercial banks. However, the withdrawal of licences was limited (65 in 1994) as their bankruptcy, it was argued, would have had even greater negative economic consequences than keeping them going.[9]

By 1995, there were 2517 credit organizations (see Zhebrak, 1999, p. 147).[10] (For a full listing of the number of credit organizations in the Russian Republic 1992–2000 see Appendix, Table A1.2). Banks were not only formed by newcomers, but also were a consequence of the destatization of the former state banks. The founders of the 'new banks' were people from diverse backgrounds. Many had been officials in the administration of the Party and state, while others were employees of financial departments of enterprises and banks. In Most bank, for instance, the leading personnel came from the offices of Vneshekonombank USSR and Promstroibank USSR.

THE OPERATIONS OF BANKS IN YELTSIN'S RUSSIA

The move to a market and the initial monetarization of the economy led to high profitability of financial operations consequent on the level of inflation and the fall of the value of the ruble against the dollar. Speculative opportunities in financial markets also arose through the privatization cheques or vouchers issued by the government to the population, on the one hand, and through short-term government bonds (GKOs), on the other. The rise in the share of government debt is shown in Table 1.1.

Clearly, by 1997 loans to the government had grown enormously since 1993 (2.1 per cent to 41.3 per cent) and, following privatization, the claims on the non-financial public sector had decreased. The high level of government debt later became a major factor in the financial crisis of 1998.

The overwhelming majority of privatized Russian banks at this time were directed to short-term speculation (see Delyagin, 1995, pp. 129–35), particularly in currency dealing and later in government stock. Bank loans to the non-financial sector fell from 25.1 per cent of total bank assets in 1993 to 18.7 per cent in 1995, or from 0.26 per cent of GDP to 0.10 per cent (Belyanova, 1995, p. 32). Company investment largely originated from retained profits of companies. For example, for the first quarter of 1999, 79.7 per cent of investment of companies came from their own capital sources: only 12 per cent of credit originated from banks and 0.8 per cent from state budgets.[11]

Table 1.1 Assets of the Russian banking system (billions of rubles)

	1993	1995	1997	1998	1999
Claims on general government	0.8	62.6	194.7	259.4	437.7
Claims on non-financial public enterprises	15.6	62.5	33.2	33.1	46.9
Claims on private sector	20.2	133.8	236.4	346.0	521.6
Claims on other financial institutions	—	0.5	8.1	7.3	13.1
Total	36.6	259.4	472.4	645.8	1019.3
	%	%	%	%	%
General government	2.1	24.2	41.3	40.2	42.9
Non-fin. public enterprises	42.7	24.1	7.0	5.1	4.6
Private sector	55.2	51.6	50.0	53.6	51.2
Claims on other financial institutions	—	0.1	1.7	1.1	1.3
Total %	100.0	100.0	100.0	100.0	100.0

Sources: *International Financial Statistics*, International Monetary Fund (Washington DC: 1996, 2000).

Developments in the banking system were concurrent with the dismantling of the centrally organized economy and the move to a market system. Prices were left to find their own level and doubled in the first six months of 1991. The value of the ruble fell from 56 rubles to the dollar to 110. In 1992, prices rose to hyperinflationary levels: 2609 per cent. From a financial point of view, most Russian enterprises became effectively bankrupt.

In 1999, lossmaking factories and organizations (excluding small businesses) in the first quarter of that year came to 43.6 per cent of the total number of factories. They made a loss of 54.5 billion rubles, compared to the profits made by other enterprises of 71 billion.[12]

No government can accept the consequences of such high levels of bankruptcy, and policy has been to maintain political and economic stability. Enterprises – even bankrupt ones – continued to function. In the monetary sphere, however, international factors limited the government's choices: a low level of internal inflation and stability of its exchange value with other currencies were crucial for Russia to enter the global economy and also to attract foreign firms and investment. The money supply was restricted, which in turn led to insufficient liquidity for companies and public institutions to pay bills and salaries. In these circumstances, a further demonetarization of the economy took place and barter and other forms of exchange occurred between enterprises. Rather than allow enterprises to close, with the subsequent social and political problems of unemployment and poverty, factories kept employees in work and bartered production for inputs and the banks played a role in these exchanges.

Many local banks (whose stakeholders included non-financial companies and government interests) started to facilitate the exchange of products and services between enterprises and institutions. By arranging barter deals (direct exchange) and issuing limited *veksels* or bills of exchange they promoted production in the ailing Russian industrial sector and enabled state taxes to be collected. (This process is documented by Woodruff, 1999, pp. 155–61.)

The ruble lost its monopoly as a means of exchange between enterprises and in wholesale trade. In February 1999, in industry, of the total quantity of exchanged goods and services, 47.3 per cent were settled through money and 52.7 per cent by other means: 12.1 per cent were resolved through bills of exchange (*veksels*), 27 per cent through settlement of mutual demands, and 7.8 per cent through barter (there was a residual of 5.8 percent). (Data for industrial production only.) Of such settlements, the electric company EES Rossii had 77.6 percent of its products and services settled by non-monetary transactions and Gazprom 46.7 per cent.[13]

Banks arranged these types of exchange. In my own survey of 163 Russian banks, 49 per cent engaged in arranging barter and other non-monetary deals. The total value of such bank involvement is significant, but not really very large. The generalizations made by Woodruff (1999, pp. 146–9) and Aukutsionek (1999, pp. 1–8) are based not strictly on barter, but on all non-monetary settlements, including *veksels* and mutual indebtedness. *Veksels*, often traded on the secondary market, are forms of money and have proved profitable for many banks.[14] These data are related to wholesale trade; they ignore small business and retail trade. The notion of a 'virtual economy' devised by Gaddy and Ickes (2001. See also Foreign Affairs, **77** (5), 1998) exaggerates the role of barter in the economy.

Interdependence of Banks, Non-Financial Companies and State Organs

In 1992, the 'new' banks, which had been formed quite independently of the branches of the state banks (which themselves had been transformed into commercial banks), comprised about one-third of the total number of credit institutions. The names of some of the major banks, differentiated by their origin, are shown in Appendix 1.3 (see also Konstantinov, 1992, p. 112). Many of the 'new banks' originated from large enterprises and were 'company banks'. These included banks such as Imperial (clients and shareholders being Gasprom and LUKOIL), Mezhdunarodny Moskovsky Bank (a group of export–import companies which had moved from Vneshekonombank), Tokobank (a number of enterprises of the oil-gas

Table 1.2 Bank ownership (% of share capital), February 1995

Type of shareholder	Total sample	Former state banks	New banks
SOE,* other state institutions	14	15	13
Privatized enterprises	26	31	21
New private companies	38	31	48
Individuals	18	18	18
Others	4	6	1

Note: * State-owned enterprises.

Source: E. Belyanova, 'Commercial banking in Russia: evidence from economic surveys', *Russian Economic Barometer*, **4** (4) 1995, p. 34.

complex, including Yuganskneftegas, Noyabrskneftegas, Kirishinneftechimeksport, Novo-Ufimskiy oil refinery) and the state corporation Goskontrakt, Avtobank (Gorky automobile plant), AvtoVAZbank (Volga automobile plant), and Neftechimbank, Yakutskzolotobank. This enabled the directors of enterprises (whether privatized or not) to control the financial flows of their companies. Here, obviously, is a possible source of corruption, as the management was able to acquire the proceeds of production for themselves.

In terms of capital ownership, the major beneficiaries of privatization were employees (31.5 per cent owning stock in 1999) (Kapelyushnikov, 2000, pp. 9–45),[15] managers (14.7 per cent), outside individuals (18.5 per cent), other enterprises (13.5 per cent), financial enterprises (10.4 per cent), the state (7.1 per cent) and other shareholders (4.3 per cent).

As indicated in Table 1.2, the capital of the commercial banks was largely owned by non-financial companies. In 1995, as much as 62 per cent of the authorized funds of the former state banks ('old banks') and 69 per cent of the new banks belonged to non-state enterprises and companies. In my own survey of 163 banks,[16] 44 per cent owned shares in other financial companies, 47 per cent had shares in the 'real sector' and 77 per cent of the banks reported that non-financial companies owned their shares.

The formation of the new Russian banks illustrates the tendency of industrial concerns to create banks rather than, as in the experience of developed Western capitalism, banks being initiators of industrial development. As noted above, the ownership share of financial companies in Russian industry in 1999 amounted to only 10.4 per cent. Non-financial companies owned the assets of commercial banks, rather than the other way around. Such developments are similar to the early stages of industrial capitalism in England, but the formation of 'company banks' on such a scale is a new phenomenon. One implication here is that non-financial companies, with a stake in or owning a bank ('pocket' banks), could transfer profits abroad leading to significant national capital loss. While the banks provided money changing facilities, they did not create deposits for the accumulation of capital in Russia. On the contrary, they facilitated capital flight. Official estimates of capital exports (for 1998) are 3999 million dollars inward investment, compared to 15194 million dollars outward payments.[17] Western estimates confidently claim that foreign capital outflows are much larger than those declared: Fitch IBCA in 1999 estimated that $136 billion of capital was exported from Russia between 1993 and 1998 (Thornhill and Clover, 1999, p. 6).

The previous administrative linkages between the Soviet state banks (particularly those such as Sberbank which has remained in state ownership and control) and their clients (non-financial companies) continued in a new context. 'De-statization' often involved government institutions taking shares in companies. Organs of government retained ownership and control over local enterprises because there were no purchasers. This, in turn, led to involvement in the privatized banks. As noted in Table 1.2, the state-owned enterprises and government institutions possessed some 14 per cent of the capital in the sample of banks under consideration. In my own survey of 163 banks, of banks owning shares in other financial companies (84), 17 per cent had a controlling interest and 63 per cent had small packages of shares. Of 89 banks owning shares in the 'real sector', 20 per cent claimed a controlling block of shares and 60 per cent a small packet (the remainder had a 'blocking package').

The banks were also a source of credit for local government (regions and city) administrations. Powers had been devolved to regional administration allowing them to 'authorize' banks in their localities. 'Authorized' banks were formed which had a special relationship with organs of state power and gave a financial base to regional governments.[18] The linkages with local (and sometimes national) politics took the form of incumbent administrations utilizing bank resources to fund personal projects and election campaigns.[19] The interpenetration of government interest and private corporate capital in the new corporations, though different in origin, was not unlike the evolution of corporations in the early days of the industrial revolution in the West. In Britain, for example, the corporations of the eighteenth century were 'effective mechanisms for blending the economic interests of the state and of private groups in mutually beneficial ways' (Baskin and Miranti, 1997, p. 132).

These forms of mutual ownership between banks, non-financial companies and government authorities have often taken the institutional form of 'financial industrial groups' (FIGs). Such groups (from December 1993) were constituted by presidential decree and given certain benefits. There are principally three types of such groups: those in which the bank is a dominant partner, those in which industrial companies are pre-eminent and others in which state institutions are hegemonic. It must be noted, however, that much of the analysis of the interrelationship between the different constituencies in the FIGs is either legalistic or speculative, derived from journalistic accounts, rumour and ex-post rationalization. The following are examples based on information concerning inter-ownership rather than the process of decision-making within the companies and the analysis must be considered as tentative (Puzyrev and Puzyrev, 1999, pp. 202, 205).[20]

OWNERSHIP PROFILES OF FINANCIAL COMPANIES

Russian companies are structured in a similar way to those in continental Europe rather than as in the UK or USA. There is a *Sovet Direktorov* (Board of Directors) (sometimes called the *Nabyudatel'ny Sovet* [Supervisory Board]), in addition to the *Pravlenie* or Executive Board. The former is constituted from the major owners of the company and it takes the strategic decisions. The Executive Board is composed of full-time employees of the company responsible to the Board of Directors; the Chairman of the Executive Board is able to, and often does, sit on the Board of Directors. While it is asserted that 'oligarchs' 'control' large segments of Russian industry, the ways this 'control' affects the strategic commercial and industrial decisions of individual companies is unspecified. It may be that the *Sovet Direktorov* 'takes decisions' which are effectively 'made' by interests on the Executive Board.

Ownership by individuals is relatively small and the denial of large personal holdings by 'oligarchs', such as Chernomyrdin, is probably authentic. Vladimir Potanin, for example, President of Interros and Uneximbank and reputably one of the most powerful of the 'oligarchs', has no recorded personal share of ownership in excess of 5 per cent of the companies in this group. Typically, as far as published data are concerned, members of the boards of companies own less than 5 per cent of shares in the authorized capital.

Sberbank is the largest bank in Russia. (See study in Chapter 4 below.) It remains 58 per cent in the ownership of the Central Bank of Russia, making it effectively state owned. Investment companies own 21.4 per cent, including a stake of 7 per cent owned by Kreditanshtal't-Grant (which in turn is owned by CA IB Investment Bank, Austria), other firms own 8 per cent and individuals 11.9 per cent.[21] Control is maintained by the Central Bank through its representatives on the Board of Directors. In January

2001, there were 17 people on the Board of Directors: eight had positions in the Central Bank and another represented the Moscow Executive of this bank, four were representatives from the Executive Board of Sberbank, and there was one representative from the Ministry of Finance, one from the Metallurgy Investment company, one from Kreditanstadt-Granit and one from the Russian Electrical Company (EES). These directors were representatives of institutions rather than being large shareholders themselves: 13 directors had no shares at all and the remaining four had a total of 0.1061 per cent of the capital: the President of the Bank, Andrey Kazmin (former Deputy Minister of Finance of the RF from January 1995 to February 1996) owned 0.037 per cent and the largest shareholder (with 0.045 per cent) was Aleksandr Solovev, Deputy Chairman of the *Pravlenie* (Executive Board) (previously Chairman of the Voronezh Bank of Sperbank from 1995).[22] Share ownership of members of the *Pravlenie* is much higher. All were shareholders, with a total of 0.313 per cent of the shares. The largest stake was owned by Gennadi Soldatenkov, with a holding of 0.052 per cent, followed by Andrey Kazmin, also a member of the *Sovet*. Soldatenkov, a Deputy Chairman of the Pravlenie, had previously (1995 to 1996) been vice-president of the Russian Sberbank and President of Moscow Bank. These figures illustrate nicely the role of managerial capital in the leading cadres of the new state banks.

Consider again Uneximbank, which was originally founded by 30 export–import companies, previously clients of Vneshtorgbank which initially used Unexim as a clearing agency. It became part of the officially constituted 'Interros' financial-industrial group on 28 October 1994.[23] One cannot infer, however, that Unexim controls these companies, rather than the other way round. The positions of members of the board of directors of Unexim, the companies they represent in 2000 and their positions in these companies are shown in Table 1.3.

While the President of Interros and the Chair of the Executive of Uneximbank (Potanin) is usually given the status of 'oligarch', as far as the commercial policy of Uneximbank is concerned, he (like other 'oligarchs') must be constrained to a considerable degree by the representatives of other, mainly non-financial companies on the board of directors. Hence the ascendancy of bank capital in Unexim is problematic. Obviously, as representatives of stake-holder companies, people such as Potanin have considerable power, but it is corporate power rather than personal power.

Exceptional is Alfa Bank, founded by Mikhail Fridman, who had been an entrepreneur in the cooperative period of the late 1980s and was later joined by Peter Aven in 1994. While Aven and Fridman in 2000 remained leading members of the board of directors, Alfa Bank's annual report states that their share capital is zero, as indeed is that of all the directors of the

Table 1.3 Composition of Board of Directors of Uneximbank, 2000

Company	Represented Position on Company	Name
Tekhnostroyeksport	Deputy Chair of BofDV	I. Velichko
Soyuzpromeksport	Chairman	V. V. Ignatov
Surgutneftegaz	Deputy general director	N. V. Kiselev
Mashinostroitelny zavod	General Director	B. A. Mezhuev
Interros	President	V. O. Potanin
Uneximbank	Chair of the Executive Board, Member of BofD	M. D. Prokhorov
Glavnoe proizvodstvenn-kom. Upravlenie pri MID RF	Head (Nachal'nik)	V. S. Fedorov
Roskhleboprodukt	President	L. S. Cheshinski

Note: None of the above directors owns shares in the authorized capital of the company.

Source: Website of Central Bank: www.cbr.ru.

bank. However, 77 per cent of the shares of Alfa are owned through companies which are in turn owned by AB Holdings, which is registered in Gibraltar.[24] One might reasonably infer that AB Holdings has significant ownership by such people as Aven and Fridman. One might also hypothesize that, as it has no share capital owned by Russian enterprises, its business orientation might well be different to that of other banks.

Provincial banks follow a similar pattern of corporate ownership. In Tula, the 9 members of Priupbank owned in total 5.04 per cent of the stock, the largest portion being in the hands of its President (0.57 per cent).[25] In 1997, 16 out of the 18 members of the board of Uralpromstroibank owned shares totalling 6 per cent, the largest holding being 1.24 per cent.[26] In 1990, in Sverdlovsk, companies in the military industrial complex founded URalKIBank, Tagilbank in 1991 and Pervouralsk in 1992, which later made up the Uralski Kommercheski Industrialny Bank. The Urals energy complex founded the Energokombank in 1992 and, in 1993, enterprises of the gold industry constituted the Zoloto-Platina-Bank. By 1999, the Ekaterinburg Bank had 11 corporate members owning over 85 per cent of its assets.[27] As to board membership, in Zoloto-Platina Bank, of nine members, two owned shares which totalled only 0.008 per cent of authorized capital. Typically, board members represent corporate interests which own large packets of stock.[28]

State involvement may also be defined in terms other than ownership of the major state banks (such as Sperbank). It may take the form of control by the administration at the level of President of the Republic, the ministries and lower-level regional state powers. Examples are Zheldorbank (the Ministry of Railways),[29] the City of Moscow (Bank of Moscow)[30] and the Republic of Tatarstan.[31]

One implication of this high level of non-financial company involvement is that banks are called to give credit not only for investment but also to pay wages when income is low. Uralpromstroybank, which traditionally serviced heavy industry in Sverdlovsk, in 1995 advanced 93 per cent of its credit in the form of short-term loans (principally for wages); only 1 per cent was directed to long-term investment and 5 per cent went to discounting of bills.[32] In my own study of bankers, I asked what influence representatives of non-financial companies had over the taking of strategic decisions at their banks. Twenty per cent said 'a large influence', 26 per cent 'some influence', and 15 per cent reported that such companies were not represented on their boards. When we disaggregate these answers by area, we find that those answering in favour of 'a large influence' and 'some influence' came to 50 per cent of respondents in Kaliningrad, 60 per cent in Nizhni Novgorod and 65 per cent in Ekaterinburg (the figure for Moscow was 45 per cent). (Proportions of all those answering the question, including those with no representatives on the board.)

These data would suggest that the greater public visibility of 'oligarchs' amplifies their importance and influence. This is not to deny either that the political elites received support in elections or that they have received preferential treatment with respect to the authorization of contracts, real estate and the purchase of commercial and industrial assets. The 'banking elites', however, are to be defined not by personal ownership of shares, but include representatives of other non-financial companies and government organizations.

THE BANKING SYSTEM AND THE ECONOMY

Russian banks, ten years into the period of transformation of state socialism to capitalism, lack the capacity significantly to create 'mobile' money to facilitate the growth of wealth. They do not facilitate the formation of capital accumulation, they only marginally act as autonomous intermediaries evaluating the risk potential of investments. Major activities of the banks, especially before the crisis of 1998, were to speculate in foreign exchange, to provide a conduit for the export of capital, to buy government bonds, and to facilitate the interests of client companies by the provision of funds and by facilitating non-monetary exchange of commodities.

The reciprocal ownership of assets by banks, non-financial companies and state institutions has led to the evolution of a depersonalized and corporate form of capitalism in Russia. The privatization of companies, both financial and non-financial, led to a dominant pattern of corporate control in which clients of banks are significant shareholders. Individual ownership is small in scale though significant for bank management which is represented on the executive board. An important conditioning factor of bank development has been the way in which privatization enabled non-financial companies to acquire the assets of the state banks and also to found new ones. Banks then became settlement centres rather than generalized credit institutions, in effect continuing the weak budget constraints characteristic of state socialism. This was facilitated (especially in 1998 and 1999) by the Central Bank advancing large amounts of liquidity to the commercial banks. Properly directed such financial support could give a long-term commitment to the non-financial sector, rather in the way in which German banks have sustained industrial development. The legacy of the Soviet system is also apparent in continuing government ownership and control of the major banks (such as Sberbank, Vneshtorgbank and Most-Bank), as well as the interpenetration of ownership and control of commercial banks and non-financial companies by ministries, Republics and local government authorities. The close links between state and non-financial companies, which in turn have stakes in commercial banks, leads to the conclusion that the banking system is not an autonomous sub-system of the economy.

A typology of types of economy under capitalism is suggested in Figure 1.1. It shows the familiar models of Anglo-American and German capitalism. German capitalism is distinguished by its long-term investment horizon, its coordinating mechanisms of business associations and banks, by stakeholders made up of owners, the state and employees, and by the source of investment being profits and bank credit. Anglo-American capitalism is characterized by market coordinating institutions, particularly the stock market, with its short-term timescale and the dominant role of owners as stakeholders. Russia falls into neither of these patterns. The coordination of the economy is performed neither by markets nor by banks, and coordination is 'chaotic'. The major stakeholders are derived from the elites of state socialism: management, the state and, to a much smaller degree, individual owners. As to the investment horizon, this is negative in the sense that the overall level of accumulation is less than capital export. The main sources of finance are retained profits, and these are very small, given the high level of company losses. The coordinating mechanisms of money (even when bills of exchange are included) is also impaired, as witnessed by the relatively high level of non-monetary settlements of company debt.

		Leading Coordinating Mechanisms		
Investment Horizon	Deficient	Market	Bus. Assocs/ Banks	**Stakeholders**
Long term			German	Owners, State, Employees
Short term		Anglo-American		Owners
Lacking*	Russian			Management, State, Owners
	Stockmarket/ Profits	Banks/Profits	Profits	
		Source of Finance		

Note: *Banks have facilitated export of capital and rent-taking. Internal capital accumulation has a very short-term time horizon.

Figure 1.1 Types of economy

The Russian Federation is a highly modernized society in terms of its level of industrial infrastructure and population skills. The process of transition from an established industrial society of state socialism in the context of a globalized economy adds a new dimension to the Gerschenkron paradigm (1962). The Russian economy, when pitched into the global one, faced widespread bankruptcies giving rise to economic collapse. The mutually reinforcing interests of state, financial and non-financial companies have countered market tendencies which would have led to the bankruptcy of enterprises and to the collapse of local economies. The banks, with state support, have given short-term loans to meet wages and facilitated exchange of products enabling enterprises to continue to work. 'Barter' is only one form of this process. Non-financial companies, having been formed prior to the banks, themselves became important stakeholders in, and owners of, banks. In the macroeconomic context of imminent large-scale bankruptcies, the Central Bank has allowed weak budgetary controls of commercial banks. It appears that the Soviet system is in some respects reconstituting itself, though in quite a different market context. Russian capitalism is likely to develop into a more corporate, state-centred type with state institutions guiding investment at a macro level and state-dependent enterprises accumulating capital from profits. In this respect, banks have played and, in the future, are likely to play a relatively unimportant autonomous role.

APPENDIX

Table A1.1 List of the first commercial banks in Russia (registration of 1988)

No.	Date of registration	Licence no.	Name of business	City	As of 1998
1	26.08.88	2	Leningradski kooperativny bank 'Patent'	Leningrad	KAB 'Viking'
2	29.08.88	3	Moskovski kooperativny bank 'Moskoopbank'	Moscow	MAKB 'Premier'
3	21.09.88	5	Moskovski kooperativny bank 'Kredit-Moscow'	Moscow	'Kredit-Moscow'
4	26.09.88	6	Kooperativny 'Poliservbank'	Kazan	Lost licence
5	29.09.88	9	Kooperativny bank 'Zarya'	Perm	Lost licence
6	11.10.88	11	Mezhregionalny kooperativny bank 'Kontinent'	Nabereznye Chelny	Lost licence
7	28.10.88	14	Kooperativny bank 'Saniya'	Karachayevsk	Lost licence
8	04.11.88	17	Aktsionerny kommercheski bank mezhotraslevoi integratsii 'AMBI'	Moscow	Lost licence
9	05.11.88	18	Kooperativny bank 'Stroikredit'	Moscow	'Stroikredit'
10	05.11.88	19	Kooperativny 'Assbank'	Grozny	Lost licence
11	10.11.88	21	Primorski territorialny koperativny bank	Vladivostok	'Primorski territorialny kommercheski bank'
12	11.11.88	22	Innovatsionny kommercheski bank 'Inkombank-Interznanie'	Moscow	'Inkombank'
13	16.11.88	23	Promyshlenny kommercheski AvtoVAZbank	Tolyatti	'AvtoVAZbank'
14	23.11.88	26	Kooperativny bank 'Vostok'	Moscow	Lost licence
15	29.11.88	29	Kommercheski bank razvitia promyshlennosti stroimaterialov 'Strombank'	Moscow	Lost licence

16	06.12.88	30	Bank razvitia avtomobilnoi promyshlennosti 'Avtobank'	Moscow	'Avtobank'
17	19.12.88	33	Kooperativny bank 'Severny'	Vologda	Lost licence
18	22.12.88	34	Kooperativny bank 'Garant'	Makhachkala	Lost licence
19	22.12.88	35	Moskovski aktsionerny innovatsionny bank	Moscow	'MAIB'
20	27.12.88	36	Aktsionerny kommercheski bank 'Aeroflot'	Moscow	Lost licence
21	27.12.88	37	Lenningradski innovatsionny bank	Leningrad	Lost licence
22	28.12.88	38	Kommercheski bank razvitia neftekhimicheskoi promyshlennosti 'Neftekhimbank'	Moscow	'Neftekhimbank'
23	28.12.88	39	Novosibirski innovatsionny bank	Novosibirsk	Lost licence
24	28.12.88	40	Aktsionerny bank innovatsii nauki i sotsialno-ekonomicheskoi tekhnologii 'ABINSET'	Leningrad	Lost licence
25	29.12.88	41	Kommercheski innovatsionny bank nauchno-tekhnicheskogo progressa	Moscow	Menatep

Source: *Rozhdenie kommercheskikh bankov ili moment istiny rossiyskoi bankovskoi reformy (svidetelstva uchastnikov)*, ed. A. Krotova and V. Lapshova (Moscow: Bankovskoe delo, 1998).

Table A1.2 Growth of credit organization in Russian Republic, 1992–2000

Year (1 Jan.)	No. of organizations
1992	1215
1993	1713
1994	2019
1995	2517
1996	2605
1997	2029
1998	1697
1999	1401
2000	1338

Sources: *Byulleten' bankovskoy statistiki* (Moscow). Various issues 1998–2000.

Table A1.3 Types of commercial banks in Russia

	Old (former special banks)		New banks	
	Banks	City	Bank	City
Business[a]	Narodny bank	Moscow	Inkombank	Moscow
	Optimum	Moscow	Kredobank	Moscow
			Vostok	Moscow
			Stolichny	Moscow
			Finistbank	Moscow
			Biznes	Moscow
			Menatep (AKIB NTP)	Moscow
			Rosinterbank	Moscow
			SKB-Bank	Yekaterinburg
			ELBIMbank	Moscow
			Moskovia	Moscow
			Aeroflot-bank	Moscow
			RNKB	Moscow
			Delovaya Rossia	Moscow
			Tekhnobank	Moscow
			Avtrokombank	Moscow
			Uralski kombank	Yekaterinburg
			Kredit-Konsensus	Moscow
			Most-bank	Moscow
			KEIbank	Moscow
Universal[b]	Promstroibank	Moscow	Srednevolzhski kombank	Samara
	Mosbiznesbank	Moscow	Permkombank	Perm
	Promstroibank (S-Pb)	Sankt-Peterburg	SVAK-Bank	Magadan

Table A1.3 (cont.)

	Old (former special banks)		New banks	
	Banks	City	Bank	City
	Zapsibkombank	Tyumen	Tekobank	Petrozavodsk
	Sankt-Peterburg	Moscow	Petrovski	Sankt-Peterburg
	Moskovski mezhregionbank	Moscow	Enisei	Krasnoyarsk
	Kuzbasprombank	Kemerovo		
	Bashprombank	Ufa		
	Uralpromstroibank	Yekaterinburg		
	Sibirski bank	Novosibirsk		
	Vost-Sib.kombank	Irkutsk		
	Evrazia	Izhevsk		
	KOMIBANK	Syktyvkar		
	Kubanbank	Krasnodar		
	Ekonombank	Saratov		
	Zapaduralbank	Perm		
	Unikombank	Moscow		
Branch central[c]	Sberbank	Moscow	TOKObank	Moscow
	Roselkhozbank	Moscow	NGSbank	Moscow
	Avtobank	Moscow	Aviabank	Moscow
	Orbita	Moscow	Elektrobank	Moscow
			Gasprombank	Moscow
			Konversbank	Moscow
			Effektkredit	Moscow
			Morbank	Moscow
			Neftekhimbank	Moscow

			Stankinbank	Moscow
			Izdatbank	Moscow
			Promradtekhbank	Moscow
			Zeldorbank	Moscow
			Rosmedbank	Moscow
			Khimbank	Moscow
Branch regional[d]	AvtoVAZbank	Tolyatti	Mosstroibank	Moscow
	Mosstroiekonombank	Moscow	Kubinbank	Krasnodar
	Vozrozhdenie Rostovski	Moscow	Dalrybbank	Vladivostok
	Komagrobank	Rostov-na-Donu	Yakutzolotobank	Yakutsk
	Agroprombank	Volgograd	Tsentrokredit	Moscow
	Lenagroprombank	Sankt-Peterburg		
	Kompleksbank	Saratov		
	Kuibyshevagrobank	Samara		

Notes:
[a] Banks which only have business customers or deal with business.
[b] Banks which deal with all banking activities.
[c] Banks in the centre with branches, as defined in the source.
[d] Banks in the regions with branches, as defined in the source.

Source: '100 krupneishikh kommercheskikh bankov SNG', *Izvestia* (13 February 1992). Kommercheskie banki Rossii: litsom k miru, Moscow-New York, 1993.

NOTES

1. This work was financed from Grant R000222954 of the British Economic and Social Research Council. I acknowledge the research assistance of VEDI (Moscow), P. Kuznetsov and Heiko Pleines who provided some of the sources used in this article. The author also acknowledges advice, assistance and materials given him by bank executives and local government officials in Moscow, Kaliningrad, Tula, Nizhny Novgorod and Ekaterinburg.
2. Taiwan, Israel, Venezuela, Kuwait, Libya and socialist countries are noted by Cameron.
3. Such as India, Yugoslavia and China. 'O razvitii reformy bankovskoy sistemy' (On developing reforms of the bank system) submitted on 6 June 1986 to the CPSU Central Committee and USSR Council of Ministers by M. S. Zotov, Chairman of the Board of USSR Stroibank.
4. The initiators of the reforms were M. S. Zotov (Chairman of the Board of USSR Stroibank), Prime Minister Ryzhkov and Dementsev (then Chairman of USSR Gosbank).
5. Leningradski kooperativni bank 'Patent' licensed on 26 August 1988, and the Moskovski bank Moskoopbank on 29 September 1988.
6. *Ekspert* (1999), p. 3.
7. *Byulleten' bankovskoy statistiki*, No. 11 (1998), pp. 77 and 78.
8. Sberegatel'ny Bank Rossiyskoy Federatsii, *Godovoy otchet i balans za 1994g* (Moscow 1995), p. 30.
9. See Tsentral'ny Bank Rossiyskoy Federatsii, *Godovoy otchet za 1994g* (Moscow 1996).
10. Byulleten' bankovskoy statistiki za 1994–96gg (Moscow 1997). See also: *Bankovskaya sistema Rossii: problemy i perspektivy razvitiya*, ed. V. A. Zhebrak (Moscow, 1999), p. 147.
11. *Sotsial'no-ekonomicheskoe polozhenie Rossii (Yan–Apr 1999)* (Moscow: Goskomstat, 1999), p. 159.
12. Ibid., p. 217. In 1997, 50.1 per cent of enterprises had made a loss. *Rossiyski statisticheski ezhegodnik* (Moscow: Goskomstat, 1998), p. 672.
13. *Sotsial'no-ekonomicheskoe polozhenie Rossii (Yan–Apr 1999)* (Moscow: Goskomstat, 1999), pp. 237–8.
14. See, for example, the annual report of Forte Bank, which records that the bank issued notes with a face value of 90 million rubles in 1998 and carried out transactions of 30 million rubles for its clients. Annual Report Forte Bank 1998, p. 14.
15. Data based on a sample of 100 enterprises.
16. 104 were located in Moscow, 18 in Tula, 19 in Ekaterinburg, 14 in Kaliningrad and 9 in Nizhny Novgorod.
17. *Sotsial'no-ekonomicheskoe polizhenie Rossii (jan–apr 1999g)* (Moscow 1999), p. 153.
18. Banks with this status included Menatep and Most-bank, authorized by Moscow in 1992 and Bank of Moscow in 1995–96; others were: Stolichniy, Promradtechbank, Delovaya Rossiya, Orbita, Sayany, Technobank and Natsionalny Kredit.
19. Most-bank, for example, is often said to have been instrumental in furthering the interests of Yu. Luzhkov, the mayor of Moscow. The bank's credit could be used for commercial schemes of the administration (such as the Manezh shopping precinct). The international economic forum which met in Davos in 1996 (attended by leading bankers, such as Gusinski, Berezovski, Potanin, Smolenski, Khodorovski and Aven) supported Yeltsin's election campaign.
20. I. R. Puzyrev and R. F. Puzyrev (1999), *Rossiyskie banki v sfere pokitiki i vlasti*, Ivanovo, 1999, pp. 202, 205; *Ekspert*, 23 March 1998.
21. Annual reports of Sberbank are available at www.sbrf.ru (2001).
22. Data from www.cbr.ru (January 2001).
23. In 2000, Unexim had stakes in the following companies:
   1. Subsidiary banks: KabbUneximbank, BaltUneximbank, Yarbank, IKB, Volzhskiy investing bank;

2. Companies: Interros (holding company), MFK-Renessans, Svyzinvest, Sidanko, Norilsknikel (later transferred to Rosbank which owns 55 per cent of its stock), Surgutneftegas, Agrokhimeksport, Raznoimport, Raznoexport, Permmotors. Media Interests: *Russkiy telegraf*, *Komsomolskaya pravda*, *Izvestiya*, *Ekspert*, Radiostantsiya Evropa Plyus;
3. Partnerships with: AVPK Sukhoy, Rosvooruzhenie (from 1997).

24. www.cbr.ru.
25. Data derived from Tsennye Bumagi database, 1992–99.
26. Loc. cit.
27. Ekaterinburg City administration (22 per cent), municipal enterprise Upravlenie kapital'noe predpriyatie (5 per cent), Betfor zavod (10 per cent), Uraluglesbyt (6.5 per cent), 'Mir Med Layn' (6 per cent), Ural Domstroitelny kombinat (5.5 per cent), Uralelastotekhnika (5 per cent), Uraltransspetsstroy (5 per cent), and 'Sangvis' (5 per cent). Tsennye Bumagi database.
28. In 1996, Uralpromstroibank's Board of Directors was composed of a Chairman from Uralelekromel, a Deputy Chairman from Sverdlovskglavsnab and Uralenergstroy, a Secretary from Sverdlesprom, and other directors represented Sinarski trubny savod, Metallurgicheski savod imeni Serova, the Kirovgradski medepravil'ny kombinat, the Ekaterinburgskoe kommercheskoe obshchestvo, the Egorshinsk radiozavod, the Reshski nikelski zavod, Uralvagonzavod, Sredneuralski medeplavilny zavod, 'Mikhalgum', and one director was from Uralpromstroibank itself (*Godovoy otchet Promstroybanka za 1995g*, p. 9). Data for 1 January 1996.
29. Zheldorbank is composed of a coalition of railway organizations and the Ministry of Railways. Ministry of Railways of Russia constituent railway companies: Gorkovsk Railway, Eastern-Siberian Ry, Oktyabrsk Ry, Zabaykal Ry, Privolozh Ry, Moscow Ry, South-Urals Ry.
30. The City of Moscow has a controlling interest in the Bank of Moscow and AFK Sistema. In turn, AFK Sistema has the following subsidiaries: Komstar, Moscow Mobile Telephones, Moscow Oil Refinery (partner), Health Insurance Co. (ROSNO), Radio Page-Plus, Sistem Galo (construction), Petrovskoe podvore, Tourist Agency Roza Vetrov, Tourist Agency Begem OT, Guda Bank, Moscow Bank of Reconstruction and Development. And under the bank of Moscow are two other subsidiaries: RenTV and TV-Tsentr.
31. The government of Tatarstan has controlling interests in Tatneft, AK BARS and Tataro-American Investment and Finance. These in turn have overlapping ownership and representation as follows: Tatneft in Bank ZENIT and AK BARS. AK BARS (Holding Company) controls the following subsidiaries: Chelny Bank, Volzhsko-Kamski Bank. In AK BARS are representatives from: Naberezhnychelninsk Furniture Factory, Kazankomprssormash, Kazan Motor Engine Factory, Nizhnekamskneftekhim. Tataro-American Investment have representatives on the boards: AK BARS, Nizzhnekamskneftekhim, Nizhnekamskshina, Interkamabank and Nishnekamski Refinery.
32. *Uralstroybank Godovoy otchet* (1995), pp. 21–4.

REFERENCES

Annual Report Forte Bank 1998 (1999), Moscow.

Arnold, A. Z. (1937), *Banks, Credit, and Money in Soviet Russia*, New York: Columbia University Press.

Aukutsionek, S. (1999), 'Barter: new data and comments', *The Russian Economic Barometer*, No. 3.

Barkovski, N. D. (1998), *Memuary bankira 1930–1990*, Moscow: Finansy i statistika.

Baskin, J. B. and P. J. Miranti Jr (1997), *A History of Corporate Finance*, Cambridge: Cambridge University Press.

Belyanova, E. (1995), 'Commercial banking in Russia: evidence from economic surveys', *Russian Economic Barometer*, **4** (4).

Byulleten' bankovskoy statistiki za 1994–96 gg (1997), Moscow.

Byulleten' bankovskoy statistiki, No. 11, 1998.

Cameron, R. (ed.) (1972), *Banking and Economic Development*, New York: Oxford University Press.

Cassis, Y. (ed.) (1992), *Finance and Financiers in European History, 1880–1960*, Cambridge: Cambridge University Press.

Delyagin, M. (1995), 'Bankovski krizis v svete osnovnykh tendentsiy ekonomicheskogo razvitiya Rossii', *Voprosy ekonomiki*, No. 11.

Dickson, P. G. M. (1967), *The Financial Revolution in England: A Study in the Development of Public Credit 1688–1756*, Macmillan: Basingstoke.

Ekspert (1999), No. 38.

Ekspert (1998), 23 March.

Foreign Affairs, **77**, No. 5, 1998.

Gaddy, C. G. and B. W. Ickes (2001), 'The virtual economy and economic recovery in Russia', *Transition Newsletter*, **12** (1).

Garvy, G. (1968), 'East European credit and finance in transition', in Gregory Grossman (ed.), *Money and Plan*, Berkeley: University of California Press.

Gerschenkron, A. (1962), *Economic Backwardness in Historical Perspective: A Book of Essays*, New York and London: Praeger.

Gerschenkron, A. (1962), 'Russia: patterns and problems of economic development, 1861–1958', in A. Gerschenkron, *Economic Backwardness in Historical Perspective*, New York and London: Praeger.

Godovoy otchet Promstroybanka za 1995g.

Grossman, G. (ed.) (1968), *Money and Plan*, Berkeley: University of California Press.

Gurley, J. G. (1967), *American Economic Review*, **57**.

Ingham, G. (1999), 'Capitalism, money and banking: a critique of recent historical sociology', *British Journal of Sociology*, **50** (1).

International Financial Statistics (1996, 2000), Washington D.C.: International Monetary Fund.

Kapelyushnikov, R. I. (2000), 'The largest and dominant shareholders in Russian industry: evidence of the Russian Economic Barometer Monitoring', *Russian Economic Barometer*, No. 1.

Konstantinov, Y. (1992), 'Kommercheskie banki: stanovlenie i razvitie', *Voprosy ekonomiki*, No. 4–6.

Matovnikov, M. Yu. i dr. (1998), *Rossiyskie banki: 10 let spustya*, Moscow: MakTsentr.

'O razvitii reformy bankovskoy sistemy' [On developing reforms of the bank system], submitted on 6 June 1986 to the CPSU Central Committee and USSR Council of Ministers by M. S. Zotov, Chairman of the Board of the USSR Stroibank.

Ol, P. V. (1922), *Foreign Capital in Russia*, cited in A. Arnold (1937), *Banks, Credit, and Money in Soviet Russia*, New York: Columbia University Press.

'100 krupneishikh kommercheskikh bankov SNG' (1992), *Izvestia* (13 February 1992), Kommercheskie banki Rossii: litsom K miru, Moscow-New York, 1993.

Puzyrev I. R. and R. F. Puzyrev (1999), *Rossiyskie banki v sfere pokitiki i vlasti*, Ivanovo.

Rossiyski statisticheski ezhegodnik (1998), Moscow: Goskomstat.

Sberegatel'ny Bank Rossiyskoy Federatsii (1995), *Godovoy otchet i balans za 1994g*, Moscow.

Sotsial'no-ekonomicheskoe polozhenie Rossii (Jan.–Apr. 1999), Moscow: Goskomstat.

Thornhill, J. and C. Clover (1999), 'Robbery of nations', *Financial Times* (London), 21 August.

Tilly, R. (1992), 'An overview on the role of the large German banks up to 1914', in Youssef Cassis (ed.), *Finance and Financiers in European History*, 1880–1960, Cambridge: Cambridge University Press.

Tsennye Bumagi database, 1992–99.

Tsentral'ny Bank Rossiyskoy Federatsii (1996), *Godovoy otchet za 1994g*, Moscow.

Uralstroybank Godovoy otchet (1995).

Woodruff, D. (1999), *Money Unmade: Barter and the Fate of Russian Capitalism*, Ithaca: Cornell University Press.

Zhebrak, V. A. (ed.) (1999), *Bankovskaya sistema Rossii: problemy i perspektivy razvitiya*, Moscow.

Zotov, M. S. (1998), 'Kommertsializatsiya bankov -vplot' do "partizanskikh" metodov', in A. Krotova and V. Lapshova (eds.), *Rozhdenie kommercheskikh bankov ili moment istiny rossiyskoy bankovskoy reformy (svidetel'stva uchastnikov)*, Moscow: Bankovskoe delo.

Websites

Annual reports of Sberbank 2001: www.sbrf.ru.

Annual reports of Central Bank: www.cbr.ru.

2. Bank sector restructuring

Satoshi Mizobata

The Russian financial crisis in August 1998 caused a great deal of damage to the banking sector. However, the oligarchic financial groups have not lost their power. The financial groups have strengthened their influence on the Russian Union of Entrepreneurs and Industrialists, whose member-firms accounted for more than 80 per cent of GDP (*Segodnya*, 25 November 2000), and maintained their presence in the (central and local) governments. In addition, the financial crisis and the subsequent economic recovery in Russia confirm that the development of financial institutions, which intermediate between the owners of the means of production and innovators, is indispensable for the capitalist economic system (Schumpeter, 1962). Financial system reforms in the aftermath of the crisis have also helped improve our understanding of the peculiarities of the Russian economic system.

FINANCIAL FLOWS AND THE ROLE OF THE BANKING SECTOR

I will describe financial flows by sector, focusing in particular on the role of the banking sector in financial circulation (see Figure 2.1, Vedev, 1999, pp. 53–69).

First of all, households and non-residents can be regarded as net creditors, or surplus sectors, as they offer funds through deposits and loans. As these funds and banks' own funds are lent to firms and governments, the latter become net debtors, or deficit sectors. The 1998 crisis did not cause any fundamental changes in these financial flows. But the following characteristics can be added: 1) although banks are net creditors in rubles, in foreign currency they may be considered net debtors; 2) after the crisis, the inflow of foreign currency drastically diminished.

Moreover, financial flows in Russia include payment arrears and non-monetary settlements such as barter, promissory notes (veksels), money surrogates and others. While governments can be regarded as a deficit sector according to the official statistics, in fact they are a surplus sector

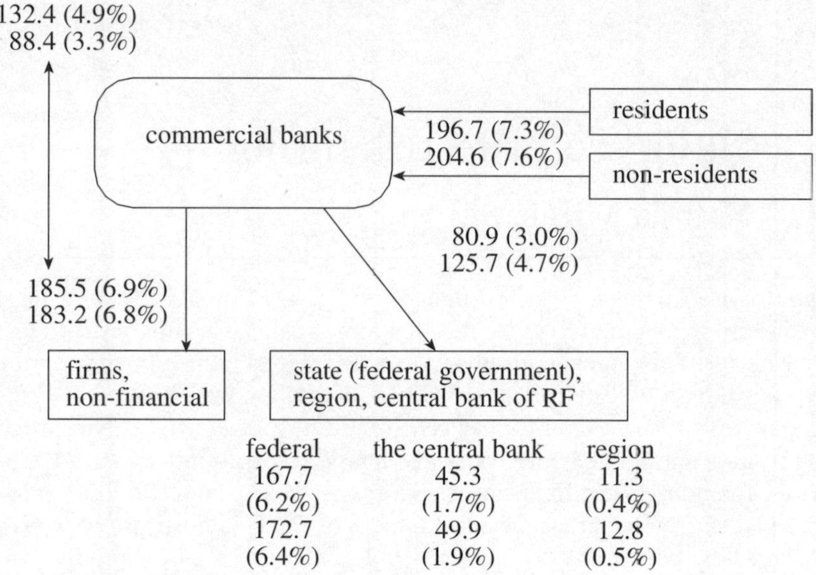

federal	the central bank	region
167.7	45.3	11.3
(6.2%)	(1.7%)	(0.4%)
172.7	49.9	12.8
(6.4%)	(1.9%)	(0.5%)

Note: All arrows indicate the financial flow, and numerical data (billion denomination ruble) are values of the financial flow at the beginning of May 1998 (the upper column) and the beginning of 1999 (the lower column). Percentage is a ratio divided by 1998 annual GDP (%). An arrow of commercial banks means they become net-creditors.

Source: Vedev (1999).

Figure 2.1 Financial flows in Russia

because they provide various subsidies to non-financial corporations and financial institutions. Table 2.1 illustrates the correlation among government securities, subsidies, bank loans, payment arrears and barter. As the volume of government securities grows, banks' capital and assets increase. At the same time, larger issues of government securities go hand in hand with increases of subsidies, payment arrears and barter, and a decline of bank loans. In particular, figures show a fall in official subsidies but an extraordinary large increase in hidden subsidies.

Funds flow from financial institutions and non-financial corporations to government bond markets. When bank loans to non-financial corporations are restricted, the corporations' financial position gets worse. To compensate for the lack of working capital, they expand barter and payment arrears. There is a mutual causal relationship between payment arrears and bank loans. Fragility and inefficiencies of the tax collection system reduce

Table 2.1 Finance, government securities and transactions in Russia (R bn. denomination, end of period)

	1992	1993	1994	1995	1996	1997	1998	1999	2000
GDP (nominal)	19.0	171.5	610.1	1540.5	2145.7	2478.6	2741.1	4757.2	7063.4
Government securities									
GKO/OFZs total	—	0.2	10.6	76.6	237.1	384.9	385.8	270.3	185.1
% of GDP	—	0.1	1.7	5.0	11.1	15.5	14.1	5.7	2.6
GKO/OFZs total trading	—	0.2	17.5	159.5	430.5	502.0	258.6	172.8	20.5
% of GDP	—	0.1	2.9	10.4	20.1	20.3	9.4	3.6	0.3
GKO/OFZs net income	—	0.2	5.7	26.8	35.2	32.7	−50.4	−67.8	−73.0
% of GDP	—	0.1	0.9	1.7	1.6	1.3	−1.8	−1.4	−1.0
Commercial banks									
Total capital	—	—	—	66.7	123.8	143.9	157.6	292.4	437.3
% of GDP	—	—	—	4.3	5.8	5.8	5.8	6.5	6.2
Total assets	—	—	200.6	342.3	497.7	622.7	933.1	1549.7	2257.3
% of GDP	—	—	32.9	22.2	23.2	25.1	34.6	34.1	32.0
Credits									
% of GDP	26.8	17.5	13.7	8.7	9.4	11.1	15.4	12.5	13.5
Subsidies (% of GDP)									
Official budget subsidies	—	—	10.2	8.6	7.9	8.6	5.9	—	—
Implicit subsidies	—	—	0.7	3.1	7.6	7.4	10.4	—	—
Total subsidies	—	—	10.9	11.7	15.5	16.0	16.3	—	—

Arrears	—	—	14.8	15.1	23.4	29.2	39.3	29.8	23.7
Arrears to governments	—	—	3.2	4.9	9.5	12.8	17.6	12.6	9.5
Share of barter in sales, industry (%)	6.0	11.0	18.0	26.0	40.0	47.0	49.0	36.0	19.0

Note: GDP is shown in billion denomination rubles. Implicit subsidies mainly include tax arrears, tax payment in barter and others. They do not include individual exemptions, overdue late charges and penalties. Implicit subsidies and total subsidies in 1994–1995 do not include local ones. Arrears are calculated in the economic sector: before 1997, arrears of industry, construction, transportation and agriculture are included, and after 1998, the above-mentioned sectors and communication, housing, and commercial are included. Arrears to governments include arrears to budgets and non-budgetary funds.

Source: *National'nyie scheta Rossii v 1992–1999 godakh*, Goskomstat Rossii (2000), *Rossiiskii statisticheskii ezhegodnik 1999, 2000, 2001* (Moscow, Goskomstat Rossii, 1999, 2000, 2001). The World Bank (2000), p. 19, Institute of World Economy and International Relations (2001), RECEP (2001).

government revenues. Tax authorities seize accounts of firms with tax arrears, and the collected revenues are directed toward compensation of arrears. Thus, a tight monetary policy, a predominant use of funds to buy government securities, an increase of funds' outflow from the real sector, an output decline, weak tax collection and tax evasion are closely connected (Seregina, 1999, pp. 72–3).

The structure of subsidies, arrears and barter from the viewpoint of financial institutions is as follows: a weak intermediary function and rent-seeking incentives expand payment arrears and non-monetary settlements. This leads to larger subsidies and budget deficit, which has to be financed by larger issues of government securities. This, in turn, strengthens speculative behaviour. The result is a vicious cycle embodied in Russia's financial flows. Though the classical intermediary function of banks is far from being sufficient, banks carry out their own 'intermediary function' between governments and firms.

Earlier discussions of the role of Russia's commercial banks (Tompson, 2000, p. 611) have shown that banks have gained profits not from their classical intermediary role of reducing transaction costs, and selecting and monitoring borrowers, but from rent seeking, speculative activities and acquisitions of state property. This kind of behaviour has taken root since the banks' establishment and can be considered typical of Russian banks.[1] Moreover, as Sberbank remains under the control of the CBR, the government has also gained from the handling of government securities (Seregina, 1999, pp. 71–2). In a sense, the government itself induced the banks' peculiarities. Thus, bank behaviour may be regarded as a result of economic policies to fight inflation and reduce the budget deficit, as well as a response to general political instability and the weakness of the Russian state.

BANK SECTOR RESTRUCTURING AND ECONOMIC POLICY AFTER THE CRISIS

Economic Policy after the Crisis

The financial crisis drastically changed bank asset and liability structure in the second half of 1998. Both total assets and net assets diminished, with net assets in particular declining by more than 20 per cent for about two weeks (beginning of August–17 August 1989). Bank equity capital indicated a sharp decline that can be attributed to the ruble's depreciation, and the capital-to-net-assets ratio decreased from 20 per cent at the beginning of August to 10 per cent at the beginning of November 1998. Banks' financial position worsened and all commercial banks, except Sberbank, went into the red. Household deposits were either frozen, or withdrawn and transferred to Sberbank. Firms' demand deposits fell too. A large amount of debt to non-residents remained on bank balance sheets. Payments on short-term government securities were frozen indefinitely and virtually turned into bad loans for the banks. Part of the government securities were purchased by the CBR or used as collateral. Bank lending to firms decreased (in August 1998 alone lending declined by 41 per cent), as possibilities to borrow from the inter-bank market became much smaller. As a result of the rapid decrease of assets and increase of bad loans, the banking sector stood on the edge of bankruptcy. One-fifth of Russia's banks had gone bankrupt by mid-2000 (*Ekonomika i zhizn*, 2000, No. 43). It was obvious that the banking sector needed a large amount of funds for its rehabilitation.

There were two main political ideas on how to reform the financial system: the left-wing insisted on stronger state control and the right-wing argued for a large-scale privatization of the financial sector (*Ekonomika i zhizn*, 2000, No. 43). While the result is common to all countries stricken by the crisis, state control over the financial system in Russia has been strengthened.

The first stabilization measure taken by the CBR was ensuring the safety of residents' deposits. Household deposits at six troubled banks designated by the CBR were either transferred to Sberbank or frozen. Secondly, the CBR lowered reserve requirements and used the freed funds for the repayment of arrears. Thirdly, the CBR extended loans to commercial banks in need of liquidity. Moreover, the CBR classified banks into four types: 1) banks with a sound financial position; 2) banks experiencing some financial difficulties; 3) banks in serious financial trouble; and 4) banks hurt most heavily by the crisis. The number of banks belonging to the first type decreased, whereas that of the third and the fourth increased. Banks were also divided into those that needed government support and those that could manage without it (the latter accounted for 70 per cent of all banks).[2]

Concerning the post-crisis restructuring of the banking sector, the following four policies are regarded as fundamental.

First, the CBR encouraged mergers among large banks to create new independent holding banks: for example, ONEKSIMbank, Menatep, and Most-bank established Rosbank, which held a 51 per cent stake in the three banks. The enterprises of each of the three financial–industrial groups also became shareholders. The accounts government offices and large companies used to keep in the three banks were transferred to the new bank, which served as a bridge bank. The main shareholder of the new bank was ONEKSIMbank. Other examples are Moscow Bank, Rossiyskiy Kredit and Dialogbank.

Second, the CBR fined or withdrew the licences of banks hurt most heavily by the crisis, namely banks that could not match reserve requirements. The Law on the Bankruptcy of Credit Organizations of 25 February 1999 was the legal basis for bank sector restructuring. However, the CBR policies toward banks whose licences had been withdrawn lacked clarity: bankruptcy proceedings were started against some banks, but others managed to escape from bankruptcy.

Third, through stabilization loans, restrictions on capital flight and other measures the government strengthened its control of the banking system. For example, the government took capital participation in some banks. The state-owned Sberbank and Vneshtorgbank (the Foreign Trade Bank) expanded the scope of their operations to the commercial banking field. In addition, government financial institutions such as the Export Credit Insurance Organization, the Organization for Savings Guarantees, the Development Bank, and the Agricultural Bank carried out various government programmes (*Ekonomika i zhizn*, 2000, No. 40).

One of these was the establishment of the Russian Development Bank (RDB), which aimed to stimulate investment in the real sector. The RDB was to be involved in project financing under conditions that ruled out the possibility of unfair competition with the commercial banking sector. The concept of this bank was approved in 1999, with its capital being set at 375 million rubles.[3] At the time of its establishment, the Federal Property Fund owned 75 per cent plus one share of its capitals. As a rule, the RDB was protected from political interference. According to the 1999 budget, the bank was supposed to have a development budget and start offering investment guarantees (up to a ceiling of 50 billion rubles). However, the development budget was not sufficient for project financing.

Furthermore, as a result of intense lobbying by the Lower House and the Ministry of Agriculture, the concept of a state agricultural bank (Rosselkhozbank) was finally approved by the government at the end of 1999. The new bank, established with capital of 327 million rubles, took over the assets (including the branches) of the former agricultural commercial bank (SBS-Agro), which used to be the government's agent for disbursing agricultural loans. The central government acquired a 51 per cent controlling stake, while regional governments and others held the rest of the shares.

The establishment of specialized government banks met with some difficulties due to both political conflicts within the government and lack of funds. The reorganization of the existing commercial banks was also fraught with political negotiation and lobbying by interest groups, an environment contributing to the non-transparent nature of the decision-making process. According to some analysts, the formation of two banks discussed above was deterred not just by a lack of state funds but also by 'a state failure' (*Segodnya*, 2 June 2000).

Another financial institution set up by the government in the wake of the 1998 crisis was ARCO. The latter was founded in March 1999 with the goal of creating an efficient banking system. ARCO was a non-profit public corporation owned by the Federal Property Fund and the CBR. The main tasks of ARCO, according to the Law on the Restructuring of Credit Organizations of July 1999, were supervision of troubled banks, acquisition of bank assets based on restructuring schemes and participation in the liquidation process. The agency selected priority regions where more than thirty financial institutions prepared restructuring plans. Though ARCO controlled commercial banks through the provision of financing and management, ARCO itself was supervised by the CBR. The CBR extended loans to ARCO, with bank shares serving as collateral (Tekeeva, 1999, p. 185).

Fourthly, foreign banks were encouraged to expand their operations. The maximum limit of foreign ownership of Russian bank shares was established by the CBR at 12 per cent of bank capital but that limit was expected to be relaxed as the share of bank capital owned by foreigners exceeded 10 per cent at the beginning of 2000.[4] The share of foreign capital was less than 4.5 per cent in 1996–1998 and 5.3 per cent in October–December 1998. In addition, the CBR published the instruction which permitted the transfer of individuals' money to foreign banks (less than 75 thousand dollars) (*Kommersant-Daily*, 21 September 2001).

Financial Sector Restructuring under the Putin Government

After taking power, the Putin government drew up its own policy report. 'The Strategy of Russia's Development until 2010'[5] was prepared by the Centre for Strategy Development, according to which Russia's goal was economic modernization based on liberal principles but with a strong role for the state. The report said the target of 5 per cent annual GDP growth until 2010 could be achieved through the formation of strong legal institutions, the overhaul of social welfare policies and the adoption of a new budgetary system. The following economic policy goals were also included: 1) protection of shareholder rights; 2) establishment of fair competitive conditions (abolition of direct and indirect privileges); 3) deregulation and cutting 'red tape' (simplification of administrative procedures for firm registration, and others).

In the financial field, solid financial infrastructure and tax preferences were deemed indispensable to create a favorable investment environment. Policy proposals included simplifying permission procedures for investment projects, improvement of bank insolvency procedures, implementation of government audits and better enforcement of legal rules in securities markets.[6] These recommendations were similar to the ones made by S. Glaz'ev (Glaz'ev, 2000), the chair of the Lower House committee on economic policy and entrepreneurship.

S. Glaz'ev argued that the Russian government should be more active in promoting economic growth through higher investment. His focus was on the state banking system, which should channel savings to investment in priority production sectors. For him, two linkages were of the utmost importance: personal savings–Sberbank–the RDB–industrial companies, and the CBR–the RDB–industrial companies. In his view, the Russian Export–Import Bank, the Agricultural Bank and the RDB have not yet started functioning. RDB lending should be based on market principles and be done jointly with commercial banks (Glaz'ev, 2000, pp. 13–26). Glaz'ev also criticized the government for the lack of progress on banking reform in 2000, and claimed that it cannot effectively implement its economic policies (*PlanEcon Report*, 2000, 16, 22).

BANK SECTOR RECOVERY

Performance of the Financial Institutions

Since the 1998 financial crisis, industrial output has grown rapidly and there are signs of recovery in the financial sector. The following evaluations can be quoted here: '1999 was the year when banks adapted to the new conditions in the Russian banking system'; 'The normalization of the banking system is on its way' (CBR, 1999); 'The first stage of bank restructuring has been completed as a whole' (Gerashchenko, 2000).[7]

Total capital of commercial banks increased by 2.8 times in the first quarter of 2000, compared to the bottom of March 1999, thus exceeding the pre-crisis level. The reasons for this were the net capital increase and the withdrawal of problem bank (those with negative capital) licences. During January–October 1999, the share of problem banks fell[8] and that of stable banks rose.[9] During 2000–2001, bank capital and profits increased further, and the number of crisis banks (according to CBR's definition) was almost halved (from 113 at the beginning of 2000 to 58 at the beginning of August 2000).

Total banking assets also grew rapidly:[10] at the end of 2000, their value reached 2 trillion 260 billion rubles, or 3.6 times larger than at the end of June 1998. Average bank assets (excluding Sberbank) increased from 442 million rubles at the beginning of July 1998 to 1 billion 56 million rubles at the beginning of 2000 (2.4 times) (*Ekonomika i zhizn*, 2000, No. 40). Though the growth rate of foreign currency assets was higher, ruble assets also rose thanks to low inflation and the stable exchange rate.

As for asset composition, bank lending has expanded, with banks lending mainly short-term and in rubles. The amount of bad loans fell as a result of debtors' financial recovery. The ratio of overdue bad loans to total loans decreased from 11.7 per cent at the beginning of 1999 to 5.8 per cent in the first quarter of 2000. In spite of this, the danger of a recurrence of bad loan problems is high because the quality of loan application screening has not improved. The inter-bank market also recovered but securities transactions by banks declined sharply.[11] Bank deposits of firms and individuals gradually increased. On the liabilities side, government deposits and loans by monetary authorities have shown the highest increases. This reiterates the point that financial sector recovery has been led by the state. However, rent-seeking incentives of the banking sector have been kept. For instance, 13 main banks participated in the competition for Pension Funds (*Kommersant-Daily*, 11 April 2001).

Financial institutions' recovery can be observed at the regional level too. For example, in the Rostov oblast total bank capital increased 1.9 times between August 1998 and July 2000. The ratio of overdue debts to total bank assets dropped from 12.9 per cent in early July 1999 to 1.6 per cent at the beginning of March 2000 (Basko and Karakai, 2000, pp. 16–17).

To recapitulate, as bank capital and assets exceeded pre-crisis levels, 'the first stage' of the reform can be judged successful. At the same time, government intervention has become stronger, and there have been no significant changes in the banks' role (toward the classical intermediary function) or in the way banks are being managed.

The Consequences of Government Intervention

Financial sector restructuring has been accompanied by a strengthening of government intervention. The CBR recapitalized large banks which transferred their assets to the newly established bridge banks. Legislation treating bank insolvency came to a standstill in the Russian parliament after major objections were raised by the CBR. It became evident that ARCO did not possess enough political and economic authority to carry out radical reforms. Pressures by the Russian political elite limited foreign investment in the banking sector. As a result, the share of foreign ownership was restricted to 8 per cent of bank assets.

The government intensified its control of the banking system through various channels such as the CBR, ARCO and government financing. Between early July 1998 and the beginning of 2000 the federal government's

Table 2.2 Ownership structure of Russian banking capital (% of the total, beginning of period)

	All banks		Banks in Moscow		Regional banks	
Shareholder	July 1998	2000	July 1998	2000	July 1998	2000
Federal authorities	2.0	16.1	1.8	18.2	0.4	0.1
Federal subjects authorities	2.7	2.0	0.9	0.4	7.4	13.4
State enterprises	7.2	4.3	3.6	2.4	18.3	16.0
Non-state enterprises	75.3	64.1	82.7	65.9	55.6	54.4
Individuals	6.8	4.0	8.0	2.3	15.4	14.0
Non-residents	6.0	9.5	7.2	10.8	2.6	2.1

Note: The original source from the CBR.

Source: *Ekonomika i zhizn*, 2000, No. 40.

share in total banking capital surged, whereas that of non-state enterprises plummeted (see Table 2.2). Moreover, the share of non-residents marked a slight increase, while those of state enterprises and of residents diminished. This trend is most valid for Moscow-based commercial banks where the federal government's share jumped by ten times. In addition, the share of federal authorities in regional banks' capital fell, while that of regional governments doubled (*Ekonomika i zhizn*, 2000, No. 40. The federal government intervened strongly in Moscow-based banks but had less influence in regional banks which did not suffer as much from the 1998 financial crisis. At the beginning of April 2000, the Russian government participated in about half of all (1 333) banks (Mikhailov, Suicheva and Timofeev, 2000, pp. 64–67).[12] State shareholding varied across banks: more than 80 per cent of the state shareholding was concentrated in Vneshtorgbank, Bashkreditbank, Bars and Sberbank, and the rest was dispersed in smaller banks.

In short, the Putin government put a great deal of effort not into liberalism but into the strengthening of government control over the CBR and commercial banks.[13] The CBR was prohibited from engaging in commercial banking activities and was to 'be transformed into a federal state institution acting in accordance with federal policy'. Moreover, the CBR had to dispose of its shareholdings in Sberbank[14] and Vneshtorgbank, and of its (the CBR's) overseas subsidiaries.[15] The CBR's 'decommercialisation' may be regarded as an important measure aimed at reducing corruption and conflicts of interest (*PlanEcon Report*, 2000, 16, 19).

The changes at Sberbank deserve special attention because of the bank's dominant position (more than 1 600 branches and 80 per cent of personal deposits) in Russia's banking sector. Sberbank shifted its emphasis from dealing in government securities to corporate finance. Its share in corporate financing tripled for two successive years after the crisis (*Ekspert*, 2002, p. 25). In particular, it started lending to large corporations in petroleum and other export-oriented industries and expanding its financing to the regions. Optimizing its branch network helped cut costs and improve profitability. For instance, branches in Rostov, Krasnodar and Adygeya were to be merged into southwest Sberbank by the beginning of December 2000.[16] Kamchatka and Chuktka offices were merged into Primorskii Sberbank, and Karachev-Cherkes and Kalmykia branches were integrated into Stavropol bank. The bank's branches were also amalgamated in the Leningrad region, Saint Petersburg, Ulyanovsk, Samara, Mordovia and Nizhgorod. On the whole, 69 local branches were integrated into 18 large regional branches, implying a higher concentration of branches in better-developed regions and the closure of loss-making branches. All these changes freed funds, thus enabling Sberbank to expand loans to the industrial sector (*Rossiiskaya gazeta*, 14 November 2000). Moreover, to attract more capital Sberbank's general meeting of shareholders decided to abolish the 5 per cent limit on foreign ownership.

ARCO's Activities and the Reform of the Banking System

I have shown how the Russian federal government has increased its influence over the banking sector and reorganized state-owned banks to enhance investment.[17] Regional governments have also strengthened their control through cooperation arrangements with regional banks.[18] Here, by examining ARCO's activities (ARKO, 2000a, 2000b), I illustrate the process of bank restructuring.

At the end of 1999, ARCO participated in the equity capital of 11 banks, and in the first half of 2000, it carried out 15 projects at 20 banks located in 12 regions. By the end of 2001 ARCO intended to complete its work with collapsed banks. In 2001, ARCO reported 447 million rubles profit and 12.5 billion rubles assets.

The eight banks where ARCO dispatched directors to carry out restructuring programmes (AvtoVAZbank, Vyatka-bank, Evraziya, Investbank, Kuzbassugol'bank, PeterPervui, Chelyabkomzembank and Vozrozhdenie)[19] have stabilized their financial positions. In addition, ARCO backed the creditor agreements of three banks (Rossiyskiy Kredit, Dal'ruibbank, and Voronejzh), paving the way for their approval by the courts. In the case of SBS-Agro, ARCO implemented so-called 'soft liquidation'. SBS-Agro's agreement with creditors envisaged purchasing their claims for the first 20000 rubles and drawing bills with no interest for three years to the rest of the deposits.[20] 'Soft liquidation' is considered better than the real variety because the government budget has to shoulder a smaller part of the losses.[21]

Furthermore, seven regional banks under ARCO's control improved their finances, which enabled them to repay overdue debts to governments and other creditors.[22] These banks were successful because they managed to boost their capital, agree with creditors on debt repayment and regain their former customers. In 1999, tripartite agreements on bank restructuring were concluded between the Chuvash Republic, ARCO and AvtoVAZbank, and between the Kirov region, ARCO and Vyatka-bank.

SBS-Agro was the largest bank to fall under ARCO's control. This bank was known as Stolichnybank till 1994 and as Stolichnybank Sberezhenii (SBS) till 1996. It changed its name to SBS-Agro after acquiring the controlling stake of the state agro-industrial bank, Agroprombank. It developed a nationwide branch network and specialized in loans to agriculture and small businesses, as well as housing loans in metropolitan areas. In July 1997, SBS-Agro and 'Alliance Capital Management', an American institutional investor, established a financial–industrial group in which the management company 'Al'yans SBS-Agro' held a 51 per cent stake. However, as a result of the 1998 financial crisis, the group's capital dropped down to a negative figure and it became the recipient of the largest stabilization loan package from the CBR and the Moscow city government. After the establishment of ARCO, SBS-Agro fell under its control.[23] At the end of 1999, ARCO decided to set up Rosselkhozbank, an agricultural bank, in place of SBS-Agro which was expected to go bankrupt in accordance with its creditors' agreement (*Segodnya*, 22 December 1999). In May 2000, deposits of less than 5 000 rubles could be freely withdrawn, and withdrawals reached 90 per cent of depositor claims.

ARCO's control did not necessarily imply successful rehabilitation of all problem banks for the sake of insufficient management and the lack of financing from the federal budget. ARCO sometimes entered into conflicts with the former managers of banks under its control. For example, ARCO's behaviour was the cause of a conflict over the dismissal of Investbank's managers, and in many cases, ARCO's activities were strongly influenced by political interests.

ORGANIZATIONAL CHANGES IN THE BANKING SECTOR

Of the initial authorized banks only one (Alfa-bank) has managed to keep its pre-crisis position. Gazprombank and Sobinbank have retained some of their positions too, but they only play supplementary roles within their groups. The CBR has withdrawn the licences of the outsider-controlled Inkombank and ONEKSIMbank. However, the view that 'bank bankruptcies have started in 1999' (*Segodnya*, 31 December 1999) is too optimistic. In fact, there is a strong tendency to evade bankruptcy for three reasons: (i) bankruptcy proceedings are very complicated and inefficient; (ii) bank reorganization is preferred to bankruptcy as debt repayment would be better guaranteed by the former; and (iii) there are strong political interests that lobby against bank restructuring.

Some banks, such as SBS-Agro and Rossiyskiy Kredit, have made use of ARCO as their guardian without having their licences withdrawn. Other banks have followed even more diversified paths of restructuring. For example, ONEKSIMbank transferred its assets to the bridge bank and reached an agreement with creditors, making the CBR suspend the withdrawal of its licence. Menatep and some others have started bankruptcy procedures. Rossiyskiy Kredit has made Impeksbank, an ARCO-controlled bank, its bridge bank and also achieved a settlement with creditors. In spite of receiving political support from the Lower House and stabilization financing from the CBR, SBS-Agro's shares have been transferred to ARCO and the bank designated for division and liquidation (Pappe, 2000, pp. 41–47).

The above cases show a peculiar Russian path of bank reorganization. Russia's financial institutions did not accept mergers of weak and strong banks. Political interests and parent company or group strategies, rather than the opinions of ordinary shareholders, creditors and depositors, influenced bank restructuring. Moral hazard in bank behaviour is likely to persist.

Moreover, many banks have concentrated and enlarged their capital. As a result, the following four financial centres have been created: Rosbank, the Gazprom-controlled banks, the CBR-controlled Sberbank and Vneshtorgbank, and Moscow bank. Bank capital concentration was, in part, a by-product of the concentration of financial–industrial groups. Besides, the merger of Konversbank with MDM-bank was anticipated because in this case both banks could rely on stronger support by nuclear power authorities.[24] This is a classical example of political influence on bank restructuring. In fact, the biggest 16 banks, 1 per cent of the total number, held 60 per cent of the total assets. The scale gap within the banking sector is huge (*Ekspert*, 2001, 34, p. 78).

CHANGES AND INERTIA IN BANK BEHAVIOUR

Using the results of studies by *The Russian Economic Barometer* (Institute of World Economy and International Relations, 2000) and by the

Economic and Business Centre (Ostapkovich, Glisin and Kitrar, 2000), I examine bank behaviour after the 1998 financial crisis.

First of all, from commercial bank activities (Institute of World Economy and International Relations, 2000)[25] two trends toward the fall of deposits and inter-bank dealings on the one hand, and the rise of hard currency assets on the other, can be discerned. Moreover, dealings in securities and government bonds have declined, whereas foreign currency transactions and loans to industrial corporations have grown. The ratios of loans to total bank assets (about 40 per cent) and of industrial loans to total loans (about 15 per cent) have been rather stable.

The most noteworthy changes in bank behaviour, according to *The Russian Economic Barometer*, may be seen in the spectacular increase of the long-term (over one year) loans-to-total-loans ratio (from 2 per cent in 1997 to 13 per cent in 1999) and the large decrease of the number not financing credits out of the total number (from 34 per cent in 1997 to 21 per cent in 1999). The share of overdue loans in total loans has also declined (from 19 per cent in 1997 to 8 per cent in 1999). It seems that firms have tried to construct a more stable relationship with banks since the crisis. As a result of stable lending to industrial corporations, the share of profit-earning banks has increased (from 74 per cent in 1997 to 83 per cent in 1999), and bank losses have diminished. We can conclude that Russian banks' adaptability to market conditions has improved remarkably since the 1998 financial crisis.

Next, research results released by the Economic and Business Centre also serve to prove the point that financial institutions have become more stable.[26] The recovery of the real sector has been reflected in bank finances, with both the number of depositors and the total value of deposits marking a substantial growth. Long-term loans to private firms have increased and overdue loans diminished. According to the Economic and Business Centre, loans to industrial firms in September 2000 surged by 5.7 per cent, a rate that exceeded the monthly average increase on a year-on-year basis (3.1 per cent) (*Nezavisimaya gazeta*, 30 November 2000).

The above survey, however, states that 'in spite of the positive tendency toward more lending by the commercial banks, about a half of industrial and three-quarters of construction and marketing firms did not borrow' (Ostapkovich, Glisin and Kitrar, 2000, p. 53). The following two explanations could be offered here. First, banks did not have sufficient information on some debtors, whereas lending to others would have been quite risky. Second, banks perceived Russia's legal system and government policies as unstable and lacking the capacity to protect investors and creditors. On the other hand, banks were encouraged to boost lending due to anticipated preferential treatment from loans to the real sector and due to capital participation by the government. In other words, banks strengthened their market adaptability but maintained their dependence on the state.

The above changes in commercial bank behaviour should not lead the reader to believe that there have been huge changes in the banks' role in financial flows. An increase of the banks' capital does not go hand in hand with motives of risk diversification (*Ekspert*, 2001, 34, p. 76). Despite the surge in lending, investment financing through bank loans is still limited and most investment is financed from internal sources. In 1999, 72 per cent of total industrial enterprise investment was financed from internal sources. The shares of budget and external financing were respectively 4.7 per cent and 23.7 per cent. The share of bank loans was 4.3 per cent and fell below that level in 2000 (Vodyanov and Smirnov, 2000).[27] According to the findings of the Economic and Business Centre, the behaviour and interests of banks are incompatible with those of industrial firms. Banks have neither performed successfully their role as intermediaries between depositors and the real sector nor rid themselves of the moral hazard problem.

CONCLUSIONS

Russian financial institutions have developed, generally speaking, through speculative activities rather than by playing the role of intermediaries. In the process of the post-crisis bank restructuring, networks, political interests, bargaining among governments and other economic and political actors have played a much stronger role than market institutions (such as bankruptcy).

After the financial crisis, the improvement of banks' market adaptability has gone hand in hand with the strengthening of government intervention. Banking sector reorganization has been not only market-led but also state-driven. On the surface at least, there seems to be a correlation between bank restructuring and their financial recovery. Bank capital, debt and assets exceed pre-crisis levels, bringing some analysts to argue that Russia has completed the first stage of its financial recovery. In particular, the increases of bank profits and long-term loans are regarded as the most important achievements of banking sector reforms.

However, both government experts and bank managers have pointed out the persistent instability of the financial system.[28] Although the degree of speculative activities has been relatively lower, the negative attitude of banks toward lending to industrial corporations and their continuing focus on foreign currency dealings and securities investment reproduce the kind of speculative behaviour which was the main cause of the 1998 crisis. Lobbyists have put steady pressure for subsidies and loans on new financial institutions such as ARCO, the RDB and the Agricultural Bank. Political interests have also ensured that ARCO, the driving force of bank restructuring, was established with only limited responsibilities and funds. Moreover, political pressures on the CBR have intensified. There is a danger that stronger state intervention in the banking sector may give rise to a new series of 'government failures'.

The Putin government has been criticized for lack of balance between liberal market policies and its positive stance toward stronger state intervention (*Segodnya*, 29 June 2000), and for the absence of government-led industrial policy that would bring an increase of private investment (L. Abalkin, *Nezavisimaya gazeta*, 18 August 2000). However, even if these recommendations were translated into concrete economic policies, the basic structures and mechanisms that caused the 1998 financial crisis would not magically disappear overnight. The cozy ties between financial institutions and governments, representing a kind of state-led corporatism,[29] will most likely continue to shape the course of banking sector reforms.

NOTES

1. Concerning the internal characteristics of banks, the following issues have been raised: 1) as bank capital and assets are insufficient, banks do not have enough credit resources; 2) audits of customers and creditors are insufficient; 3) banks are under constant pressure to service short-term debt; 4) banks have a strong incentive to gain from speculative activities; 5) bank management is poor. As for the external characteristics of banks, their high dependence on government budgets, poor control and auditing standards, poor legal institutions and other factors are pointed out (Tekeeva, 1999, pp. 181–3).
2. Many medium-size banks could neither channel their funds to governments bonds nor borrow from abroad and from the risky inter-bank market. In this sense, medium-size banks can be regarded as stable and with high chances of survival (Tekeeva, 1999, p. 184). However, the opposite has also been argued. In spite of the general understanding that the Russian financial crisis damaged mainly the large banks that were closely connected to the government, a look at bank assets shows that regional banks and medium-size banks were also damaged, and the growth gap between large banks and all others increased (Kazantsev, 2000, pp. 68–80). According to the classification of banks in 1999–2000, the number of sound banks increased and that of problem banks diminished (RECEP, 2000c, p. 60).
3. The idea of the establishment of the Russian Development Bank was developed at the end of 1998. However, owing to lack of funds, this idea was not realized and a new concept was prepared after the appointment of V. Putin in 1999. The establishment methods included a requirement of the Primakov concept (new creation) and restructuring of the insolvent bank Promstroibank (RECEP, 2000a).
4. RECEP (2000a), p. 80. The permitted share of foreign ownership in Russian bank assets is less than 8 per cent, and political pressure aimed to protect Russian banks from takeovers by foreigners remains strong (*PlanEcon Report*, 2000, 16, 19).
5. In May 2000, the draft of 'The Strategy of Russia's Development until 2010' was debated by the government. After revisions by the IMF and the World Bank, the strategy was officially approved as 'Fundamental directions of the socio-economic policy of the Russian Federation toward a long-term perspective' and 'The priority tasks of the

Russian Federation in 2000–2001'. Following the strategy, the government adopted federal laws on taxation and budgets and developed the 'Working programme of the Russian Federation in the field of social policy and economic modernization in 2000–2001'. The economic policy of the Putin government is based on liberalism, a strong state and integration into the world economy.

6. In October 2000, the conference on 'Russian financial institutions' stated that Russia could not achieve investment and stable growth without well-developed financial markets. The conference also pointed out that without an increase of investment it would be difficult to achieve the government's economic growth targets. Foreign investors have much interest in Russia but are also increasingly wary of difficulties with the protection of investors' rights and other problems. The Russian economy cannot be considered liberal because of a lack of competition (*Nezavisimaya gazeta*, 27 October 2000). In September 2001, a draft 'Joint strategy of the CBR and the government RF on the development of the banking sector' was prepared (*Vedomosti*, 17 September 2001). The aim of the draft is to consolidate and strengthen the banking sector in order to accept international accounting standards. This draft also includes a positive role for the government and the CBR.
7. See CBR (1999), Gerashchenko (2000), RECEP (2000a, 2000b).
8. The share of problem banks in total assets and in personal deposits respectively decreased from 45.5 per cent to 20.1 per cent and from 13.9 per cent to 7 per cent in 1999.
9. During the same period the share increased from 65.4 per cent to 76.5 per cent.
10. Bank assets increased by 51 per cent in 1999 and by 14.5 per cent in the first quarter of 2000. If Sberbank and Vneshtorgbank are included, banking assets increased by 66 per cent in 1999. The ratio of bank assets to GDP remained at one-third. Foreign exchange transactions accounted for more than 60 per cent of total profits in the banking sector at the beginning of 2000.
11. The share of securities dealings to total assets decreased from 29.9 per cent at the beginning of August 1998 to 21.6 per cent in early October 1999. However, banks' trust business cannot regain confidence.
12. The government participated in 469 banks (of which 76 were problem ones) as a shareholder. With the exception of 19 banks controlled by ARCO, it was reported that the government and the CBR participated in 30 banks (*Nezavisimaya gazeta*, 21 October 2000). Of the 800 banks founded by the state in the end of the 1980s–beginning of the 1990s, 335 banks survived and the share of capital participation by the state in those banks was high (Mikhailov, Suicheva and Timofeev, 2000, pp. 64–67). In September 2001, 30–40 per cent of total bank assets was owned by the government banks (*Vedomosti*, 12 September 2001).
13. The CBR's Chairman Viktor Gerashchenko argued that ensuring CBR's independence from the federal government was an urgent task (Gerashchenko, 2000).
14. Sberbank is 58 per cent owned by the CBR. According to Glaz'ev (2000), however, Sberbank is owned 51 per cent by the Federal Government.
15. *Nezavisimaya gazeta* (21 October 2000). Sberbank would be spun off by 2005, Vneshtorgbank by 2003 and the subsidiaries by 2002. Divesting the CBR of its holdings in the five overseas subsidiaries was set as a condition for IMF loans. The IMF wanted to deter the CBR from intervening both directly and indirectly in commercial banks.
16. Southwest region's Sberbank was located in Rostov-on-Don, and the president of Rostov Sberbank was reappointed as the president of the newly established bank.
17. The tasks of insufficient risk management and lack of transparency have not yet been dealt with. Takeovers of loss-making banks by the state foreign trade bank are regarded as a method of entering the commercial banking sector.
18. For example, an agreement between the Khabarovsk regional government and NOMOS bank (*Rossiiskaya gazeta*, 28 September 2000).
19. Vozrozhdenie took measures to maintain liquidity. Its deficit disappeared after the purchase of the bank's bad assets by ARCO. The latter's support made sure the bank kept its branch network and functions in the Moscow region (ARKO, 2000b, p. 26).
20. According to the head of ARCO, SBS-Agro could guarantee more than 75 per cent

deposit withdrawal within one year and a half in case it reached an agreement with creditors. In the case of bankruptcy, the bank guaranteed just 40 per cent within two years, that is, bank reorganization was more beneficial both for creditors and depositors (*Izvestiya*, 15 November 2000).

21. Tyumenev (2000). Based on a government decision of April 2000, ARCO strongly pressed for a creditor agreement. In the first quarter of the year 2000, only deposits of less than 5000 rubles could be withdrawn from Kuzbassprombank and Progressprombank. In ARCO-controlled banks with no overdue claims, withdrawal of all deposits was guaranteed.
22. *Vedomosti* (30 November 1999), claimed that ARCO was focused more on the restructuring of the regional financial system than on the reconstruction of large banks (the so-called 'system-forming banks').
23. The equity capital of SBS-Agro was one billion 20 million rubles in August 1999, and its shareholding structure was as follows: the management company of SBS-Agro (27.3 per cent), the SBS trade union, the regional social organization (19.5 per cent), STB-KART, a closed joint stock company (8.7 per cent), Zoloto-Platina Bank (8.7 per cent). The bank and its affiliates owned the controlling stakes (*Vedomosti*, 5 November 1999).
24. *Kommersant'-Daily* (11 April 2001). The chairman of the auditors' board of Konversbank (bank of the Ministry of Atomic Energy Industry) argued the merger had no alternative (*Segodnya*, 1 November 2000).
25. This study was carried out in 1997–1999 with a sample of 20 to 40 medium-size banks located in the Russian regions. The average value of bank assets in the sample was 350 million rubles, and the average number of employees 160. The former specialized banks and the newly established commercial banks accounted respectively for about one-half and one-third of the banks in the sample.
26. This research on banks and insurance companies was carried out in the first half of 2000. It includes not only a comparison with 1999 but also a forecast for the second half of 2000. Questionnaires were sent to the managers of 87 banks and 119 insurers of various sizes.
27. According to data released by the Ministry of Economic Development, the share of firm investment financed from internal sources decreased from 57 per cent in January–March 2000 to 53.5 per cent in June 2000. Meanwhile, the share funded from external sources increased from 43 per cent to 46.5 per cent. The shares of budgets and banks remained relatively stable: around 20.6 per cent and 4 per cent (in June 2000) respectively (*Segodnya*, 1 November 2000). However, bank loans to industrial corporations increased by 75 per cent in the third quarter of 2000, in comparison with the same period of 1999. At the very least, in 2000 both commercial banks and industrial corporations strengthened their market adaptability, based on the economic recovery. In September 2001, while the ratio of bank assets to GDP was 20 per cent, only 3 per cent of investment came from bank loans (*Vedomosti*, 12 September 2001).
28. A. Illarionov (an economic advisor of President Putin) criticized the CBR's regulation that exporters must sell 75 per cent of their foreign currency earnings. He argued that this regulation generated a constant reproduction of the crisis in the monetary sphere (A.Illarionov, *Izvestiya*, 26 October 2000; *Nezavisimaya gazeta*, 27 October 2000).
29. The view that the present economic system in Russia is a kind of state-led corporate capitalism is close to those proposed by Kosals (2000) and Mizobata (1998).

REFERENCES

ARKO (2000a), 'Itogi deyatel'nosti ARKO za 9 mesyatsev 1999 goda', *Den'gi i kredit*, 1.

ARKO (2000b), Agentstvo po restrukturizatsii kreditnykh organizatsii v pervom polugodii 2000 goda', *Den'gi i kredit*, 8.

Basko, V. N. and N. V. Karakai (2000), 'Nekotorye aspekti kreditovaniya regional'noi ekonomiki', *Den'gi i kredit*, 8.

The CBR (1999), *Osnovnye napravleniya edinoi gosudarstvennoi denezhnokreditnoi politiki na 2000 god.*

Gerashchenko, V. V. (2000), 'O sostoyanii i perspektivakh razvitiya bankovskoi sistemy Rossii', *Den'gi i kredit*, 7, http://www.cbr.ru.

Glaz'ev, S. (2000), 'Gryadet li novyi finansovyi krizis v Rossii', *Voprosy ekonomiki*, 6.

Institute of World Economy and International Relations (2000), *The Russian Economic Barometer*, 2.

Institute of World Economy and International Relations (2001), *The Russian Economic Barometer*, 1.

Kazantsev, S. (2000), 'Kakye banki sil'nee zatronul avgustovskii krizis', *EKO*, 1.

Kosals, L. (2000), 'Rossiiski put' k kapitalizmu: mezhdu Kitaem i Vostochnoi Evropoi', *Mirovaya ekonomika i mezhdunarodnye otnosheniya*, 10–11.

Mikhaikov, L., L. Suicheva and E. Timofeev (2000), 'Kazennaya pomoshch', *Ekspert*, 22.

Mizobata, S. (1998), 'Financial Relations in the Russian Financial-industrial Groups: A Comparison of Russia and Japan', Kyoto University, *KIER Discussion Paper*, No. 480.

Ostapkovich, G. V., F. F. Glisin and L. A. Kitrar (2000), 'Delovaya aktivnost' organizatsii finansovogo sektora Rossii', *Voprosy statistiki*, 10.

Pappe, I. S. (2000), *Oligarkhi ekonomicheskaya khronika 1992–2000*, Gosudarstvenny universitet Vuishaya shkola ekonomiki.

Russian European Centre for Economic Policy (RECEP) (2000a), *Russian Economic Trends*, 9, 1.

RECEP (2000b), *Russian Economic Trends*, 9, 2.

RECEP (2000c), *Russian Economic Trends*, 9, 3.

RECEP (2001), *Russian Economic Trends*, 10, 1.

Seregina, S. F. (1999), 'Vzaimosvyaz' fiskal'noi i monerarnoi politiki', ed. V. V. Gerasimenko and D. E. Gorodetskii, *Rossiiskaya ekonomika: finansovaya sistema*, Teis.

Shumpeter, J. (1962), *The Theory of Economic Development*, translated from the German by R. Opie, Harvard University Press.

Tekeeva, A. K. (1999), 'Problemui poslekrizisnogo razvitiya kommercheskikh bankov Rossii', ed. V. V. Gerasimenko and D. E. Gorodetskii, *Rossiiskaya ekonomika: finansovaya sistema*, Teis.

Tompson, W. (2000), 'Financial Backwardness in Contemporary Perspective: Prospects for the Development of Financial Intermediation in Russia', *Europe-Asia Studies*, Vol. 52, No. 4.

Tyumenev, V. (2000), 'Po pravu sil'nog', *Ekspert*, 39.

Vedev, A. (1999), *Bankovskaya sistema: Rossii krizis i perspektivi razvitiya*, Vedi.

Vodyanov, A. and A. Smirnov (2000), 'Pautina rosta', *Ekspert*, 42.

The World Bank (2000), 'Razrushenye sitemy neplatezhei v Rossii sozdanie uslovii dlya ustoichivogo rosta', *Voprosy ekonomiki*, 3.

3. The present and future of banking reform

William Tompson

The Russian banking system in 2001 presented a paradox. Russian banks were, on the face of it, healthier than they had ever been. They were also, both politically and economically, more of an irrelevance than at any time since the early 1990s. The aim of this chapter is to examine this paradox in an attempt to understand the place of the banking system within the Russian polity and economy, as well as to assess the prospects for banking reform. The discussion begins with an assessment of the state of the sector in early 2001, before turning to consider in turn the banks' political and economic role in Russia since the August 1998 financial crisis. This will be followed by an examination of the outlook for banking reform, a look at the interim 'coping' strategies being devised to compensate for the weakness of the banking sector and a brief conclusion.

THE STATE OF THE SECTOR

Assessing the health of Russia's banking sector remains notoriously difficult.[1] While the overall quality of Russian economic data has improved in recent years, there remain particular problems with banking data. First, there are good reasons to doubt the completeness and accuracy of banks' reporting of their positions to the Central Bank of Russia (CBR). Secondly, the data are based on Russian rather than international accounting standards. Russian accounting standards (RAS) leave the banks much greater freedom to decide whether or how to classify problem loans and do not generally require assets such as securities to be marked to market.[2] Thirdly, the official data do not fully cover banks' off-balance sheet exposure, including the ruble–dollar forwards concluded before August 1998 and subsequently defaulted on by many banks.[3] In early 2001, the CBR, after a two-year delay, began exploring steps to resolve the forwards issue, suggesting that this exposure was not the irrelevance that many had thought it to be (*Vremya novostei*, 7 February 2001;

Vedomosti, 7 February 2001). Nevertheless, even if one makes generous allowance for these data problems, it is likely that the trends they reveal are genuine. Moreover, if they are read with other evidence in mind, then the overall picture of developments since mid-1998 is both consistent and plausible.

That picture is of a steady recovery of capital, assets and profits from the beginning of 1999, when the sector as a whole was, as the CBR acknowledged, effectively bankrupt (Agentstvo RosBiznesKonsalting, 14 April 1999). Total capital rose by 120.1 per cent in real terms from 1 January 1999 to 1 November 2000, with 87 per cent of Russian banks recording increases in capitalization. Gross assets increased by 53.1 per cent in real terms over the same period. Total assets actually declined slightly at the end of 2000, but this appears to have been a year-end tidying of balance sheets, since all categories of asset continued to grow except reserves and claims on other financial institutions. The sector's capital-to-asset ratio rose from 7.3 per cent at 1 July 1999 to 10.7 per cent at 1 July 2000. Return on assets and capital for the twelve months to 1 July 2000 recovered to 0.7 per cent and 7.1 per cent respectively, from –3.4 per cent for ROA and –44.0 per cent for ROC for the year to 1 July 1999.

The quality of banks' portfolios also improved in 1999–2000. Overdue credits as a share of total ruble credits outstanding fell from 13.2 per cent at 1 January 1999 to 3.1 per cent at 1 November 2000. The corresponding figures for credits granted in foreign currency were 10.2 per cent and 6.3 per cent respectively. The proportion of 'non-standard' loans declined from 7.2 to 4.8 per cent, the share of 'doubtful' loans from 6.0 to 1.9 per cent and that of 'hopeless' ones from 11.3 to 5.0 per cent. Thus, 11.6 per cent of bank credits outstanding were problematic to some degree at the end of 2000, as against 24.6 per cent at end-1998. These indicators doubtless understate the share of problem assets in banks' portfolios, but the declining trend they reflect is real enough. This improvement in loan portfolios is chiefly a result of the dramatic improvement in the financial condition of non-financial enterprises. The term structure of banks' balance sheets also improved during 1999–2000, although long-term assets continued to exceed long-term liabilities. The CBR's preferred indicator for assessing the risks posed by this gap is to compare the gap between long-term assets and long-term liabilities to the total of attracted funds with terms of less than one year. The logic here is that the excess long-term assets must be financed by short-term liabilities: the greater the share of short-term liabilities set against long-term assets, the greater the risk of liquidity problems. This indicator fell from 21.1 per cent at end-1998 to 11.1 per cent at 1 November 2000. In other words, a far smaller share of short-term liabilities was required to cover long-term assets.

Most indicators of banking activity were, at the end of 2000, still below pre-crisis levels, but they were rising fast and would appear to have overtaken their pre-August 1998 peaks in early 2001 (*Segodnya*, 12 April 2001). Moreover, many of the pre-crisis strains that emerged from late 1994 as the banks struggled to cope with the consequences of government stabilization policies are no longer an issue.[4] Thus, the share of banks reckoned by the CBR to be in 'critical condition' fell from 18.6 per cent at the end of 1998 to 3.0 per cent at 1 November 2000. The proportion suffering 'serious financial difficulties' dropped from 14.0 to 8.8 per cent over the period.

The banks' recovery largely reflects the CBR's decision to bail the sector out after August 1998,[5] but it also reflects the very conservative strategies the banks themselves adopted in the wake of the crisis. Instead of lending to real-sector borrowers – or even to each other (the inter-bank market remains very small) – banks sought to minimize risk and maximize liquidity. According to one estimate based on data covering the top 100 banks (by assets) in the first half of 2000, funds placed in foreign banks, correspondent accounts or super-short-term (up to 7 days) deposits accounted for 13 per cent of the top 100's assets, up from 10 per cent a year earlier. Another 13 per cent was in government securities, and 12 per cent was held in correspondent accounts and deposits with the CBR. If foreign exchange on hand and other highly liquid assets were included, then around two-thirds of the top 100's total assets took the form of highly liquid reserves. One of the most marked indicators of this tendency was the steady increase in commercial banks' deposits with the CBR, from Rb64.1 billion at end-1998 to Rb264.2 billion at 1 January 2001. The balances in their CBR correspondent accounts rose from Rb28–30 billion in early 1999 to Rb76–77 billion in April 2001 (*Reuters*, 12 March 2001). This accumulation of funds with the CBR, usually at negative real rates of interest, highlighted banks' preference for low risk and high liquidity.

Not all banking risks declined after 1998. Many banks continued to lend heavily to shareholders and to firms in which they held stakes. Indeed, the resurgence of the 'pocket bank' was one of the most noticeable responses to the crisis, as large non-financial companies shifted their business back to banks over which they exercised a substantial degree of control (*Profil'*, 22 February 1999). This trend was reflected in the CBR's estimate that around 30 per cent of sector assets in early 2001 were accounted as large credit risks. The banks were also vulnerable to any liberalization of the currency control regime, since much of their new-found liquidity consisted of short-term deposits necessitated by the requirement that exporters sell 75 per cent of their foreign exchange earnings for rubles.[6] Finally, it is crucial to note that the banks' improved health was chiefly a result of the broader improvement in economic conditions rather than aggressive restructuring or other behavioural changes on their part. Russian banks were healthier than they had been, but they were not as sound as they appeared, and they remained highly vulnerable to an economic downturn. Nevertheless, the sector was in much better shape in early 2001 than it had been two years earlier, and the CBR had good reason to believe that the risk of a systemic crisis had been substantially reduced.

Ironically, the banks' recovery coincided with a marked decline in their political and economic importance. This is far from coincidental: many of the factors that contributed to the banks' improved financial health were closely linked to both their reduced political influence and their limited impact on the non-financial sector. The following sections explore these two issues in turn.

POLITICAL IRRELEVANCE: THE RISE AND FALL OF THE BANKS

Politically, Russian banks are no longer the force that they were. While conflicts among Russian business 'clans' remain a feature of political and commercial life, the 'banking wars' of the 1990s have given way to 'oligarch hunting', and to conflicts among powerful groupings in various industrial sectors. It is battles among oil companies, metals producers and other industrial concerns – not bankers – that dominate the headlines where commerce and politics meet. The politically prominent bankers of the 1990s who remain major players are those who used their banking bases to secure positions in other sectors. Thus, Vladimir Potanin is more closely involved with Interros and, in particular, Norilsk Nickel, than with Uneksimbank or Rosbank. Even before the August collapse, Mikhail Khodorkovskii had left Bank Menatep to head the Rosprom Financial–Industrial Group. Today, he is more closely identified with Rosprom and Yukos than with any of Menatep's 'successor' banks. And for Vladimir Gusinskii, Media Most and NTV were always more important than Most Bank. At the same time, leading bankers such as SBS-Agro's Aleksandr Smolenskii and Inkombank's Vladimir Vinogradov, who failed to establish themselves as dominant players in other sectors, proved far more vulnerable after the crisis.

The authorities' attitude towards the banking sector further underscores its irrelevance. The Kasyanov government showed scant interest in the issue of banking reform in its first year. The government's medium- and long-term plans barely addressed it, and President Vladimir Putin failed even to mention it in his annual message to the Federal Assembly in April 2001 – a speech that touched on virtually every other structural reform issue (Putin,

2001). In general, the government has left banking reform to the CBR, which has done little other than bail out the banks in the immediate aftermath of the collapse. 'Restructuring' was largely confined to the issuing of stabilization credits and other liquidity injections. Once the crisis was past and the normal operation of the payments system restored, bank restructuring declined rapidly in salience. The pace of licence withdrawals slowed, allowing those in charge of failed banks to siphon off assets (frequently into new banks), leaving little more than an empty shell for creditors. Nor did passage of a law on the bankruptcy of credit institutions in March 1999 lead to the anticipated upsurge in licence withdrawals and bankruptcies. Instead, the CBR began to play down the need for such measures (RIA-Novosti, 14 April 1999; *Finansovaya Rossiya*, 8 April 1999). CBR chief Viktor Gerashchenko, who had predicted after the crisis that the post-restructuring sector would comprise some 200–300 institutions, told the State Duma in March 1999 that more than 1 000 were likely to remain (RIA-Novosti, 19 March 1999). The CBR's February 2001 report on 'conceptual questions' of banking system development (CBR 2001) can only be described as a manifesto of 'don't-rock-the-boatism'. The report addresses many of the sector's problems and rightly identifies much that needs to be done, but it commits the CBR to very little – most of its proposals are addressed to the government and the Federal Assembly – and it stresses the need to proceed with caution.

How can we explain the banks' political marginalization? In fact, it is not their decline but rather their period of (apparent) hegemony that needs explaining. The first point to emphasize is that the banks' power was never as great as it appeared. Even at the peak of their political influence, Russian banks were small and not terribly stable. Their liquid liabilities were small relative to GDP, as were their claims on the private sector; their survival depended chiefly on the patronage of the state, to which they were closely linked in every sphere of activity (Sutela, 1998a, p. 99; Tompson, 1997, pp. 1170–78; Tompson, 1998a, pp. 215–34). Indeed, although the banking sector in the mid-1990s was regarded by some as the sector 'most advanced as far as the progress of market reforms is concerned' (Zhuravskaya, 1995, p. 167), it actually had a strong claim to being the most subsidized in the Russian economy. The subsidies it received persisted even as state support for other sectors dried up – partly because they were usually implicit rather than explicit. The much-vaunted influence of Russia's banks in the mid-1990s must thus be viewed alongside this very dependent position *vis-à-vis* the state. The relationship between major banks and the government was often presented as one in which powerful banks dominated a weak state. In fact, both were weak. The state's reliance on the banks reflected its inability to perform a number of basic functions, while the banks' reliance on the state reflected their limited ability to survive without easy access to state funds. What the scandals of 1996–98 highlighted was the extent to which the banks' future depended on this access. The so-called 'banking wars' of 1997 reflected banks' vulnerability more than their strength. Tighter monetary policies, exchange rate stabilization, falling yields on government securities and lower inflation all hit banks hard. Central bank credit became more expensive, tougher reserve requirements were imposed and access to budgetary funds was curtailed. With so many sources of state subsidy drying up, the battle for those that remained, and especially for control of state assets still to be privatized, could not but escalate.

Nevertheless, Russia's major banks appeared for a time to dominate the political scene, persuading or compelling the government to sell them the state's most valuable assets at bargain-basement prices. The loans-for-shares deals of 1995 and the ensuing privatization auctions in 1996–97 appeared to confirm the impression that real power in Russia rested with the banks. While this impression was exaggerated, there was much substance to it. How, then, did the banks come to achieve, for a time at least, this apparent hegemony? The answer to this question, which goes a long way to explaining the banks' subsequent political decline, involves a number of factors, including cabinet politics, state weakness, fiscal crisis, electoral pressures and generalized illiquidity. In essence, for a brief period in the mid-1990s, the banks were able to exploit a peculiarly favourable – and, as it turned out, transitory – set of political and economic circumstances.

Banks in the early 1990s were not an especially powerful lobby at federal level. This was the period when industrial lobbies came to dominate the government. The government's industrial lobby grew steadily more influential in the cabinet from June 1992, as growing resistance to the 'market Bolshevism' of the Gaidar government led to the promotion of 'industrialists' like Viktor Chernomyrdin, Oleg Soskovets and Oleg Lobov, who favoured a retreat from radical reform. Ironically, this trend became particularly pronounced in the last quarter of 1993. As the conservatives in parliament were crushed by Yeltsin, the conservative wing of the cabinet grew more powerful – a shift that was reinforced by the results of the December 1993 elections. The banks, for their part, were making easy profits from trade finance, foreign exchange speculation and the handling of state accounts, soft credits, and so on. They did not at this stage evince much interest in using their rapidly growing wealth for political ends, beyond ensuring that these activities continued. The government's remaining liberal reformers, who were later identified very closely with the leading banks, at this stage viewed them with suspicion. This was partly because so many banks were such obviously shaky (and shady) institutions; partly because they were closely tied to the CBR, then headed by the reformers' *bête noir*, Gerashchenko; and partly because they were perceived as enemies of stabilization. It was no accident that the architects of Russian privatization policies in 1992–93 sought to limit the banks' role in the privatization process. The privatization programme confirmed on 24 December 1993 stated that banks could not purchase equity stakes in enterprises undergoing privatization and limited banks' shareholdings to 10 per cent of the shares of any given company and 5 per cent of the banks' own assets (RF Government, 1994).

Things changed dramatically in 1995, chiefly as a result of the tightening of liquidity throughout the economy as a result of stabilization policies. The government's fiscal problems grew more acute, as did the real sector's problems with access to finance. While there had been widespread complaints about inflation's erosion of working capital in 1992–93, the flow of soft credits and other official support to enterprises was still substantial during this period, and industrial enterprises were net beneficiaries of credit emission, at least in the short term (Layard and Richter, 1994). Industrial firms' problems with access to capital became acute only as policy was tightened. Inflation ceased to erode the value of their debts, the flow of soft CBR credits ceased and high yields on government paper drew banks towards the GKO market. The share of bank credit among all sources of enterprise financing fell from 20.6 per cent in the last quarter of 1994 (already well below the levels of 1992–93) to 10.9 per cent in January–March 1997 (RECEP, 1997, p. 110). Since other sources of finance were also shrinking, the absolute decline was even more dramatic. This was also the period in which barter and non-monetary exchange began to grow most rapidly and payment arrears exploded. Banks, too, felt the strain of stabilization, but, with a near-monopoly on ruble liquidity in a liquidity-starved economy, they found it easy to exploit the situation. As Gaddy and Ickes (1998) observed, 'in the land of the cashless, the man with pocket change is king, or at least an oligarch. . . . It is the Russian tycoons' relatively cash-rich status in a cashless economy that gives them so much power.'

Other factors strengthened the banks further. The beleaguered position of Boris Yeltsin's Kremlin in 1995–96 left it particularly vulnerable to bank lobbying, while the government's remaining liberal reformers searched for allies to help them shore up their positions in a cabinet dominated increasingly by the likes of Chernomyrdin and Soskovets. At the same time, leading industrialists began to develop their own links to major banks (other than the pocket banks already created by many big firms). Corruption, too, appears to have played a role. While official corruption was hardly a phenomenon unique to the Russia of the mid-1990s, the instability and uncertainty of 1995–96 do appear to have fuelled it, particularly at the highest levels. In late 1995, officials in the government apparatus claimed that the main problem they faced in dealing with the Kremlin was that their colleagues in the presidential administration were busy planning for 'life after Yeltsin', arranging jobs for themselves outside the Kremlin and establishing contacts in the business community.[7] Officials who believed the Yeltsin era would soon end would have made far easier targets for the banks' lobbying efforts.

It would, nevertheless, be a mistake to view the give-away privatization deals of the mid-1990s solely in terms of the banks' political muscle.[8] Such deals generally took place when the banks had managed to forge alliances with key industrial companies: hostile acquisitions were rare and were fiercely contested. Even prior to the collateral auctions, banks had generally preferred acquiring stakes in enterprises with whose managers they had close relationships (Freinkman, 1995, p. 61). Despite their enormous financial problems, the industrialists' position was far from weak. In the absence of a credible bankruptcy threat, they did not need to surrender control to outsiders simply because their finances were a mess, nor were they inclined to do so. Indeed, the vast majority of enterprises originally slated for inclusion in the infamous loans-for-shares auctions were able to lobby their way out.[9] In the end, only nine of the original list of 64 actually ended up on the auction block. Of these, three had the funds to secure control of their own shares, albeit in auctions that effectively excluded other participants, and five were acquired by banks to which they had very close links. The only major exception was the non-ferrous metals giant Norilsk Nickel. Oneksimbank acquired a controlling stake in this concern against its managers' wishes and had to fight a protracted legal, commercial and political battle to secure real control.

Viewed in the light of the above, the banks' political decline appears relatively straightforward. The most important factor of all was clearly the passing of the extreme illiquidity that afflicted the economy during 1995–98. The situation was transformed so completely in the aftermath of the August devaluation that the main problem afflicting the financial system in 2000 was *excess* liquidity. The re-monetization of the real sector and the related dramatic turnaround in the fiscal position greatly reduced the banks' political leverage. At the same time, the political situation stabilized under Vladimir Putin and the government's liberal wing grew much stronger. The corporate balance of forces also changed. In the post-devaluation recovery that began in 1999, money was made chiefly from the economic rents associated with the exploitation of natural resources. Control over oil, gas and metals, rather than mere liquidity (which was no longer such a scarce commodity), represented the keys to real wealth. This coincided with the maturing of the superstructures of the more dynamic groupings such as Rosprom and Interros. The banks' management of company shares became less direct, and the centre of gravity within these groupings shifted from the banks to the parent holdings.

This shift in the internal balance of power within the groupings also reflects the shift in the sources of their profits. In the mid-1990s, super-profits were earned in the government securities markets, where real yields on short-term GKOs reached triple-digit annual rates. In this environment, the incentives to strip industrial assets and accumulate payment arrears in order to play the GKO market were enormous. This is precisely what many managers did. In the post-crisis recovery, however, it was exports, particularly oil exports, that generated super-profits. Even many of Russia's processing industries returned to profit. In this environment, the banks' role as profit-generators was dramatically reduced. While it was encouraging that profits were being generated by real activity rather than financial speculation, rent-seeking formed the primary basis for profit in both instances. Using assets acquired through shady privatization deals to extract and export raw materials in 2000 was only marginally more entrepreneurial an activity than lending the state its own money had been in the 1990s. Neither had much of an impact in terms of wealth-creation.

ECONOMIC IRRELEVANCE: BANKS THAT (STILL) DON'T BANK

Economically, banking remains a vitally important sector, at least in a negative sense: a banking crisis that paralysed the payments system for even a short time could have serious knock-on effects for the rest of the economy. Memories of the paralysis that followed the 1998 financial collapse remain fresh, and the authorities' approach to the sector cannot be understood without reference to that experience.[10] The maintenance of financial stability and, in particular, the smooth functioning of the payments system have been the chief objectives of the CBR in managing the sector since 1998.

If the consequences of a banking crisis are potentially dire, the sector's potential *positive* impact on the real economy is limited. It remains very small, both in international comparison and relative to GDP. According to the CBR, the gross capitalization of the banking sector at 1 January 2001 did not exceed 4 per cent of GDP. Gross assets amounted to no more than about 35 per cent of GDP. Nor do Russian banks engage much in lending to the non-financial private sector. In early 2001, such lending was only slightly above 30 per cent of the sector's total assets, not much changed from pre-crisis levels.[11] The share of bank credits in the total volume of investment in fixed assets in 2000 has been variously estimated at between 3.9 per cent and 10 per cent (CBR, 2001, prilozh. 1; *Vedomosti*, 23 January 2001). This disconnection between the financial and real sectors is, of course, both cause and consequence of banks' preference for the conservative, high-liquidity strategies described above. Such strategies keep banks safe but make them less relevant to the real sector.

Ironically, managerial surveys suggest that this state of affairs does not particularly trouble real-sector companies.[12] They have long been used to doing without bank lending, and their improved financial condition means that they are better able to finance both working capital and investment from retained profits. Moreover, the rapid real growth in bank assets has meant that access to credit has improved despite the limited share of bank assets devoted to enterprise lending. Most lending is in any case for relatively short terms, while the real problem for real-sector companies is the dearth of resources available for investment over the long term. Given the term-structure of their liabilities, most banks are still in no position to do much long-term lending even should they wish to do so. Long-term liabilities (that is, those with terms of over one year) amount to about 8 per cent of total liabilities. Long-term assets constitute about 30 per cent of total assets. The largest share of long-term assets consists of government paper, which is liquid enough to hold for relatively long periods and can easily be realized in the event of a liquidity squeeze. Few banks could or would risk extending long-term loans to real-sector enterprises on any scale.

This is hardly surprising. The underlying obstacles to the banks' development as real financial intermediaries have not been addressed since the crisis, so there is no reason the banks should be much more effective at financial intermediation than they were before August 1998.[13] Most of these obstacles have little or nothing to do with the banking sector itself. Part of the problem is to be found in the dearth of borrowers who are good credit risks.[14] It can be extraordinarily difficult to assess a would-be borrower's financial health given problems with RAS accounts and the difficulty of making valid assessments on the basis of historical financial information in what is, after all, a very rapidly changing economic environment. Most potential borrowers simply do not have long credit histories, and large numbers of Russian borrowers have shown a marked tendency to view debt repayment as optional. Russian corporates also tend to be a good deal more secretive than Western companies. While the situation appears to be improving, it will be some time before lenders forget the non-payments crises of the 1990s. Moreover, even where an apparently creditworthy borrower can be identified with confidence, the inadequacy of the legal framework can make lending difficult. Procedures for realizing collateral or pursuing bankruptcy are not particularly creditor-friendly. Finally, most Russian banks still lack the skills needed for credit assessment.

The banks' connection to the rest of the economy is similarly limited on the liability side of the balance sheet. One of the major functions of the banking system is supposed to be to mobilize and aggregate savings not otherwise available for investment, assuming the costs of collecting deposits and reducing informational asymmetries in order to make savers comfortable with the idea of relinquishing immediate control over their funds (Levine, 1997, p. 699). This the Russian banking system remains manifestly unable to do. Trust in banks remains low, particularly among households, which continue to hold a large share of their savings in foreign (mainly dollar) cash and remain deeply suspicious of the commercial banks. According to the CBR, household deposits in the banking system as of 1 November 2000 stood at just 68 per cent of their pre-crisis levels in real terms. As before the crisis, the overwhelming preponderance of these deposits are held with the state-owned Savings Bank of the Russian Federation (Sberbank). In April 2001, Sberbank held 86.2 per cent of household ruble deposits and 49.4 per cent of household deposits in foreign currency (Reuters, 12 April 2001).

The absence of any form of deposit insurance makes it virtually impossible for commercial banks to compete with Sberbank in the retail market, because the state guarantees Sberbank deposits. This allows Sberbank to dominate the retail market despite the fact that interest rates on its deposits are often negative in real terms. The higher interest rates offered by commercial banks are generally insufficient to offset the security to be found in Sberbank. In any case, the extent to which higher interest rates would make households more inclined to bank their savings is limited. The real disincentive to banking private savings is that it exposes them to the tax organs. Sberbank, for its part, continues to operate credit policies that reflect the requirements of economic policy as much as, if not more than, commercial expedience. Thus, in the first half of 2000, Sberbank's ruble deposits grew by Rb60 billion, while its credit portfolio expanded by just Rb17.6 billion (Polit.ru, 2000b). In general, the bank in 2000 pursued a strategy that effectively removed a considerable volume of liquidity from the economy – precisely what the CBR, which holds a majority stake in Sberbank, wanted it to do.

Despite these problems, banking reform has not been an urgent priority. Despite many reports and much discussion, little was done in the two-and-a-half years following the August crisis about the transition to IAS accounts, the formation of a system of deposit insurance or the strengthening of the CBR's supervision and regulation of the sector – issues that have been on the policy agenda since long before August 1998. Nor, despite repeated promises to the contrary, was anything done about easing foreign access to the sector. The reasons for this lack of urgency will be explored below. First, however, it is necessary to consider the consequences of this neglect. Russia badly needs an efficient, effective, sound banking system in which banks engage in financial intermediation on a commercial basis. The thinness of Russian financial markets and the underdevelopment of the banking system mean that the economy is ill-equipped to channel investment resources to their most efficient uses. There is little capacity for allocating capital across, rather than merely within, sectors. Thus, the investment recovery that began in 1999 appears to have remained concentrated in a few highly profitable sectors. The fuel and energy complex in 2000 absorbed over 60 per cent of total investment in fixed capital (Putin, 2001). This is all the more worrying given that Russia's medium- to long-term prospects depend on investment-based growth even more than do those of most other transition economies (Sutela, 1998a, pp. 100–105), largely owing to the greater severity of the structural distortions inherited from central planning.[15] The development of a banking system capable of mobilizing and efficiently allocating domestic savings will be critical to Russian growth prospects, particularly given its size, its limited attractions for foreign investors and the limits on its firms' capacity to finance investment from retained earnings (Sutela, 1998a, pp. 107, 120).

THE OBSTACLES TO BANKING REFORM

In the immediate aftermath of the financial crisis, the Russian authorities evinced little interest in pursuing the sort of bank reform agenda that would facilitate the emergence of a network of real financial intermediaries. Their principal concerns were using the banks more effectively as agents of the fisc, ensuring the smooth operation of the payments system (and the processing of budgetary payments in particular), and using the banks to support the government's attempts to formulate and implement some form of 'industrial policy' (Tompson, 2000a, pp. 65–93). These priorities have changed. The turnaround in the fiscal position has greatly lessened the urgency of the tax-collection issue, while the banks' recovery has eased concerns about a banking crisis and its possible implications for the payments system. Elements of the third priority remain prominent in the government's thinking, although the Kasyanov government is generally more liberal than the Primakov cabinet was, and its ambitions in the field of industrial policy are consequently rather less ambitious. Nevertheless, neither the government nor the CBR appears interested in forcing the pace of bank reform. Indeed, when the State Duma approved a trio of bank reform bills at second reading in April 2001, over 18 months after the government had introduced them, Gerashchenko remarked that the issues the bills addressed 'had lost their earlier urgency' (*Vremya-novostei*, 19 April 2001), while First Deputy Finance Minister Sergei Ignat'ev stated that it would be at least another 18 months before any further measures to improve banking legislation were passed (*Vedomosti*, 19 April 2001).

Politically, the low priority attached to banking reform by the Russian authorities makes sense. First, the government's agenda is already crowded with politically contentious structural reform issues; it can easily leave banking reform to one side at present. The CBR bears primary responsibility for the state of the sector, and the government can argue, with some justice, that many of its other reforms will facilitate the development of financial intermediation. These include, *inter alia*, judicial reform, the creation of a legal framework that facilitates contract enforcement, the protection of property rights, accountancy reform and other measures to improve the quality and availability of enterprise-level financial information. Real financial intermediation will take some time to develop, even in the best of circumstances. Even given an ideal legislative framework, expertise, experience, confidence and meaningful credit histories would all take time to develop. The process could, of course, be accelerated by allowing foreign banks a greater role in the sector, thereby effectively 'importing' some of their expertise and credibility. However, merely opening the sector to non-resident banks will not be enough in the absence of significant improvements in both the legislation on the books and the administration of law in practice. In any case, the critical point remains that the evolution of Russia's banking sector into a real system of financial intermediation will be a very long-term project. Yet if the benefits of such a system, however great they may be, will be realized only over a long period, the same cannot be said of the costs, which will be substantial and, in many cases, up front. This in itself is a deterrent to reform.

A further problem is that the short-term requirements of political and economic management are often difficult to reconcile with the long-term structural needs of the economy. The CBR's cautious approach to reform is partly a reflection of this awareness. The CBR is keenly aware that 'hasty action in adopting and realizing important decisions' could 'destabilize' the sector and undermine confidence (CBR, 2001, para. 3.2.6). The economy is growing for the first time in over a decade and the banks appear to be relatively stable; the authorities are understandably reluctant to do anything that might jeopardize either the recovery or the stability of the sector. Hence the slow progress of accountancy reform, for example. The CBR is aware of the necessity of shifting banks onto IAS but has repeatedly postponed the transition. The problem is that the move to IAS will reveal that banks' capital-adequacy ratios are much lower than they appear and that their portfolios contain a much larger share of problem assets than is currently acknowledged. This will have an impact on both confidence in the sector and the banks' financial position. The real cost of the transition will arise not from retraining accountants or replacing computer programmes but from taking the steps needed to shore up balance sheets in light of the IAS results. A similar story obtains with respect to the proposals for liberalizing the currency-control regime. While acknowledging the problems created by currency controls, senior CBR officials fear that rapid liberalization could harm the banks, which now benefit from mandatory surrender requirements and other regulations. In short, the authorities are aware of what needs to be done to strengthen the sector in the long run, but are reluctant to press ahead too quickly for fear of the short-term consequences.[16]

Like other structural reforms, banking reform faces a more general difficulty: it is a public good. A successful reform would bring substantial long-term benefits in the form of improved economic performance. However, these benefits would be extremely diffuse and would profit economic agents whether or not they had contributed to the implementation of reforms or borne their costs. Yet these costs will have to be borne by specific interests which are aware of what real, rigorous reform would mean to them – specifically, the banks, their favoured clients and the officials at federal and regional level who remain heavily involved in resource allocation within the financial system. Each of these groups has done well out of a decade of 'banking' activity concerned chiefly with rent-seeking, political allocation and state support. The costs of reform for the banks are obvious: tighter supervision, greater transparency and the need to operate on a truly commercial footing all imply both costs and substantial risks. Many industrial managers would rather secure such credit as they receive on the basis of cross-shareholdings, personal connections and political lobbying. These are all far more familiar and, in many cases, more comfortable than the disciplines of a real market-based financial system. And the attachment of the Kasyanov government to plans for increasing the role of state banks (Grozovskii, 2000; Polit.ru, 2000a) suggests that even the relatively liberal federal government cannot quite give up on political allocation of credit.[17] Moreover, as noted above, any benefits that a successful banking reform might bring would be evident only in the very long term, and it is unclear how they would be distributed. There is good reason to suspect that credit resources would be allocated very differently than at present, so the beneficiaries of the present arrangements are right to be wary of reform. Given that the benefits of reform will be distant, diffuse and uncertain, the incentives to free ride are enormous.

In the circumstances, therefore, it is not difficult to make the case that the CBR's approach – incremental reform with the priority being to avoid disruption and conflict and thereby build trust – may be the most sensible strategy to pursue. The question is where incrementalism stops and immobilism begins. By the end of 2000, many critics had concluded that the CBR was practising the latter even as it proclaimed the virtues of the former. The end of 2000 saw the central bank launch a pilot project concerning the shift to IAS accounting, which was to involve six banks over a period of 16 months, enabling them to produce IAS accounts for 2001. Shifting the entire sector onto IAS is expected to take several more years (EIU, 2000, p. 26; UFG, 2001). Nor has there been much evidence of haste on the issue of deposit insurance, proposals for which have circulated in the State Duma since the mid-1990s. After more than half-a-decade of discussion, debate in early 2001 was focused on proposals for a pilot project involving six banks (*Izvestiya*, 17 April 2001). Even if such a system is created, Sberbank will retain a significant competitive edge unless it is a full participant: if its state guarantee allows it to avoid paying deposit insurance premia or to pay at a reduced rate – as has been proposed – then the competitive playing field will remain uneven (*Segodnya*, 13 April 2001; *Vedomosti*, 24 April 2001). In many cases, the CBR can reasonably argue that legislation and government action are required if progress is to be made – and the signals coming from the government in early 2001 did not suggest that it was inclined to make banking legislation a top priority. Indeed, one of the striking things about the CBR's February 2001 bank reform strategy is how many of its specific recommendations were directed either at the banks themselves or at other state institutions. It contained very few specifics about what the CBR itself would do and when, particularly on issues that might lead to conflict with the banks.

THE SEARCH FOR SHORTCUTS

If the foregoing analysis is correct, then banking reform will proceed incrementally and the development of a properly functioning 'normal' banking system in Russia is likely – even in the best of circumstances – to take well over a decade. Yet the problem of allocating resources across sectors remains acute. It should come as no surprise, therefore, that both the state and private agents have sought shortcuts, that is, institutional arrangements that will enable them to channel funds across sectors to where they will yield the best returns. The two major approaches both have troubling implications for Russia's long-term development: the further extension of the state's role in the banking sector, and the development of huge new industrial conglomerates along the lines of South Korea's *chaebol* – in essence, a resurgence of the financial–industrial groups (FPGs) that had begun to form prior to the August crisis, although not explicitly designated as such.

Many in the government appear to favour the further development of state banks. Despite its generally liberal orientation, the Kasyanov government has moved forward, in fits and starts, with projects for the creation of new state banks and the consolidation of existing ones, including the new Russian Development Bank (RBR), the Russian Bank for Agriculture (Rosselkhozbank), the All-Russian Bank for Regional Development (VBRR) and a new bank that is likely to be formed as a result of the restructuring of Vneshekonombank (VEB). VEB's commercial departments are to be merged with the much smaller Russian Export–Import Bank (Roseximbank) to create a new bank for export promotion. The merged bank could have charter capital of Rb22–25 billion, as compared with the Rb51 million of the under-capitalized Roseximbank. To these must be added the two large banks controlled by the CBR, Sberbank and Vneshtorgbank (VTB). The CBR is already the monetary authority, the banking regulator and the banking sector's largest single creditor, as well as the institution empowered to take most major decisions pertaining to the bankruptcy of a credit organization. Its position as owner of the sector's two largest banks is thus fraught with conflicts of interest, and the authorities have finally agreed, under IMF pressure, that the CBR's role as owner should be wound up. It is transferring its stakes in Russian state banks abroad (the so-called *Roszagranbanki*) to VTB and is now committed to disposing of its VTB shares by the beginning of 2003. The commitment to the CBR's withdrawal from Sberbank is less clear, and it will remain in control of the savings giant until at least the beginning of 2005 (*Vedomosti*, 18 and 20 October 2000). Whether Sberbank and VTB will actually be privatized also remains to be seen. It is entirely possible that the government will take control of the state shares in these banks. The presidential administration, eager to secure a role for itself in this area, has proposed that the state banks be managed by a collegium including representatives of the CBR, the government and the presidential administration, but, unsurprisingly, the CBR and the cabinet have shown little enthusiasm for this idea (*Vedomosti*, 3 November 2000).

More generally, the authorities' position with respect to the role of the state in the banking sector is somewhat contradictory. In principle, the state's presence in the sector is rather larger than the CBR or the government would like.[18] In practice, the authorities' behaviour suggests that they remain deeply attached to the control over major financial flows that a large pool of state banks gives them. The CBR is extremely reluctant to relinquish its stakes or to level the competitive playing field between Sberbank and the commercial banks. It remains attached to the use of Sberbank, in particular, as an instrument of monetary policy. In early 2001 the CBR proposed a 10–15 year transition period prior to Sberbank's full inclusion in any system of deposit insurance (*Segodnya*, 13 April 2001). The government, for its part, sees state banks as vehicles for its industrial policy, although the aims and criteria guiding that policy are not entirely clear. Thus, it has moved ahead, albeit slowly, with the development of the RBR and Rosselkhozbank without clearly indicating how they will work.

As a result, the state's already large role in the sector has expanded steadily since the financial crisis. According to the CBR, the state holds a majority stake in some 23 credit institutions, including those banks controlled by the federal government and the CBR. As of October 2000, the state's share of total banking sector capital stood at 28.4 per cent, up from 11.9 per cent in July 1998 and 22.4 per cent in January 2000. Predominantly state-owned banks accounted for 34.7 per cent of the sector's assets (Nazarova, 2000, p. 1; CBR, 2001, para. 3.2.1). These figures do not include the 15 banks under the tutelage of the Agency for the Reconstruction of Credit Institutions (ARCO), nor do they include the many privately owned regional banks under the *de facto* control of regional administrations. The federal authorities' role is larger than their capital share implies, since those figures include state stakes in banks that, while partially privatized, are still controlled by the state, like Sberbank. Sberbank and VTB, the two largest banks in the system in terms of both capital and assets, are both state banks. Together, they accounted for 30.4 per cent of total bank capital and 28.8 per cent of banking sector assets as of 1 January 2001.[19]

The predominance of state-owned banks in the sector poses two problems. The first is their tendency to act on the basis of political and/or policy considerations rather than commercial ones. This makes for inefficiencies at best and corruption at worst. In addition, the regulatory and other privileges that state banks enjoy make it more difficult for commercial banks to compete with them. The official CBR line on state-owned banks is that their purpose should be to correct market failures. Their activities should be specialized in sectoral and other niches which the market, left to its own devices will not address, such as the financing of agriculture (Rosselkhozbank) or support for regional development policies (VBRR). The CBR also maintains that granting regulatory and other privileges to state-owned banks is both bad for competition and a source of systemic risk (Polit.ru, 2000a). Yet the government remains inclined to grant privileged access to budgetary funds and other perks to state banks. Agriculture Minister Aleksei Gordeyev even proposed that Rosselkhozbank could handle all transactions involving agricultural land, controlling the prices of such transactions so as to prevent 'speculative activity' (*Vedomosti*, 21 March 2001).

The CBR's defence of Sberbank's privileges is even more striking, given that Sberbank is hardly an institution with a specialized niche. It is now a universal bank, which continues to exploit its unique political position and its carefully protected retail monopoly to extend its business in other directions. The same can be said, albeit to a lesser degree, of VTB. Indeed the CBR (2001, para. 3.2.4) acknowledges that these two banks 'have gone far beyond the bounds of the specialization that characterized their activities in Soviet times and are universal with respect to both their circle of clients and the character of the tasks they handle. A return to specialization would be mistaken for these banks, from the perspective of their development strategy, as well as inefficient in practice.'

The expansion of both banks' corporate business has been especially noticeable. State support made it easy for Sberbank to grow its corporate business very rapidly in the wake of the August collapse, as corporate customers came to see reliability as virtually the sole criterion when choosing a bank. The share of corporate deposits on the liability side of its (rapidly growing) balance sheet rose from 5 per cent in the late 1990s to 23 per cent in 2001 (*Vedomosti*, 18 April 2001). This growth was closely linked to the rapid increase in its share of the corporate lending market: like most Russian banks, Sberbank prefers to lend to enterprises whose shares and/or accounts it holds. Loans to the real sector grew from 23.2 per cent of total bank lending to the non-financial private sector at the end of 1999 to 32.0 per cent at the end of 2000. With VTB accounting for a further 3.9 per cent, this left the two CBR-controlled banks with almost 36 per cent of real-sector lending on their books. This might suggest that two state-owned giants are undertaking precisely the lending that the private sector needs. However, most of this lending is still relatively short-term, and a look at Sberbank's medium- to long-term lending activity highlights its preference for politically well connected Russian 'blue chips', like the electricity monopolist RAO EES, Russian Aluminium, the Tyumen Oil Company and leading military aviation exporters (Sberbank, 2001).

In early 2001, it appeared that a new 'shortcut' was emerging as a private-sector solution to the problem. Cash-rich exporters in 2000 began aggressively acquiring undervalued industrial assets. A great deal of this can be seen as a form of 'vertical integration', with resource exporters such as the metallurgy sector acquiring control of both their suppliers (for example, in the coal sector) and their consumers (as in the case of Siberian Aluminium's acquisition of the Pavlovsk and Gorkii Automobile Plants). There are now around 40 big industrial groups, ranging from the obvious giants like Gazprom and the new metallurgical groupings, to much smaller groups that concentrate on one particular sector. This is not simply a return to the empire-building of the 1990s, however, for there are signs that the new conglomerates are interested in developing the businesses they acquire rather than merely extracting rents and stripping assets. They are dominated not by their banks – which are usually treated as corporate treasuries – but by revenue-rich export companies.

It is not yet clear whether, or to what extent, the creation of such *chaebol*-like structures will facilitate the efficient allocation of financial resources across sectors. For the moment, at least, financial resources are being devoted more to further acquisitions than to restructuring and investment, and it is too early to say much about the long-term significance of the new groupings, as it will be some time before it becomes clear how integrated they will be or how stable. However, there is plenty of room for doubt. Their loose structure and the extent to which they rest on informal networks and personal relationships means that they may prove far less durable than they appear. Much will also depend on the attitude of the core companies in the groupings: they may prefer not to develop the businesses they have acquired but rather to use their control over those businesses to concentrate profits at particular points in the production chain, extracting value from others, a practice all too familiar to observers of Russian corporate capitalism.

CONCLUSIONS

Despite the generally downbeat tone of most of the preceding analysis, there are good grounds for ending on a cautiously – and very modestly – optimistic note. The outlook for the sector's long-term evolution towards 'normal' banking is markedly more favourable than it was in the year or so following the August crisis. First, the most problematic proposals, such as Gerashchenko's call for a central-bank-led industrial policy dominated by state-directed investment, have fallen by the wayside (*Kommersant'-Daily*, 19 March 1999). Secondly, recent central bank proposals reflect a clear sense of what must be done to develop a sector characterized by transparency, competition and openness. The CBR is also alive to the dangers of state interference in credit allocation – though it retains a blind spot with respect to Sberbank and Vneshtorgbank – and of the need to break with the practice of politically directed lending by commercial banks, particularly in the regions (CBR 2001, paras. 3.3.1–2). While implementation of the necessary changes is proceeding very slowly, the monetary authority's stance on these issues is a welcome change. Thirdly, the State Duma in the summer of 2001 finally passed the bank reform legislation drafted by the government in consultation with the IMF in the wake of the financial collapse. Three key measures introduced into the chamber by the government in 1999 finally reached the statute books in June 2001.[20]

The new measures would introduce the notion of bank holdings and bank groups into Russian law, together with consolidated accounting for such structures – although the latter will mean little until IAS accounts are adopted. They would give the CBR the right to withdraw licences from banks with capital adequacy ratios of less than 2 per cent and would oblige it to initiate the liquidation of banks that had lost their licences and could not fulfil their obligations to creditors. The amendments would also give the CBR the right to do its own evaluation of a bank's capital and to require the bank to raise new capital if the CBR assessment showed a shortfall not reflected in the bank's own reporting. All these measures could, in principle, improve both the transparency of the sector and the CBR's oversight. However, two concerns remain. The first is the tendency of the CBR to acquire an ever wider range of powers, which often involve serious conflicts of interest, and the second, ironically, is its evident reluctance to use the powers it has to tighten up on the sector.

Crucially, the government and the Kremlin have, since the accession of Mr Putin to the presidency, shown a greater commitment to structural reform than any government since 1992. This is perhaps the most important factor of all, given that banking reform in isolation can achieve little: the development of the financial sector depends largely on what happens in the rest of the economy. Lending to real-sector firms (especially industrial companies) cannot take place on a commercial basis unless and until lenders can be confident that debts will be repaid and that effective action can be taken in the event of default. This will require not only better legislation governing, for example, creditor protection and the realization of collateral, but also improved accounting standards in both the real and the financial sectors, strengthening of the rule of law, and improvements in a host of spheres from corporate governance to taxation to competition policy. Above all, real-sector firms, no less than banks, must be subjected to the disciplines of the market and must be made more financially transparent. If the government makes progress on its broader structural reform agenda, therefore, the incremental pace of banking reform may not matter so much; if it does not, then even a more aggressive approach to banking reform will achieve little.

NOTES

1. Unless indicated otherwise, all data which follow are from the Central Bank of Russia (CBR) web site (http://www.cbr.ru).

2. The problems this creates were exemplified by Inkombank's results for 1998, its last year in operation: the bank's RAS results showed a healthy profit of $422m (despite losses of $700m on their loan portfolio), while its international accounting standards results showed a loss of $355m (United Financial Group 1999, p. 6).
3. According to Granville (2001), the notional value of outstanding forward foreign exchange contracts at the beginning of 1998 was $365 billion: more than 30 times the capital of the entire banking system.
4. For a look at the impact on the banks of the exchange-rate based stabilization strategy pursued by the authorities from 1995 to 1998, see Tompson (1997, pp. 1174–6).
5. For a description of the CBR's handling of the immediate aftermath of the crisis, see Tompson (1999, pp. 126–41) and (2000a, pp. 170–74).
6. For discussion of the link between liberalization of the currency control regime and the health of the banks, see *Vedomosti* (19 February 2001 and 14 March 2001) *Segodnya* (19 March 2001).
7. Private information.
8. For the best available account of the collateral auctions, see Duncan Allan, 'The "Loans-for-Shares" Auctions: Russian Banks as Lobbyists' (Centre for Russian & East European Studies, University of Birmingham: mimeo, 2001). See also chapter 6 in this collection.
9. The initial bank proposal for the scheme involved a list of some 64 enterprises. Yeltsin's 31 August decree included a list of 44, but within a fortnight this was reduced to 29, then 26 and, finally, by mid-October, just 16 (mainly in oil, metallurgy and river transport). For an excellent analysis of the collateral auctions, focusing on their dubious legality, see *Nezavisimaya gazeta* (27 January 1998).
10. For a close look at the CBR's unblocking of the payments system in late 1998, see Tompson (1999), pp. 132–4, and Tompson (1998b).
11. The CBR's *Byulleten' bankovskoi statistiki* 3 (94) (March 2001), p. 23, gives a figure of 33.81 per cent for claims on the non-financial private sector and households. Deducting the household share would yield a figure closer to 30 per cent.
12. See the surveys of the Institute for the Economy in Transition (http://www.iet.ru/) and the quarterly surveys published in the *Russian Economic Barometer*.
13. For a detailed discussion of the obstacles to the banks' development as real financial intermediaries, see Tompson (2000b).
14. This was one of Prime Minister Kasyanov's chief complaints when addressing the Association of Russian Banks in April 2001 (*Segodnya*, 12 April 2001; *Kommersant'-Daily*, 12 April 2001).
15. On the problems posed by Russia's inherited structural distortions, see Gaddy and Ickes (1999), pp. 95–7; Ericson (1998), p. 622; and Sutela (1998b), p. 4.
16. This dilemma is not by any means confined to banking reform. The need to maintain the current recovery constitutes a disincentive to reform in other areas as well, such as the liberalization of domestic energy prices.
17. This is not a view universally shared within the government; the Ministry for Economic Development and Trade is opposed to a growing role for state banks (*Vedomosti*, 3 November 2000).
18. See CBR (2001), para. 3.1–3.2. The April 2001 joint statement on economic policy issued by the government and the CBR (RF Government 2001) promised that no more new state banks would be created.
19. The former figure partly reflects VTB's high (28 per cent) capital-to-assets ratio: Sberbank alone accounted for 14.9 per cent of capital but 24.1 per cent of assets, while the corresponding figures for VTB were 15.5 per cent and 4.7 per cent respectively.
20. The texts of the amendments to the laws 'On Banks and Banking', 'On the Central Bank of the Russian Federation (Bank of Russia)' and 'On the Insolvency (Bankruptcy) of Credit Organizations' may be accessed via the links at http://www.akdi.ru/gd/proekt/GD01.HTM.

REFERENCES

CBR (2001), 'Kontseptual'nye voprosy razvitiya bankovskoi sistemy Rossiisskoi Federatsii', *Vestnik Banka Rossii* 12 (512).

EIU (2000), *Russia: Country Report*, London: Economist Intelligence Unit, December.

Ericson, Richard E. (1998), 'Economics and the Russian Transition', *Slavic Review* 57, 3.

Freinkman, Lev (1995), 'Financial-Industrial Groups: Emergence of Large Diversified Private Companies', *Communist Economies and Economic Transformation* 7, 1 (March), pp. 51–66.

Gaddy, Clifford G. and Barry W. Ickes (1998), 'Beyond a Bailout: Time to Face Reality about Russia's "Virtual Economy"', unpublished paper, June 1998, http://www.brook.edu/fp/articles/gaddy/gaddick1.htm.

Gaddy, Clifford G. and Barry W. Ickes (1999), 'An Accounting Model of the Virtual Economy in Russia', *Post-Soviet Geography and Economics* 40, 2.

Granville, Brigitte (2001), 'International Financial Architecture: A Russian Perspective', paper presented to the conference 'The Russian Banking Sector: Evolution, Problems and Prospects', Emmanuel College, Cambridge, 6 April.

Grozovskii, Boris (2000), 'Gosbanki: men'she no bol'she' (http://www.polit.ru/documents/362950.html).

Hellman, Joel (1996), 'Russia Adjusts to Stability', *Transition* (17 May), pp. 6–10.

Layard, Richard and Andrea Richter (1994), 'Who Gains and Loses from Credit Expansion?' *Russian Economic Trends* 2, 4.

Levine, Ross (1997) 'Financial Development and Economic Growth: Views and Agenda', *Journal of Economic Literature* 35, 2.

Nazarova, L. (2000), 'Tikhii peredel', *Ekonomika i zhizn'* 40 (October).

Polit.ru (2000a), 'Tsentrobank prodolzhaet protivostoyat' planam pravitel'stva po usileniyu gosbankov' (1 November) (http://www.polit.ru).

Polit.ru (2000b), 'Bol'shoi pylesos prodolzhaet rabotu: Stat'ya o deyatel'nosti Sberbanka v pervom polugodii' (3 November) (http://www.polit.ru).

Putin, V. V. (2001), 'Ezhegodnoe poslanie Prezidenta Rossiiskoi Federatsii Federal'nomu Sobraniyu Rossiiskoi Federatsii', Moscow (3 April) (http://president.kremlin.ru).

RECEP (1997), 'The Banking Sector', *Russian Economic Trends* 6, 3.

RF Government (1994), *Sobranie aktov Prezidenta i Pravitel'stva Rossiiskoi Federatsii* 1, st. 2.

RF Government (2001), 'Zayavlenie Pravitel'stva Rossiiskoi Federatsii i Tsentral'nogo banka Rossiiskoi Federatsii ob ekonomicheskoi politike na 2001 god i nekotorykh aspektakh strategii na srednesrochnuyu perspektivu' (April), (http://www.pravitelstvo.gov.ru/government/minister/kas_04_23_2001.html).

Sberbank (2001), 'Ob itogakh raboty Sberbanka Rossii v 2000 godu' (17 April) (http://www.sbrf.ru/ruswin/press.htm).

Sutela, Pekka (1998a), 'The Role of Banks in Financing Russian Economic Growth', *Post-Soviet Geography and Economics* 39, 2.

Sutela, Pekka (1998b), *The Road to the Russian Market Economy*, Helsinki: Kikkimora.

Tompson, William (1997), 'Old Habits Die Hard: Fiscal Imperatives, State Regulation and the Role of Russia's Banks', *Europe-Asia Studies* 49, 7, pp. 1159–85.

Tompson, William (1998a), 'Service Providers or Servants of the State? Russian Banks in the Nineties', *Society and Economy in Central and Eastern Europe* 20, 2.

Tompson, William (1998b), 'The Future of the Russian Banking System: Liquidation or Mergers?', in Graeme Herd (ed.), *Russia in Crisis*, Sandhurst: CSRC, pp. 7–25.

Tompson, William (1999), 'The Bank of Russia and the 1998 Rouble Crisis', in Vladimir Tikhomirov (ed.), *Anatomy of the 1998 Russian Crisis*, Melbourne: CERC, pp. 108–44.

Tompson, William (2000a), 'Nothing Learned, Nothing Forgotten: Restructuring without Reform in Russia's Banking Sector', in Stefanie Harter and Gerald Easter (eds), *Shaping the Economic Space in Russia*, Aldershot: Ashgate, pp. 65–101.

Tompson, William (2000b), 'Financial Backwardness in Contemporary Perspective: Prospects for the Development of Financial Intermediation in Russia', *Europe-Asia Studies* 52, 4, pp. 605–25.

United Financial Group (1999), *Russia Morning Comment* (17 March).

United Financial Group (2001), *Russian Morning Comment* (24 April).

Zhuravskaya, Elena (1995), 'The First Stage of Banking Reform in Russia is Completed: What Lies Ahead?', in Jacek Rostowski (ed.), *Banking Reform in Central Europe and the Former Soviet Union*, Budapest: CEU Press.

4. The view from the ground: case studies of three major banks (Sberbank, Uneximbank/Rosbank, Bank of Moscow)

David Lane and Irene Lavrentieva

Reminiscent of the early days of the Industrial Revolution in the West, at the beginning of the period of marketization, the number of commercial banks in 1992 was 1 215 and the number grew to reach 1 605 by 1996. By 2 000, there were 1 338 banks ('credit organizations' as they are defined by the Central Bank of Russia), of which 21 were completely foreign owned. (For details see Appendix 1.2, Chapter 1 of this collection). While large in number by contemporary European standards, the USA, due to legal and other constraints, has an even larger number of banks. In the 1920s in the USA there were over 20 000 banks and even today the number still runs into five figures. In 1995, there were 10 958 FEIC-insured commercial banks, 2 262 savings institutions and 12 317 credit unions. (Data from US Bureau of the Census, Statistical Abstract of United States for 1995. Washington DC 1995, 518.) These banks vary tremendously in size of assets, liabilities, capital and number of branches. A small number of banks dominates the banking sector and there is a long tail of very small banks. Appendix 4.1 to this chapter ranks the top 50 Russian banks by size of assets in 2001. The table lists their location, number of branches and employees, assets, capital, levels of retail and corporate deposits.[1]

It is clearly impossible to give an account of the structure and evolution of all of these organizations. In this chapter, we focus on three banks: Sberbank of the Russian Federation, Uneximbank/Rosbank, and the Bank of Moscow. Ranked by assets in 2001, these banks are respectively first, eighth and ninth. Basic comparative statistical data are included in Table 4.1. We focus on their origins, ownership, forms of adaptation to a market system and future prospects. We do not claim to provide a comprehensive account of the banks, but an outline of their salient features to illustrate some of the realities of the evolving banking system.

Sberbank, still largely in state ownership, is the biggest Russian bank by number of branches and employees, size of assets, capital, amount of commercial credit and profits; it has the largest base of individual depositors. Uneximbank illustrates the merging of banking and industrial capital and is the centre of a financial–industrial group. The study shows how it faced ruin after the financial crisis of 1998 and then was merged into Rosbank. The Bank of Moscow exemplifies a bank associated with a regional government power, the City of Moscow.

SBERBANK OF THE RUSSIAN FEDERATION

Sberbank has its origin as a state bank founded under the Tsars. On 30 October 1881, Emperor Nicholas II issued a decree opening savings' offices in Russia.[2] These offices came under the control of Russia's State Bank supervised by the Ministry of Finance and, after 1895, under Minister of Finance Sergei Witte, they began to be called 'state savings offices'. In the Soviet period, these continued as a state savings bank, as noted in Chapter 1. They were owned by Gosbank USSR and their major task was to pay wages and accept savings deposits from the population. Under Gorbachev, in 1988 Sberbank became an independent lending institution and was called Sberbank of the Soviet Union. After the disintegration of the Soviet Union and the dismantling of USSR State Bank (Gosbank) in 1990, units of Sberbank in the RSFSR[3] became the property of the Russian Federation and were reorganized into a joint-stock commercial bank. On June 1991, Sberbank was registered as an independent bank by the Central Bank of the Russian Federation.

In the early period of post-communist transformation, Sberbank faced competition from the new banks which were favoured by corporate capital, as they gave their owners (non-financial companies) control unimpeded by the government. Sberbank's major activities included the preservation of Sberbank's national structure, retention of its position on the retail banking and deposit service market, and improvement of the quality of its client services.[4]

As noted in Table 4.1 Sberbank has assets which are five times greater than the next highest bank (Vneshtorgbank), while its individual (*fizicheskikh lits*) deposits are greater than the total of all other banks put together and represent some two-thirds of its liabilities. As Sergei Alexashenko, former deputy chairman of Russia's Central Bank, has put it: 'Sberbank occupies a special place in Russia's financial system. The size of its operations on the deposit market has no parallel in our country.'[5] Sberbank has the largest number of personnel and branches. In July 2000, the total number of employees was some 200000 and the number of offices 21778 (see Table 4.1). The next

Table 4.1 Data on Sberbank, Rosbank and Bank of Moscow, March 2001 (ranked by assets)

		Number of branches	Main location	Number of employees	Assets*	Capital*	Retail Legal deposits*	Entities' deposits*
1	Sberbank of Russia (1 July 2000)	21 778	Moscow	199 896	596 081 075	43 495 214	348 038 432	149 691 114
8	Rosbank, successor bank to Uneximbank	13	Moscow	—	44 912 616	7 061 292	2 675 777	27 072 172
9	Bank of Moscow	38	Moscow	2 968	36 363 109	3 318 671	3 409 576	30 445 008

		Loans and advances to customers*	Loans and advances to banks*	Balance and profit*	Government securities*
1	Sberbank of Russia (1 July 2000)	274 093 646	8 095 874	17 444 055	60 348 987
8	Rosbank, successor bank to Uneximbank	32 453 556	6 495 383	3 230 733	981 577
9	Bank of Moscow	20 683 769	9 409 893	314 964	45 285

Note: * Thousands of rubles.

Source: Rating Information Centre. Cited in *Moscow Times*, *Business Review*, Vol. 98, No. 2 (March 2001).

largest bank, by number of branches, is Svyaz with 128. It has a network of 71 territorial banks in the republics and regions, 1612 branches and 154 agencies, which is a large network even by international comparison.[6]

The Bank is a single legal entity that includes all its branches and subdivisions in all parts of Russia. Sberbank's branches in Russia's republics, regions and territories, and in the cities of Moscow and St Petersburg are called territorial banks, while its offices in other cities and administrative regions are branches. The branches, however, vary greatly in power and resources. In 1997, for instance, five of them (Moscow, St Petersburg, Krasnodar, Samara and Voronezh banks) accounted for 50 per cent of Sberbank's profits and 30 per cent of its capital.[7]

Ownership and Control

The ownership of shares in Sberbank in 2000 was as follows: banking sector, including Bank of Russia 58.9 per cent, investment companies 21.4 per cent, other legal entities 8 per cent, private individuals 11.9 per cent.[8]

As the Bank is legally required to reveal publicly those owning over 5 per cent of shares, the only information we have is that until 1999, the second largest shareholder was Kreditanschtaldt-Grant investment company.[9]

Study of the composition of the Supervisory Board (Board of Directors) brings out the preponderance of government representatives, both from ministries and also from the Central Bank of the Russian Federation itself. At various times, the persons in charge of strategic management of Sberbank were Victor Gerashchenko, Anatoli Chubais, Sergei Dubinin, Sergei Alexashenko, Mikhail Zadornov, Alexander Livshits and other well-known Russian economists. The government either directly through representatives or ministries or the Bank of Russia or indirectly through pressure on the Supervisory Board effectively controls the Bank. The operational management of Russian companies is performed by an Executive Board, staffed by professional managers employed in the company, many of whom also serve on the Supervisory Council.

Andrei Kazmin is president of the bank, as well as being a member of its Supervisory Board and chairman of the Executive. Early in 1996, Kazmin came to the post of chairman of Sberbank from the Ministry of Finance. He brought several bankers with him, including Alla Aleshkina from Menatep, where she was deputy chairman of the Executive Board, approximately at the same time. Later, a number of senior government ministers and officials joined the executive. They included Gennadi Melikyan, who was Russia's Minister of Labour and Social Development until July 1997, and Andrei Pogodin, an advisor at one of Russia's Ministry of Foreign Affairs departments until the summer of 1997. In 1999, three members of

Table 4.2 Sberbank's portfolio of ruble-denominated government securities ($ billion)

	Total outstanding government securities (market value)	Sberbank's investments in government securities	Sberbank's investments as % of total outstanding government securities
06.01.95	3.14	0.81	26
03.01.96	15.89	5.82	37
01.01.97	42.64	14.94	35
01.01.98	57.14	15.56	27

Source: Central Bank statistics: www.cbr.ru.

the Executive – Alla Sleshkina, Andrei Kazmin and Alexander Solovev – were also on the Supervisory Board.

Sberbank's policy

As a government bank, Sberbank offers (or should offer) a high level of security to its depositors. A legacy of the Soviet era is that Sberbank continued as the traditional 'people's bank' and retained a very large individual deposit base. Such a position enabled it to fix deposit rates fairly autonomously. By mid-summer 1998, Sberbank had accumulated 120 billion rubles (about $20 billion) and $2.4 billion in individual deposit accounts, or 84 per cent of total ruble deposits and 42 per cent of total hard-currency deposits in all Russian banks.[10]

Sberbank is not only a commercial bank but also acts as the 'government bank'. It has been an agent of the Federal Government in financing programmes and has handled the accounts of the Ministry of Finance. It administered the government's compensation scheme to account holders for the gross devaluation of their savings in the early period of transition. It also supports such schemes as the State Housing Certificate programme which helps retired army officers to purchase their own accommodation. It is also the government's agent for government savings bonds (OGSZs).

The Bank implements the market policy thought appropriate by the financial authorities (the Central Bank and the Ministry of Finance). The best known example here is its operations in the market for GKOs (short-term government bonds) and OFZs (longer term government bonds issued to finance budget deficits). It was a market-maker and itself a major operator in this market. As shown by Table 4.2, Sberbank took from 26 per cent to 37 per cent of government bonds.

In December 1997, when non-residents were selling, Sberbank increased its GKO portfolio by 2.3 billion rubles (about $400 million) and thus compensated the government for the withdrawal of Western investors from the market. 'We played our role of market stabilizer to the full,' said Sberbank's chairman when assessing its activities during that time.[11] This example highlights the conflict of interest between its duty to the government and to its depositors.

By mid-summer 1998, Sberbank's investments in ruble-denominated government securities reached 100 billion rubles (the equivalent of $16 billion). In July 1998, the bank partially restructured its portfolio of ruble-denominated government securities, converting part of them into Russian government eurobonds. It is quite possible that Sberbank's management foresaw the coming ruble devaluation and sought to hedge Sberbank from foreign-exchange risks.

In July 1998, the government devised a plan for the voluntary restructuring of ruble-denominated government securities. Foreign and Russian holders of GKOs were invited to exchange their GKOs with maturities before 1 July 1999 for US dollar-denominated eurobonds with fixed rates and maturities in 2005 and 2018. In all, the government purchased 27.2 billion rubles' worth of securities ($4.4 billion) from investors. Sberbank accounted for 40 per cent of these exchanges.

However, even after the restructuring, Sberbank's investments in ruble-denominated government securities were huge. They accounted for the greatest part of Sberbank's liquid assets. Following the 1998 crisis, Sberbank's liabilities – including a large number of ordinary account holders' deposits and significant investments in government securities (see Table 4.3) – should have led to insolvency.

Sberbank, however, could not be said to have acted speculatively. Government securities are traditionally regarded as 'low-risk assets'. Not

Table 4.3 Sberbank's investments in government securities and individual account holders' deposits before the 1998 crisis[12]

	01.04.98	01.07.98	01.10.98
Total investments in Russian government securities*	17.3	17.0	6.7
Government securities investments†	56.0%	54.9%	50.2%
Total individual account holders' deposits*	22.8	23.0	8.6
Individual account holders†	74.0%	74.2%	64.4%

Notes: * $ billion; † % of Sberbank's assets.

long before the beginning of the crisis, Bella Zlatkis, head of the Securities and Financial Market Department of Russia's Ministry of Finance, said: 'If you consider Sberbank's activities during the last two years, you will see that it implements a rather prudent policy. Ordinary Russians' deposits in Sberbank are protected because they are all invested in government securities, which means they are guaranteed by the state.'[13] This, of course, is what many Western investors also thought.

However, the government froze ruble-denominated government bonds on 17 August 1998. The consequent collapse of the ruble and numerous failures of Russia's largest banks had a negative effect on Sberbank which suffered massive deposit withdrawals from Russian depositors. (The rates of ruble/dollar exchange, 1993–2001, are listed in Appendix 4.2 below.) Between January and September 1998, Sberbank lost 16 per cent of individual account holders' ruble deposits and 30 per cent of hard-currency deposits. It managed to meet its liabilities only thanks to support from the Central Bank, which not only actively lent to Sberbank, but also announced that deposits in Sberbank were covered by state guarantees. Moreover, additional powers were extended to Sberbank during that period. The Central Bank worked out a programme to enable depositors of insolvent banks[14] to transfer their deposits to Sberbank. Personal deposits at Sberbank began to grow, with Russian pensioners accounting for most of them.[15]

Consequences of the 1998 crisis

Consequent on the 1998 crisis, Sberbank of Russia was one of the few Russian banks that continued operations and fulfilled all of its deposit and client liabilities. Though most Russian banks reported huge losses, Sberbank ended 1998 with a profit that significantly exceeded profits of other large Russian commercial banks.[16] This was possible again only because of significant support from its major shareholder, the Central Bank of Russia. But Sberbank's financial position deteriorated significantly during the crisis and post-crisis period.

After rising to their highest level ($2.6 billion) in 1996, Sberbank's profits, in dollar terms, decreased significantly in the following years. They decreased to $0.8 billion in 1997 and to $0.5 billion in 1999.[17] The decline of Sberbank's performance was explained mostly by the worsening of the situation on Russia's financial market. Government securities, a reliable and profitable instrument in the past, disappeared from the market, while lending to industries still involved high risks. The value of the bank's capital also decreased significantly. In less than two years, it decreased by more than 66.7 per cent in dollar terms and 300 per cent in ruble value.

The 1998 crisis, however, aided Sberbank's leadership in retail banking. At the end of 1998, Sberbank accounted for about 85 per cent of all deposits in

Russian commercial banks, compared to 78 per cent at the start of the year. In 1998, individual account holders' deposits at the bank grew 21 per cent to 126.8 billion rubles and $1.3 billion at the start of 1998. When implementing its Outlook for Sberbank's Development to the Year 2000 (which was worked out in 1996),[18] the bank paid special attention to developing services to corporate clients. The Outlook defined 'the transformation of Sberbank into a universal commercial bank' through 'the development of banking services to corporate clients' as one of Sberbank's priority goals. The establishment of long-term mutually beneficial relations with corporate clients and the provision of a full range of banking services meeting their requirements helped Sberbank create a stable client base.

At the beginning of 2000, Sberbank's major corporate clients included Rostelekom, subdivisions of Gazprom and RAO UESR, the Lukoil company, TNK, the Sibneft and Severnaya Neft oil companies, Transneft, the oil pipeline operator, Severstal, the Norilsk Mining and Metallurgical Company, Rosvooruzhenie, the VGTRK television and broadcasting company, ALROSA, Aeroflot, Krasny Oktyabr, a confectionary and the Baltika Brewery. Other clients included 'enterprises in all industries, of all types of ownership and of all sizes, from small businesses to Russia's major companies, and also various financial institutions and government organizations and bodies of state administration'.[19]

Government organizations which were clients included Russia's State Pension Fund, the Ministry of Fuel and Energy, various departments of the Ministry of Defence, the Ministry of Internal Affairs, Russia's Federal Border Protection Service, the Ministry of Emergency Situations, the State Customs Committee, and the Court Marshal Service of the Ministry of Justice. Sberbank also handled accounts of various work and project-implementation groups established within the framework of Russia's cooperation with the International Bank for Reconstruction and Development (IBRD) and the European Bank for Reconstruction and Development (EBRD).

Prospects for Sberbank's further development

In 2000, Sberbank published its 'Outlook for Sberbank's Development to the Year 2005'. It defined Sberbank's strategic goal as 'reaching a qualitatively new level of client services and preservation of Sberbank's position as that of a modern, first-class, competitive bank in Eastern Europe'. In addition, Sberbank planned to pay more attention to lending to ordinary Russians. It intends to increase its share of this market to 30 per cent and increase lending to individual account holders at least twofold. The Bank proposes to intensify its work with corporate clients, which has always been its weakness. Its plan also acknowledges its role as a bank of 'national significance' and it intends to continue helping the government with the implementation of its investment and export-support programmes. It also aims to optimize the network of Sberbank's branches 'with consideration of both economic and social factors'.[20] Accordingly, the network of Sberbank's branches will retain its four-level structure, but the number of territorial banks will be reduced: 18 new territorial banks will be established on the basis of 70 old ones.

Sberbank proposes to change the structure of its equity capital. In 2000, non-residents officially held only 0.11 per cent of Sberbank shares. According to Andrei Kazmin, however, the actual figure was much higher as 15 per cent of Sberbank shares were held by Russian companies which were 100 per cent owned by foreign entities. In the early summer of 2000, the article in Sberbank's Charter limiting non-residents' participation in Sberbank's equity capital to only 5 per cent was removed. The government's stake will be reduced, while the share of non-residents will increase. According to Russian legislation, the Central Bank's stake in Sberbank must amount to 50 per cent plus one share. It seems likely that the Central Bank could (and will) shed up to 7 per cent of its surplus shares. Alexander Shokhin, head of the State Duma's Banking Committee, believes that the Central Bank must withdraw its stakes from Sberbank and Vneshtorgbank.[21] According to other would-be reformers of Sberbank, its deposits should be used for long- and medium-term loans to the Russian Bank for Development and then used for financing enterprises. However, opponents point out that personal savings accumulated at Sberbank are already invested in various projects and industries. Also, under current Russian conditions, active lending to industries involves high risks of delays in interest and principal repayments which would not be acceptable to bank depositors.

There is also a possibility of a more radical reorganization of Sberbank. The International Monetary Fund has long expressed its dissatisfaction with Sberbank's monopoly position on the market for deposit services. In view of this, it was decided to ask PriceWaterhouseCoopers to carry out an additional audit of Sberbank. Results of the audit should show whether Sberbank will continue as Russia's largest bank or whether it will be divided in several financial institutions.[22] However, Sberbank's management in its 'Outlook' document ignores discussion of such radical moves. A greater emphasis on 'state led' economic activity is a component of President Putin's policy and it seems more likely that state involvement in Sberbank will continue.

UNEXIMBANK (UNITED EXPORT-IMPORT BANK)/ROSBANK

Uneximbank (Obedinennyi Eksportno-importnyi Bank)[23] was established on 20 April 1993 by several former Soviet foreign-trade associations. After establishing itself as one of Russia's major commercial banks, following the financial crisis of 1998 the bank faced considerable financial problems and in September 2000 it merged with Rosbank. The history of the bank illustrates how one major bank dealt with the financial crisis by dissolving itself.

Its initial equity capital amounted to a modest 50 million rubles ($30,000) which was contributed by many of Russia's largest foreign-trade associations,[24] including Exportkhleb, Raznoimport, Rosvneshtorg, Obshchemashexport, Soyuzpromexport, Sovintorg, Purneftegaz, Rosnefteimpex, Prodintorg and GLAVPUDK (an institution of the Ministry of Foreign Affairs). Uneximbank was originally headed by Vladimir Potanin, who formerly worked at the Ministry of Foreign Economic Relations and Mikhail Prokhorov, a former employee of Comecon's Bank for Economic Cooperation. They were assisted at the top management level by a team of Prokhorov's former associates from the Moscow Institute of Finance. Before the establishment of Uneximbank, Potanin worked at the USSR Ministry of Foreign Trade (1983–1990). His last job there was that of a senior engineer of the Soyuzpromexport All-Union Foreign Trade Association under the Ministry of Foreign Trade. In 1990, he established the Interros Foreign Trade Association, on which the Interros Holding was formed in 1994.[25] Potanin was an important link between Interros and Unexim. By 1995, the Interros Holding had been set up and Uneximbank was one of its principal companies. Potanin's major partner on the financial markets was Boris Jordan, an American of Russian origin who came from the United States to head the Moscow office of Credit Suisse First Boston and to act as consultant to the Russian government on privatization of state property.

Between 1990 and 1992, the Interros Foreign Trade Association engaged in a wide range of export transactions, which were very profitable. After the disintegration of the Soviet Union many of Potanin's transactions involved the division of financial assets and liabilities between the former Soviet republics, which also earned him significant profits in the form of commissions. In the summer of 1991, Potanin met Mikhail Prokhorov, head of the foreign-exchange and export transaction department of the International Bank for Economic Cooperation. Initially, Prokhorov provided consulting services to Interros but later, in 1992, he became an employee and brought other banking colleagues with him.[26]

Uneximbank emerged because former Soviet foreign trade associations were eager to find a new bank able to do their transactions. These were clients of the previous Soviet bank, Vneshekonombank and/or the International Bank for Economic Cooperation. Its founders were Russia's largest companies engaged in foreign trade. Uneximbank's equity capital was divided between a large number of shareholders and it is difficult to

Table 4.4 List of shareholders that owned more than 5 per cent of Uneximbank shares in the period between 1996 and 2000 (%)

	1996	1997	1998	1999	2000
Surgutneftegaz	19.96	19.96	10.51	10.51	9.46
Interros Estate			15.00		
Norilsky Nikel			11.35	11.35	
Investfinance				10.00	10.00

Source: Quarterly equities' reports for the Central Bank of RF, 1996–2000, www.cbr.ru.

determine who actually controlled the bank. For several years, one of Uneximbank's largest shareholders was Surgutneftegaz which, in 1996–1997, owned nearly 20 per cent of Uneximbank's shares (see Table 4.4). Later (in 1998–99) its stake in Uneximbank decreased to 10.5 per cent. Concurrently, Norilsk Nikel emerged in the group of Uneximbank's large shareholders with an 11 per cent stake.

The 1998 crisis had a significant effect on Uneximbank's shareholder structure. In 2000, Uneximbank had only two large shareholders with more than 5 per cent of the bank's shares. They were Surgutneftegaz (9.46 per cent) and Investfinance (10 per cent). However, the latter company itself is 100-per cent owned by Uneximbank. Other shareholders, who jointly own 80.54 per cent of Uneximbank, each held less than 5 per cent of the bank's shares. Potanin could be a major shareholder in Investfinance and through this connection exert influence over Uneximbank.

Table 4.5 lists the composition of the Supervisory Board in 1999–2000. The data shown indicate the importance of interlocking directors with other important companies which are members of the Interros Group. What the table does not show is that Uneximbank is controlled by the Interros Holding (which has control of its affiliated companies which own small packets of its shares) and the position of its head Vladimir Potanin.

Vladimir Potanin held the post of Uneximbank's President for many years until the middle of 1998, when he took up a post at Interros and his position, in turn, was occupied by Mikhail Prokhorov.

Uneximbank's rapid development was a consequence of its participation in various government programmes. In 1993, Uneximbank became official dealer in government bonds (GKOs), a payment agent for domestic hard-currency denominated bonds (OVVZs), an authorized depository and payment agent for Treasury bonds (the debt of the Russian government), an authorized agent of the Federal Department for Bankruptcy (Insolvency), an authorized bank of the Russian government for transactions with Chechnya,

Table 4.5 Members of Uneximbank's Board of Directors in 1999 and 2000

Company	1999	2000
Technostroyexport	Velichko, V. I., President, Vice-Chairman of Board of Directors	Velichko, V. I., President, Vice-Chairman of Board of Directors
Soyuspromexport	Ignatov, V. V., President	Ignatov, V. V., President
Surgutneftegaz	Bogdanov, V. L., General Director, Member of Board of Directors	Kiselev, N. B., Vice-President, finance and taxation
Machinostroitelny zavod (machine building plant)	Mezhuev, V., General Director	Mezhuev, V., General Director
Interros		Potanin ,V., President Ushakov, D. L., General Director
Uneximbank	Prokhorov, M., Chairman Governing Board, Member of Board of Directors Ushakov, D, Member of Board of Directors Potanin, V., President	Prokhorov, M., Chairman Governing Board, Member of Board of Directors
Commercial Division of servicing of Diplomatic Corps under Ministry Foreign Affairs		Fedofov, V., Director
Roskhlebproduct	Cheshinsky, L., President, Member of Board of Directors	Cheshinsky, L., President
Nafta-Moskva	Kolotilin, A., Chairman, General Director	

Source: Quarterly equities' reports for the Central bank of RF, 1996–2000. www.cbr.ru (2000).

for the State Property Management Committee, for the government's and the Moscow city government for servicing their foreign economic relations. The acquisition of all these functions was possible through Vladimir Potanin's good connections with various government ministries and agencies, whose recommendations made it possible for Uneximbank to take part in such profitable government programmes. Uneximbank also managed to expand its client base even during its first years. In addition to the largest foreign trading associations, its clients included the State Customs Committee and Rosvooruzhenie, a state-owned arms exporter.[27]

Uneximbank's activities in Russia's regions were based on its special agreements with regional governments and governments of the Republics within the Russian Federation.[28] Though there were no legal restrictions on the establishment of regional branches, any bank wishing to set up such branches had to receive a license from the Central Bank's regional department, which took into account the local authorities' attitude to a particular bank when it considered issuing a license to it. Local authorities were very reluctant to admit Moscow-based banks to their region, blaming them for their 'barbarian' attitude to regions, which meant 'exporting capital' from the region. Consequently, local authorities preferred to establish their own banks which were completely under their control. Uneximbank established subsidiaries preparing their own balance sheets rather than branches of Moscow-based banks in Russia's regions. This policy enabled Uneximbank's regional subsidiaries to attract new clients among large regional companies and local governments.

Uneximbank's domestic success was supplemented by measures to create a favourable image on international markets. For instance, Uneximbank registered a subsidiary bank in Switzerland (Banque UNEXIM Suisse). In May 1996, the US Securities and Exchange Commission gave Uneximbank the status of a reliable foreign depository (Uneximbank was Russia's first financial organization to acquire such status), enabling it to attract American mutual funds to Russia.

Participation in Financial Associations

By 1994–95, Uneximbank had gained a foothold in all segments of the financial services market and occupied a leading position in most of them. In one of his interviews, Potanin gave reasons for the rapid growth of his business as follows: 'We had a good team and worked very well. We also had a good strategy. On the other hand, we worked under conditions of general [economic] instability and the absence of clearly defined legislation. This made it possible for us to become rich much faster than if we had worked under normal conditions, like those in developed countries.'[29]

In September 1994, Uneximbank became one of the founders of the Interbank Credit Union, an organization that later became a main intermediary between the Russian government and foreign buyers of GKOs. In July 1995, it concluded an agreement with the Russian Export–Import Bank on guaranteeing and insuring foreign-trade transactions. In September, Uneximbank signed an agreement with the Stolichny Saving Bank on the establishment of the STB-Russia company, a major project in the area of plastic card settlements. At the same time, Vladimir Ryskin, Uneximbank's deputy chairman, was placed on the Board of Directors of

Table 4.6 Results of auctions won by Uneximbank

Company	Block of shares acquired, % of equity capital	Loan to the government, $ mn
Norilsk Nickel	38.00	170.10
SIDANCO, an oil company	51.00	130.00
Surgutneftegaz*	40.12	88.00
Novolipetsk Metallurgical Plant	14.84	31.00
Nafta-Moskva	15.00	20.01
North-Western river steamship Co.	25.50	6.05

Note: * Uneximbank acted as a guarantor, the winner was Surgutneftegaz's non-government pension fund.

Source: Official data received from GosKomUmuschestvo, 1995. VEDI data bank.

the Depository and Clearing Company (DKK). In November 1996, Uneximbank acquired a controlling stake in the UCS processing company, which held exclusive rights for servicing Diners Club card holders through its network until 1 October 1999.

Uneximbank's participation in the Consortium of Commercial Banks played a special role in its development and in the advancement of the Interros Holding. The Consortium was established for the purpose of lending to the Russian government against the security of government stakes in Russia's largest industrial companies. Potanin was generally regarded as the initiator of the establishment of the Consortium, which was set up early in 1995.

The subject of loans for shares is covered in detail in the chapter in this collection by Duncan Allan. As far as Unexim is concerned, Table 4.6 shows that, as a consequence of the auctions, the Bank had acquired a significant number of shares in large Russian companies. Since the government did not repay the loans, the right of ownership was transferred to Uneximbank or Interros.

Interros Holding

Having established Uneximbank, Potanin then expanded into the adjacent sectors of the financial services market. While Russia's banking system was already relatively well developed at that time, other sectors of the financial services market were only beginning, and Potanin was a pioneer in many of them. The Interros-Soglasie insurance company was established in

September 1993 and Interros-Dostoinstvo, a non-government pension fund, was established in December of the same year. It was the first officially licensed non-government pension fund in Russia. The Interros financial and industrial group (FIG Interros) was established in October 1994 and included, in its major activities, industrial investments, company reorganizations and consulting. One of Russia's first leasing companies, Interrosleasing, was established in November 1994. All these companies were members of the Interros group until April 1998, when Interros Holding was established to manage assets of the Interros group on a commercial basis.

The Holding's president is Vladimir Potanin who has the reputation also of being a key figure in the political sphere. Boris Berezovsky, for instance, has named him as one of the oligarchs who runs Russia. For Potanin, however,

> The notion 'oligarch' is rather artificial. There is no oligarchy in the country. It is a conventional term. The concept 'oligarchy' was introduced by Boris Berezovsky in his interview with the *Financial Times* in the autumn of 1996. It is the authorities who decide whether to invite them as consultants or not, or whether to carry out a dialogue with them or not. The authorities are primary to any kind of business.[30]

But Potanin does not deny his political influence:

> Yes, capital concentration is high in our country, there are a few large businesses. It is understandable that they are all influential. . . . If Interros controls Norilsk Nickel, if we support the entire industrial region, if we account for more than 50 per cent of budget revenues of the Krasnoyarsk Region, then it's clear that it is politics.[31]

Interros Holding consists of four components. The banking component includes Uneximbank, the MFK bank, Rosbank, and Uneximbank's subsidiary banks. The financial services component is made up of Interros-Soglasie, Interros-Dostoinstvo, Interrosleasing and Interros-Transtur. The industrial component includes companies in which Interros Holding has significant stakes: Norilsk Nickel, SIDANCO, the Novolipetsk Metallurgical Plant and others. There is also a media component which includes Komsomolskaya Pravda and Izvestia (dailies) as well as Ekspert, a magazine popular in financial circles.

Uneximbank's Financial Policy

Since its foundation, Uneximbank has been a bank providing services to Russian companies which, as a rule, participate in government foreign-trade programmes.[32] They included large exporters and importers, and companies in Russia's key industries, including oil extraction and refining, ferrous and non-ferrous metallurgy, machine-building, and agricultural production.[33] Many foreign-trade companies remain its shareholders or clients. They include Agrokhimexport, Zarubezhneft, Mashinimport, Obzhemashexport, Prodintorg, Raznoimport, Raznotreid, Raznoexport, Rosvneshtorg, Rosnefteimpex, Sovbunker, Sovintorg, Sovrybflot, Soyuzplodimport, Soyuzpromexport, Soyuztransit, Tekhmashimport, Tekhnostroiexport, Tekhnosnabexport and Exportkhleb.

Uneximbank's lending policy was specified in accordance with Interros Holding's policy. The Bank lent mostly to companies that were members of the Holding or controlled by it. The Holding managed its member companies and made significant investments in their development. For instance, Uneximbank began lending to the Novolipetsk Metallurgical Plant (NMP) in the pre-crisis period.[34] It began to support NMP in December 1997, when the first $50-million loan was provided to it. During the first five months of 1998 the total amount of loans available to NMP grew by another $200 million. But Uneximbank had revised its lending policy and reduced the volume of lending during the periods of financial crisis in 1997 and 1998. Immediately before the 1998 crisis, Uneximbank's outstanding loans amounted to about $1.5 billion, or 40 per cent of its assets.

Uneximbank was a primary dealer on the GKO/OFZ market and the bank maintained a 500-million-ruble portfolio of government securities. During the 1997 international financial crisis, Uneximbank significantly increased its portfolio investments. As a result, its investments in Russian government securities grew from 523 million rubles (about $90 million) at the start of 1997, to 1.3 billion rubles ($230 million) on 1 October 1997. The share of government securities in Uneximbank's assets grew from 2.6 per cent to 6 per cent during that period.[35]

Uneximbank never intended to become a retail bank providing services to the public and individual account holders' deposits were insignificant. By the summer of 1998 they amounted only to a little more than $100 million, or 3 per cent of Uneximbank's liabilities. Most of these deposits were hard-currency deposits.

Uneximbank was one of the most active Russian borrowers on the international capital market. It raised syndicated loans, received credit lines and sold its eurobonds. The European Bank for Reconstruction and Development (EBRD) extended a $100-million combined credit line to Uneximbank in November 1997. According to its agreement with the EBRD, Uneximbank received $50 million for five years for medium- and long-term lending to its private-sector clients in various industries, including the petrochemical, mining, food and other industries, and for the development of infrastructure in various Russian cities. Another $50 million was provided as an instrument of controlling Uneximbank's liquidity.

Uneximbank's financial position after the 1998 crisis

In 1997 and the first half of 1998, Uneximbank met all its liabilities and never delayed client payments. At the same time, the instability of Russia's financial markets told on Uneximbank's financial position. In the first half of 1998, Uneximbank made losses (including losses from revaluation of its securities investments). However, they were not very large and were covered by earlier profits.

Many banks found themselves on the verge of bankruptcy after the 1998 crisis as individual account holders withdrew deposits. Uneximbank was in a favourable position because it did not have significant deposit liabilities and provided services to clients who were to some extent under the Holding's control. Uneximbank's financial stability during that period could partly be explained by loans from the Central Bank. During the first few days after 17 August, the average daily amount of the Central Bank's stabilization loans was estimated at 140–150 million rubles ($20–$25 million).[36] Also, Uneximbank's exposure to exchange rate risks was not large. On the contrary, its hard-currency assets exceeded its hard-currency liabilities. This difference amounted to 1.3 billion rubles (more than $200 million) at the end of the first half of 1998. As a result, a ruble devaluation was even profitable to Uneximbank, because it could increase its receipts. (These figures exclude forward contract liabilities.)

In view of this, a rapid deterioration of Uneximbank's financial position can be explained by its financial policy rather than the crisis. The Bank made significant short-term borrowings on the international market and invested the funds in long-term development projects of the Holding or to support members of the Holding. Before the crisis, Uneximbank was one of the ten Russian banks that had the highest level of overdue debt. As of 1 April 1998, it came to 201.5 million rubles, or 1.2 per cent of high-risk assets.[37]

In the midst of the crisis, in August 1998, Potanin contended,[38] in an interview to the *Financial Times*, that Russian banks would not be able to repay debts to creditors unless they loosened loan terms. He also said that Uneximbank had considered the possibility of defaulting on its forward contracts and would try to renegotiate terms of other loans. As illustrated in Table 4.7, Uneximbank's financial position deteriorated rapidly.

As a consequence of the financial crisis and ruble devaluation, significant losses were incurred ($150 million in 1998–99) and Uneximbank's capital decreased from $1000 million in early 1998 to $4 million by the start of 2000.

Table 4.7 Uneximbank's major financial indicators before and after the 1998 banking crisis ($ million)

Date	Jan. 97	Jan. 98	Jan. 99	Jan. 00	Apr. 00
Shareholders' equity	180.26	319.21	92.13	70.46	66.52
Profit	40.22	102.22	−53.88	−135.43	−127.88
Capital	599.28	1026.57	162.76	4.09	3.81

Source: Reports of Central Bank of RF (kreditnye organizatsii), www.cbr.ru.

Potanin explained the situation as follows:

> As for the GKO market, in June 1998 it was no secret that it would collapse. Those who could get rid of the paper [GKOs], did so. We didn't sell all the GKOs because we were a primary dealer, and we could not act as such without a GKO portfolio. Uneximbank's problems were caused neither by GKOs nor by devaluation. The bank must work with some national financial instruments, that is its job. It must hold a few GKOs, a few Vneshekonombank bonds, a few company shares, and so on. That's how we plan risk diversification: some prices fall, others rise. When everything falls at the same time, when there is a default on GKOs, a default on Vneshekonombank bonds, when blue chips fall by 70 per cent within a few days, then it is clear that these instruments have simply disappeared. And all our money is in them . . . Our problem was not only that we were a Russian bank and could not take it abroad. The only thing we could not foresee was future contracts. The bank's managers made mistakes here, failing to assess all foreign exchange risks. But I should point out that our debts arising from forward contracts are included in our accounts. All our forward contract associates have voted for restructuring.[39]

In late 1998, Potanin faced a difficult choice. He could either have preserved Uneximbank (and paid creditors at the expense of the Holding's industrial assets) or given up Uneximbank (and keep his industrial assets intact). Its assets, including particularly Norilsk Nickel, were still in demand. Selling them could help Uneximbank pay its creditors. However, the bank's debts were large, and it was not possible to receive a realistic price for them during the crisis. As a result, Potanin chose to keep the industrial assets. This led to the closure of Unexim and to the establishment of Rosbank.

The Disappearance of Uneximbank and the Establishment of Rosbank

After the 1998 crisis, Uneximbank made repeated attempts to improve its financial position, including mergers with other banks. It was ready to take part in an interbank settlement pool. Other participants would include Most-Bank, Rossiisky Kredit, Alfa-Bank, Sberbank of Russia, Vneshtorgbank,

Vneshekonombank, MFK, SBS-Agro, Menatep and the National Reserve Bank. It was also expected that the establishment of the pool would help improve interbank settlements, especially in view of the fact that its participants planned to receive a 700-million ruble credit from Russia's Central Bank. However, no action was taken to implement such plans.

The establishment of bridge banks was the most popular way of alleviating consequences of the crisis after August 1998. Part of a bank's assets was transferred to bridge banks and clients were advised to open accounts and carry out their settlements through them. This made it possible for old banks to negotiate debt restructuring with creditors without losing clients and to continue operations through new banks. Uneximbank decided on this strategy. Initially it was planned that a new bank would be established by Menatep, Most-Bank and Uneximbank; later, it was announced that MFK would join. 51 per cent of the shares in these banks would be transferred to the new bank (with an equity capital of $500 million). The Chief Executive Officer would be Mikhail Prokhorov, chairman of Uneximbank's Executive Board. The chairman of the new bank's Board of Directors was to be appointed by Menatep and Most-Bank. This was how Rosbank was established.[40] It immediately received all the necessary licenses, including a general banking license, a license for transactions with precious metals and the license of a professional stock-market participant. The plan for the reorganization of the above three banks through their unification was approved by the Central Bank's Board of Directors in September 1998. 'It was an attempt to create a bank that would not be associated with any of the groups.'[41]

Rosbank's shareholders were companies and organizations from Russian industries. However, large shareholders (those holding more than 5 per cent of Rosbank shares) included only Interros Estate (90.61 per cent at the moment of Rosbank's establishment and 74.86 per cent at the start of 2000) and, later, Surgutneftegaz (14.23 per cent). By July 2000, the former company was 75 per cent owned by Interros and became a member of Interros Holding. As a result, in the middle of 2000, Rosbank was fully controlled by Interros Holding. Moreover, the initial list of amalgamating banks decreased to only one bank, Uneximbank. All its attempts to amalgamate with other banks had failed. The bank had restructured its debts independently.

Its representatives met with its foreign creditors in London in the autumn of 1998. In November 1998, they agreed on the establishment of the Committee of Uneximbank's Foreign Creditors, whose members represented the interests of all groups of creditors, including international commercial and investment banks. Auditors estimated Uneximbank's debts to Western creditors at about $800 million (excluding forward contract debts, which the bank recognized and also planned to restructure).[42] The total amount of the debt to be restructured exceeded $1 billion,[43] though later estimates placed it at $1.7 billion.[44]

Uneximbank's debt restructuring plan provided for the repayment of a $105-million debt in cash and the conversion of a $130-million debt into twelve-year eurobonds (to be guaranteed by Rosbank). The remaining repayments (about $1.2 billion[45]) were to be funded by revenues of the Special Purpose Vehicle (SPV), a trust company established with the aim of managing Uneximbank's assets and distribution of profit among its creditors. The plan provided for Uneximbank's eventual amalgamation with Rosbank and the establishment of a new financial institution.

As Uneximbank's negotiations with its creditors proceeded, its business was gradually transferred to Rosbank. The transfer of securities from Uneximbank's depository to Rosbank's depository accelerated in the summer of 1999. As a result, the total value of assets kept in Rosbank's depository exceeded $1.1 billion as of 1 January 1999. In 1999, the number of Rosbank depository's clients grew from 10 to 260 legal entities and individuals. In 1999, Rosbank depository established a network of correspondents, which included settlement and authorized depositories of all major types of security traded on the stock market.[46] In September 1999, the transfer took place of its plastic cards business to Rosbank.[47] Finally, at Rosbank's shareholders' meeting held on 20 June 2000 it was agreed that Uneximbank be included in Rosbank. The merging of Rosbank and Uneximbank was announced in mid-September 2000.

Potanin recognized that the merging of the two banks and the reorganization of Uneximbank was a measure aimed at protecting the Holding's reputation. 'It was important for us to retain the Holding's moral and psychological right to stay in the banking business.'[48] As a result, Uneximbank's business continues under the aegis of Rosbank.

Rosbank's plans are ambitious: it sought to attract $0.5 billion from individual clients in the year 2001. One of Rosbank's business priorities will be reorganization of its Russian lending institutions. Such services are expected to be very much in demand in Russia's problematic banking sector. The first step in this direction has already been taken. Working together with Price Waterhouse Coopers, Rosbank provides advice to the Agency for Restructuring Lending Organisations (ARCO). Rosbank will provide services to large corporate clients and engage in private banking (particularly services to wealthy individuals). Introduction of a flat income tax on individuals is likely to stimulate personal savings. 'It will be a good opportunity for the re-emerging middle class.'[49] The group headed by Vladimir Potanin has managed to preserve its industrial assets (Norilsk Nickel, the Novolipetsk Metallurgical Plant, Permskie Motory) and has created a new financial centre, Rosbank. However, the group incurred substantial losses during the banking crisis. In particular, it had to sell Baltiisky Zavod and lost control of the Sidanco oil company.[50]

THE BANK OF MOSCOW

The Bank of Moscow was established by the City of Moscow in 1995. By the beginning of the new millennium, strategic cooperation with various financial and non-financial institutions had enabled the Bank to transform itself from an ordinary municipal bank into a large banking conglomerate.[51] By the year 2000, it was one of Russia's major banks acting not only as an instrument of Moscow's administration but conducting business on a national scale. As indicated in Table 4.1, in 2001 it was ranked ninth in terms of its asset base; it also is distinguished by having had relatively few of its assets in government securities.

From the early 1990s, the accounts of Moscow Municipal Government Agencies and Organizations were held by many authorized banks. These included Most-Bank, Menatep, SBS-Agro, Inkombank and Rossiisky Kredit, as well as, to a lesser degree, Mosbusinessbank, Unikombank, Promradtekhbank, Tekhnobank, Montazhspetsbank and Zenit. Yuri Luzhkov, Mayor of Moscow, issued a number of instructions dividing budgetary and extra-budgetary accounts between these banks and this system operated more or less effectively until the autumn of 1994.

In August and September 1994, the City of Moscow's relations with the authorized banks deteriorated. Some observers believe that this was because the City encountered unexpected problems in managing its budget as a result of uneven flows of income and expenditure. To resolve these imbalances, Luzhkov asked the authorized banks for credit. Though they did not refuse, they agreed to provide funds only at market interest rates. This appears to have been a major stimulus for the establishment of Moscow's own bank.

According to its own public statements, a municipal bank was needed to improve the management of Moscow's funds, to create a lending and financial infrastructure, to increase investment in its industries, to promote restructuring of its economy and to develop local private enterprise.[52] The City's administration also needed a bank to attract foreign investment to large-scale municipal economic development projects.

On 7 March 1995, the Moscow Joint-Stock Settlement Bank (which then carried out only an insignificant amount of business) was reorganized into the Moscow Municipal Bank, or, as it was popularly called, the Bank of Moscow.[53] The main shareholders in the bank (Moscow branch of Sberbank of Russia, Mosbusinessbank, the Moscow Industrial bank and

Mosstroibank) were to become minority shareholders and the City of Moscow would hold 51 per cent of the Bank of Moscow's shares.[54]

In addition to handling the City of Moscow's accounts, the new bank was expected to engage in transactions with the City government's other funds, including foreign exchange, money market and securities transactions, and to act as the agent for servicing the City's public loans. According to its President, Andrei Borodin, the bank was to become a 'normal universal bank'.[55]

It gradually acquired the functions of a major bank.[56] In October 1996, it became the City's general payment agent for foreign borrowings and joined the Europay International payment system. In February 1997, it became a member of the VISA Int. payment system. In April, it became the City's authorized depository and payment agent for servicing municipal loans. In September, it expanded its business through forming a strategic partnership with the Troika-Dialog Investment Company, one of the leading participants of the Russian stock market. As shown in Table 4.8, the City of Moscow is the Bank of Moscow's major shareholder, owning 62.7 per cent of its assets in 2000.

Table 4.8 List of large shareholders (holding more than 5 per cent of shares) of the Bank of Moscow (%)

	1998	1999	2000
Moscow's Property Fund	33.2		
Moscow's Property Management Committee	19.5		
City of Moscow's Department of State and Municipal Property		52.75	62.7
IKONIKA[57]	5.1		
Mosenergo[58]	5.1		
Troika Dialog Investment Company[59]	6.4		
Surgutneftegaz's Insurance Company[60]		8.33	

The City administration plays an important role in the strategic management of the Bank. Six of the 13 members of the Board of Directors represent the City of Moscow.

The President of the Bank, Andrei Borodin, has described the bank's relations with the City of Moscow as follows:

> Our relations with the City of Moscow . . . are almost ideal. . . . Our main shareholder leaves day-to-day business to the bank's top management. When plans are jointly discussed, the question that is always asked is how this or that decision will tell on the bank's financial position. Whether it is possible to implement it in principle within normal banking practice.[61]

The Bank holds approximately 30 per cent of the city's accounts.[62]

> One should not forget that the Moscow authorities work with a number of authorized banks and, therefore, can continuously compare terms offered by all their partners. When they need loans we, as a rule, do not have many competitors. But we have to compete fiercely for the budgetary funds with other authorized banks.[63]

The Bank cooperates with the Moscow Mayor's Office on most aspects of the municipal economy, including guarantees of payment for food deliveries to Moscow and the promotion of small business within the framework agreements with other interested parties (such as the City Department for the Support and Development of Small Business and the Moscow Foundation for the Development of Small Business). The Bank opened up credit to finance nearly 100 small-business projects in Moscow. It also successfully implements a $2-million programme of lending to small businesses together with the USA–Russia Investment Fund.

The Bank is a participant in all municipal programmes. One example is its joint work with the City of Moscow's Department of Science and Industrial Policy, which is aimed at financial restructuring of AMO ZIL, Russia's major truck manufacturer with headquarters in Moscow. It also works with the Moskvich car plant. As a general investment agent of Moscow's Committee for Municipal Loans and Development of the Stock Market, the Bank finances relevant programmes and implements agreements. In addition, it manages a significant number of its own investment programmes, which have been designed in accordance with the City's interests. One of them is the establishment of a network of post and banking offices. (As of 2000, in addition to 38 bank branches, there were 295 post offices in Moscow which provided some banking services, including the transfer of pensions to pensioners' bank accounts.)[64]

Despite the Bank of Moscow's close relations with the Moscow political authorities, its President, Andrei Borodin, has been cautious about the Bank's political involvement. Speaking about the Bank's participation in Russia's 2000 presidential election campaign, when the possibility of Moscow's Mayor running for the presidency was being discussed, he pointed out:

> Like all other legal entities, banks can make donations within the existing legal framework to support political parties, movements and the like. Such amounts are not very large. My credo is that banks are not the type of organization that should get involved in politics. I don't believe it is right for the Bank of Moscow to participate in the 2000 election campaign or to support one of the candidates. And no one has ever set such a task for us.[65]

The Bank of Moscow has successfully established contacts with regional administrations because of its closeness to the City of Moscow and its special status. 'Our work in the regions is facilitated by well-established relations with local administrations and presidents of republics . . . Local authorities regard us not as opponents, but rather as business partners.'[66] 'The fact that the controlling stake is in the hands of the City of Moscow does not impede our work. This is because many enterprises and local administrations regard it as a guarantee of the Bank's stability and reliability.'[67]

The Bank's presence in Russia's regions is not limited to its branches. The bank frequently signs cooperation agreements with regional administrations, including those of Keremovo, Petersburg, Murmansk, Novosibirsk, Nizhni Novgorod, Sakhalin, Kemerovo, Arkhangelsk, Perm and Astrakhan Regions, the Khabarovsk territorial administration, and Orsk and Mytishchi city governments.[68] Other areas of influence include Yaroslavl, Kaliningrad, Samara, Petropavlovsk-Kamchatsky, Kirov, Petrozavodsk, Vologda, Kostroma and Tambov.[69] In 2000, the Bank established a subsidiary bank in the Republic of Belarus, the Moscow-Minsk Bank.

Bank of Moscow's Relations with Other Financial Organizations

In the late summer of 1997, the Bank and Troika-Dialog, one of Russia's major investment companies, agreed on strategic cooperation. The Bank purchased 20 per cent of Troika-Dialog's shares from Dialog-Bank and its affiliated companies and the Bank of Moscow's head, Andrei Borodin, was appointed Chairman of Troika-Dialog's Board of Directors.[70] According to *Kommersant-Daily*,

> What is behind the deal is the City of Moscow's intention to use its Bank's funds on the stock market more actively and more effectively. Troika-Dialog's gain is also obvious: in exchange for partial loss of its independence, it will procure opportunities for access to the huge financial resources of the City of Moscow. It is already expected that the Mayor's Office will become Troika-Dialog's client. This will strengthen Troika-Dialog's leading position on the Russian stock market. In addition, it would be reasonable to assume that Troika-Dialog will participate in managing Moscow's investment projects. Now the City of Moscow has a bank, an exchange and an investment company at its disposal.[71]

Another major step towards expanding the City of Moscow's banking business was the Bank of Moscow's amalgamation with Mosbusinessbank which had a wide client base and a large number of branches. The Moscow Mayor's Office assessed the proposed merger:

> Dynamic development, successful handling of the City of Moscow's budget, . . . a significant client base, and the well-developed international relations of Mosbusinessbank will help strengthen Moscow's financial position further, the

> new financial institution will be widely represented in the regions, which will transform [the Bank of Moscow] into a bank of federal significance.[72]

In the summer of 1998, the Bank of Moscow acquired a 10-per cent stake in Mosbusinessbank and became one of its major shareholders,[73] leading to a controlling stake in the autumn of that year. The Bank worked out a financial restructuring programme which in turn was supported by the Central Bank of Russia which provided a one-year billion-ruble loan. The Bank of Moscow also used its own funds for the purpose.[74]

Though the Bank of Moscow-Mosbusinessbank was initially thought of as the first bank merger in Russia's recent history there was actually no merger at all: the municipal bank simply swallowed one of its founders.

Bank of Moscow's Equity Investments

The Bank of Moscow is one of the founders of the Moscow Stock Exchange and is its clearing bank. The Bank's subsidiaries include not only financial organizations, but also other businesses, including those in the media sector and various non-profit organizations (see Table 4.9).

The Bank's major clients include departments and subdivisions of the City of Moscow, including its Department of Finance, Department of Economic Policy and Development, Department of Science and Industrial Policy, Department of Municipal Housing, Department of Food, Financial and Business Department, Budgetary Planning Department, Main Department of Internal Affairs (GUVD) and its structural subdivisions, and Moscow's Tax Inspectorate. Other clients include Moscow departments of the Russian Federation Pension Fund, Federal and Territorial Road Funds, and Obligatory Medical Insurance Fund.[75]

Many businesses became clients of the Bank even during the early phase of its development. Moreover, as the number of its clients grew, the share of state-owned and municipal businesses in the total decreased slightly, from 76 per cent in early 1996 to 70 per cent in early 1997.[76] The Bank has also taken part in the development of the Russian Bistro fast-food chain in Moscow, which is regarded as an alternative to McDonald's restaurants.[77] Two more large investment projects were related to the reconstruction of Moscow's Luzhniki stadium and sports complex and construction of a trading complex in Manezhnaya Square in central Moscow.

Effect of the 1998 Crisis on the Bank of Moscow

Before the crisis, the Bank of Moscow was generally recognized as one of the most conservative Russian banks.[78] This, together with support from

Table 4.9 Bank of Moscow's major subsidiaries, July 2000

Organization	Date of registration	Place of registration	Bank of Moscow's share holding (%)	Sector
Imedzhin	08.02.1996	Moscow	100	
Altruist	02.08.1996	Moscow	100	
Finansovy Assistant	31.07.1996	Moscow	100	
MK-Bulvar Magazine	02.07.1997	Moscow	50	Media
Mosvodokanalbank commercial bank	25.05.1994	Moscow	34.9	Bank
Moscow International Business Association	17.11.1997	Moscow	25	Non-profit organization
TsAO Management Company	13.03.1998	Moscow	26	
Ubank Universal Bank	16.06.1994	Krasnodar, Krasnodar Territory	50	Bank
Izhkombank commercial bank	30.10.1990	Utsmurt Republic, Izhevsk	52.25	Bank
Mosbusinessbank joint-stock commercial bank	12.12.1990	Moscow	51.18	Bank
President advertising and marketing agency	08.04.1996	Moscow	49	Advertising, marketing
BM Holding Ltd	27.10.1999	Non-resident, Zurich	98	
Zareche joint-stock commercial bank	31.08.1992	Kazan, Republic of Tatarstan	53.22	Bank
Russian Land Bank	29.04.1994	Moscow Region	63.08	Bank
Bank of Khakassia	21.12.1998	Chernogorsk, Republic of Khakassia	28.57	Bank
Moscow Export–Import Bank (Moseximbank)	02.07.1992	Moscow	19	Bank
Russian National Commercial Bank	16.01.1998	Moscow	50.1	Bank

Moskva-Minsk unitary enterprise	07.04.2000	Non-resident, Minsk, Republic of Belarus	100	Bank
Non-Government Municipal Pension Fund	13.12.1995	Moscow	50	Pension fund (non-profit organization)
Aktiv Bank joint-stock commercial bank	28.12.1998	Saransk, Republic of Mordovia	51	Bank
Stolitsa, a foundation for social and cultural development of Moscow	05.03.1996	Moscow	23.8	Non-profit organization
Moscow Leasing Industrial Company	17.07.1996	Moscow	20	Leasing
Foundation for the Support of Moscow's Main Department of Internal Affairs (GUVD)	28.06.1996	Moscow	71.43	Non-profit organization
Press-Magnat	02.08.1996	Moscow	100	Media
BM-Security	02.08.1996	Moscow	90	Security

Source: Quarterly equities' reports for the Central Bank of RF, www.cbr.ru.

the City of Moscow, probably helped the bank to survive the crisis. However, the consequences of the financial crisis and ruble devaluation in the summer and autumn of 1998 had a negative effect on the Bank of Moscow's capital, which was more than $110 million before the crisis, but fell to $50 to $60 million at the beginning of 1999. The replenishment of the Bank's equity capital in the middle of 2000 (it grew by a billion rubles or $36 million in the second quarter of that year) made it possible for the bank to compensate for the 1998 losses (Bank of Moscow's capital amounted to about $90 million in the summer of 2000).

After the beginning of the banking crisis, banks close to the City of Moscow announced the establishment of a pool (guaranteed by the City of Moscow), which included the Bank of Moscow, Mosbusinessbank, MIB, Ogni Moskvy, Mosvodokanalbank and Moseximbank. The Bank of Moscow became the pool's clearing centre. Associations of banks were a popular way of trying to alleviate the consequences of the crisis at that time. In addition, it was believed that bank associations could get funds from the Central Bank more easily than separate banks. The City of Moscow also decided to support friendly banks and asked the Central Bank to provide funds for them. The Central Bank supported the Bank of Moscow by contributing about 200 million rubles during the crisis.[79]

The Bank of Moscow managed to alleviate the consequences of the crisis due to a significant reduction of its government securities portfolio, which decreased from 1.7 billion rubles ($270 million) on 1 July 1998 to 100 million rubles (about $5 million) on 1 November 1998. During the crisis, the Central Bank frequently purchased government securities from some commercial banks in an attempt to maintain their liquidity. This is probably how the Bank of Moscow disposed of its government securities, which were an illiquid asset during that time.

There was no significant withdrawal of funds from the Bank of Moscow during the crisis period. On the contrary, deposits in the bank grew, though only in ruble terms. In dollar value, they declined from $630 to $300 million within a single quarter (1 July 1998 to 1 October 1998). The Bank managed not only to survive during that difficult period but also to improve its financial position. Ranked by capital,[80] it rose from thirty-third place in June 1998 to thirteenth place in September 2000, and by assets from eighteenth to seventh (ninth in 2001).[81]

Russia's crisis forced the Bank to revise its investment policy. However, its major directions remained the same: financing the industrial sector and development of its group of companies. New clients came to the Bank during the post-crisis period and the number of its corporate clients grew to 14000 by the beginning of 2000. New clients included many large Russian companies, such as RAO UESR, Rosvooruzhenie, Surgutneftegaz,

Moscow Oil Refinery, Sukhoi aircraft design office, Kazan helicopter plant, Tula KBP and Zarubezhneft.[82]

One of the Bank of Moscow's major clients was Rosvooruzhenie, a state-owned arms exporter.[83] According to a long-term agreement on investment, signed with this company in the spring of 1999, the Bank assumed obligations to support its programmes and to optimize its cash flows. Rosvooruzhenie planned to use it to service its export and import operations and provision of cash and settlement services and to give guarantees for credits from Russia's defence companies.[84]

A major problem facing the Bank in future may be caused by Moscow City Treasury using the Central Bank as a depository for its revenues, thus reducing the Bank's potential profits. However, according to the Bank of Moscow's President, their revenues are already diversified and the Bank will continue to be used as the settlement and investment centre for all city projects.[85] Future strategy will be to expand into Russia's regions.[86]

The Bank of Moscow is an example of a successful municipal bank, managed by the City of Moscow. Established much later than most Russian banks, it survived the 1998 crisis and improved its position in the Russian banking and services sector. By the end of 2000, the Bank was a strong financial institution and the core of the Moscow Financial Group.

CONCLUSION

Whatever difficulties remain, it is no small achievement to have set up a modern banking system in such a short time. The three banks studied in this chapter portray some of the successes and failures of this transformation. The three banks illustrate that large banks provide a comprehensive service of banking facilities for customers: government, corporate and individual. Exemplified by Sberbank, services are on a national scale. But the structure of the companies again illustrates the peculiarities of the new Russian system.

The banks are influenced in many ways by the legacy of the Soviet period. The structures and processes of Sberbank have been greatly influenced by the Soviet structure of Sberbank USSR and its predecessors. This has secured its very large deposit base among the population; it also ensures its links with non- financial companies. It continues to act as a state bank and has received more than equal support for its liabilities. This was particularly so following the 1998 crisis. Support from the Central Bank even ensured that Sberbank made a profit after 1998. Both Sberbank and Uneximbank have had a very strong continuity of personnel with banks of the Soviet period. Unexim, as we have seen, developed out of earlier Soviet banks linked to the foreign-trade sector. These connections made it possible for Unexim to be part of companies involved in foreign trade, which became their major owners. It, like Sberbank, became a major operator in the purchase of government securities. Bank of Moscow is a new bank, but it too has the hallmark of state socialism. The crucial role of political control over assets in localities has led to local authorities founding their own banks.

The role of government has been predominant in the history of all three banks. All have benefited from government contracts and deposits: Sberbank from the government of the Russian Federation and the Bank of Moscow from the City of Moscow, itself a major economic and commercial entity. Unexim also had strong links with Russia's regions either directly or through subsidiaries. This development turned on receiving licences from government ministries, showing once again the role of state power over the banks. The loans-for-shares initiative also benefited Unexim in its bids for shares which gave equity in non-financial companies. State institutions, on the other hand, expect financial support from the banks for economic and commercial activities. Such backing can take the form of loans to government controlled companies, or to companies which a local authority may deem to be essential for its citizens. In 1997, for instance, 70 per cent of corporate clients of the Bank of Moscow were state-owned and municipal businesses. Involvement with politics may also include more direct support of 'government' candidates in elections, though precise information on the extent of this is lacking in our studies.

A second general characteristic of the three banks is that ownership is held by non-financial institutions: companies and government departments. Individual ownership is relatively low. Typically, non-financial companies own banks, not the other way around, although this does not exclude other ownership by banks of companies, which was particularly the case for the Bank of Moscow. Such overlapping in membership gives rise to financial industrial groups in which non-financial companies receive finance from the constituent bank, something which has been illustrated in the study of Unexim. One implication here is that a bank losing money through financial operations could utilize its non-financial assets to pay debts. Alternatively it could go out of business (with a consequent loss to its creditors) and secure its non-financial assets. As government institutions, such as the City of Moscow, own the Bank of Moscow, which in turn owns media companies, there are possibilities here for political control of the media. A major problem facing the banking system is the extent to which government holdings and influence over 'state' banks' financial policies is in the public interest; how far they have an undue advantage over other commercial banks; and how far the interests of depositors are compromised by political interests.

APPENDIX

Table A4.1 Top 50 Russian banks, ranked by assets, March 2001

	Number of branches	Location	Number of employees	Assets*	Capital*	Retail deposits*	Legal entities' deposits*
1 Sberbank of Russia (1 July 2000)	21778	Moscow	199896	596051075	43495214	348038432	149691114
2 Vneshtorgbank (Bought out Most Bank in November 2000)	32	Moscow	3555	120413797	44271708	2966616	42361903
3 Gazprombank	27	Moscow	2689	86271143	1657378	5447485	33736636
4 AlfaBank	25	Moscow	4336	75652582	22144165	4756226	19154335
5 Mezhdunarodny PromyshlennyBank	4	Moscow	466	75135117	26158542	—	4297873
6 Mezhdunarodny Moskovski Bank	—	Moscow	—	72692633	2494174	1007651	54636031
7 DIB	—	Moscow	400	49376312	3112978	3782027	39289790
8 Rosbank (Successor bank to Unexim Bank)	13	Moscow	—	44912616	7061292	2675777	27072172
9 Bank of Moscow	38	Moscow	2968	36363109	3318671	3409576	30445008
10 Citibank	1	Moscow	232	28421679	2844757	405328	9995723
11 MDM Bank	12	Moscow	1312	26020303	4569208	385491	6220424
12 Promstroibank	44	St Petersburg	—	24076212	1939513	1799089	16602657
13 Menatep St Petersburg	57	St Petersburg	2351	23011441	2673568	1320087	13273433
14 Bashkreditbank	13	Ufa	2424	22049470	3972683	1015864	10487595
15 Globex Bank	8	Moscow	137	19129608	5100966	145028	1002185
16 National Reserve Bank	1	Moscow	309	16187298	4840709	210529	4155287
17 Avtobank	27	Moscow	2911	15345074	1592367	2722261	4772117

Table A4.1 (cont.)

	Number of branches	Location	Number of employees	Assets*	Capital*	Retail deposits*	Legal entities' deposits*
18 Evrofinars	3	Moscow	295	15018333	2953225	188131	3975204
19 ABN Amro	1	Moscow	160	12491538	1203571	234602	4167685
20 Guta Bank	39	Moscow	1998	12068651	2727271	495311	6333064
21 Sobinbank	16	Moscow	—	11912612	3747121	289639	2009523
22 Nomos-Bank	1	Moscow	330	10459579	2529832	139117	2083391
23 Vozrozhdeniye	62	Moscow	3580	10428231	1450049	1419970	3712071
24 Bark Zenit	3	Moscow	54	9541811	1598706	486203	6542393
25 Bank Austria Creditanstalt	5	Moscow	212	8802535	1953454	1818222	1249557
26 ING Bank (Eurasia)	—	Moscow	192	8227116	1525923	288205	2886764
27 Konversbank	12	Moscow	956	7747012	1763000	915686	2374019
28 Moskovsky Industrialny Bank	37	Moscow	2810	7354232	1485510	764543	3983191
29 Petrovsky	17	St Petersburg	3763	6717263	619440	1367141	3046500
30 Ak Bars –	20	Kazan	1802	6583291	2593523	518790	4472990
31 Petrokommerts	14	Moscow	1062	6443982	1443099	1029134	1208596
32 Zapsibank	32	Tyumen	1442	6377639	432912	811874	4818625
33 Krasbank	0	Moscow	99	6236462	140748	423	33680
34 Metkombank	6	Cherepovets	659	5811758	364607	837268	4379131
35 Impexbank	46	Moscow	2107	5740006	1588099	1025526	2319480
36 Investitsionno-Bank. Gruppa NIKoil	6	Moscow	711	535879	1383394	691274	254682
37 Olimpiiskv Bank	1	Moscow	213	5241691	1669671	150159	709319
38 Transkretitbank	4	Moscow	370	4498471	1349461	55717	1586304
39 Avangard	—	Moscow	512	4203548	841375	52755	5068

40 Mosnarbank	—	Moscow	138	4 135 158	1 076 804	124 882	373 702
41 MIB	2	Moscow	140	4 127 412	826 776	6887	1 362 370
42 Baltisky Bank	9	St Petersburg	1241	395 639	353 656	924 934	1 646 571
43 MFK Bank	—	Moscow	159	3 899 720	1 320 143	58 850	245 060
44 Russkv Generalny Bank	1	Moscow	231	3 738 367	509 833	31 428	2 863 296
45 MBRR	5	Moscow	283	3 613 704	798 432	33 367	1 410 304
46 Chelindbank	28	Chelyabinsk	1392	3 583 707	519 451	651 587	1 906 933
47 lnkasbank	9	St Petersburg	700	3 580 945	631 150	140 893	1 492 477
48 Probiznessbank	—	Moscow	535	3 570 693	1 043 590	155 706	2 213 807
49 Visavi	—	Moscow	174	3 352 739	1 527 728	43 073	308 699
50 Garanti Bank-Moskva	—	Moscow	68	3 236 594	397 083	65 446	4224

Notes: * Thousands of rubles.

Source: Rating Information Centre. Cited in *Moscow Times*, *Business Review*, 98, No. 2 (March 2001).

Table A4.2 Exchange rates, Russian ruble–US dollar, 1 January 1993 to 1 January 2001

Date	Exchange rate (ruble/USD)
01.01.1993	417
01.04.1993	692
01.07.1993	1059
01.10.1993	1166
01.01.1994	1247
01.04.1994	1753
01.07.1994	1989
01.10.1994	2596
01.01.1995	3571
01.04.1995	4897
01.07.1995	4538
01.10.1995	4508
01.01.1996	4610
01.04.1996	4854
01.07.1996	5108
01.10.1996	5402
01.01.1997	5560
01.04.1997	5729
01.07.1997	5782
01.10.1997	5861
01.01.1998	5963
01.04.1998	6108
01.07.1998	6.2
01.10.1998	15.90
01.01.1999	20.65
01.04.1999	24.16
01.07.1999	24.21
01.10.1999	25.05
01.01.2000	27
01.04.2000	28.6
01.07.2000	28.05
01.10.2000	27.75
01.01.2001	28.16

Source: www.sky-net.ru.

NOTES

1. The journal *Ekspert* regularly publishes basic data on rankings of the major banks, derived from statistics published by the Bank of Russia. The data here are as published by *The Moscow Times, Business Review*. Another accessible source is *Ekspert*, No. 24 (25 June 2001). The journal *Profil'* also publishes lists. Though all these lists are based on Bank of Russia statistics, the figures may differ due to recalculation by the journals. Below there may be discrepancies between different figures cited.
2. Data on historical development are based on Sberbank's official website: www.sbrf.ru (accessed 20 January 2001).
3. RSFSR (Rossiyskaya Sovetskaya Federativnaya Sotsialisticheskaya Respublica). One of the constituent republics of the USSR, which under Yeltsin declared its sovereignty and then became the present Russian Republic.
4. 'Sberbank's Development until the Year 2005'. Official website: www.sbrf.ru (accessed January 2001).
5. Annual report of Sberbank (2001). www.sbrf.ru.
6. Ranked by number of branches, it is claimed by Sberbank to be the second largest bank in the world. Annual reports of Sberbank available on www.sbrf.ru (2001).
7. Source: website. Annual reports of Sberbank are available at www.sbrf.ru (2001).
8. Quarterly equities reports for Central Bank of RF, www.cbr.ru (2001).
9. This company is a fully owned subsidiary of CA IB Investment Bank AG of Austria.
10. Data derived from GosKomstat, *Sotsial'no-Ekonomicheskoe polozhenie Rossii*, January–December 1998.
11. Andrei Kazmin (Bank president), *Profil*, No. 9 (3 March 1998), p. 81.
12. Central Bank of the Russian Federation, the State Statistics Committee, 'Vedi' database, derived from www.cbr.ru.
13. Annual reports Sberbank, op. cit.
14. The six 'problematic' banks were SBS-Agro, Menatep, Mosbusinessbank, Most-Bank, Promstroibank and Inkombank.
15. According to GosKomstat, in 2001 pensioners accounted for 61 per cent of the ruble deposits in Sberbank.
16. Sberbank's official website: www.sbrf.ru (accessed January 2001).
17. Data here and in following paragraphs are derived from Sberbank's annual reports: www.sbrf.ru (January 2001).
18. Source: website www.sbrf.ru (accessed January 2001).
19. Annual report.
20. 'The Outlook for Sberbank's Development until the Year 2005', Sberbank's official website: www.sbrf.ru (accessed January 2001).
21. Finmarket, www.finmarket.ru (accessed 5 October 2001).
22. Kompaniya, No 28 (124), 25/07/00: Kontseptual'nyi Sberbank.www.sbrf.ru.
23. It is sometimes referred to as Oneksimbank, or ONEKSIMbank, this being a literal transliteration from Russian.
24. *Profil'*, No. 16 (27 April 1998), 'Udelnyi knyaz' Vladimir Olegovich.
25. Ibid.
26. Ibid.
27. *Finansovo-promyshlennie gruppy v economike i politike sovremennoy Rossii*, Moscow, Center politicheskikh tekhnologii, 1997. Agentstvo federal'nykh rassledovanyii 'FreeLance Bureau', http://www.flb.ru/potanin/7.html (September 2000).
28. Agentstvo federal'nykh rassledovanyi 'FreeLance Bureau', http://www.flb.ru/potanin/7.html (September 2000).
29. BBC World/BBC News, 'HARDTalk', 14 July 1999, interview with Potanin by Tim Sebastian.
30. 'Ya nikogda ne bil liberalom', *Kommersant*, No. 36 (9 March 1999).
31. *Novaya gazeta*, No. 47 (18 December 1999).

32. Agentstvo federal'nykh rassledovanyii 'FreeLance Bureau', http://www.flb.ru/potanin/7.html (September 2000).
33. Interros, official website: www.interros.ru (2000).
34. Novolipetskiyi metalurgicheskiyi kombinat is one of the biggest aluminum producers in the world (the largest in Russia).
35. Quarterly equities reports for the Central Bank of RF, 1996–2000, www.cbr.ru (2000).
36. 'Bankovski krizis', *Profil'*, No. 31 (28 August 1998).
37. *Profil'*, No. 20 (92) (2 June 1998).
38. Interros, official website: www.interros.ru (2000).
39. *Novaya gazeta*, 13.12.99. No. 47 (569).
40. It was officially established on 8 September 1998 on the basis of the renamed Nezavisimost bank.
41. 'Potanin – Ya borus' po lubim pravilam', *Kompaniya* (17 May 1999).
42. 'Economicheskie novosti i normativnie akti', *Finmarket* (31 January 2000).
43. *Finmarket* (4 February 2000).
44. *Kommersant-Daily* (4 July 2000).
45. *Kommersant -Daily* (4 July 2000).
46. 'Economicheskie novosti i normativnie akti', *Finmarket* (10 January 2000).
47. *Segodnya*, No. 205 (13 September 1999).
48. Artem Lebedev, 'Tol'ko dlya solidnih klientov', *Vremya novostey* (19 September 2000).
49. Nil's Iogansen, 'Rosbank zakonchil sliyanie s UNEXIMBANK', *Izvestiya* (19 September 2000).
50. Yakov Pappe, 'Oligarhi bez oligarhii', *Ekspert* (3 April 2000).
51. *Kompaniya*, No. 8 (59) (8 March 1999).
52. Bank of Moscow, official website, www.mmbank.ru (2001).
53. Ibid.
54. *Kommersant-Daily*, No. 69 (15 April 1995).
55. Ibid.
56. 'Vechernyaya Moskva' (7 March 2000).
57. 100 per cent of shares belong to Ikonnikova I.V.
58. 49 per cent of shares belong to 'EES Rossii'.
59. 100 per cent of shares belong to 'Troika Dialog'.
60. 99.8 per cent of shares belong to 'Surgutneftegaz'.
61. Interview with A. Borodin, President of Bank of Moscow, *Ekspert*, No. 34 (8 September 1997).
62. Ibid.
63. Ibid.
64. *Vechernyaya Moskva* (7 March 2000).
65. Interview with A. Borodin, *Vechernyaya Moskva* (10 March 2000).
66. Interview with A. Borodin, *Economika i zhizn'. Moskovski vipusk*, No. 14 (22 September 2000).
67. Interview with A. Borodin, *Vedomosti* (3 August 2000).
68. Interview with A. Borodin, *Economika i zhizn'. Moskovski vipusk*, No. 14 (22 September 2000).
69. Ibid.
70. Quarterly equities' reports for the Central Bank of RF, www.cbr.ru.
71. *Kommersant-Daily* (2 August 1997).
72. Moscow government press-release (9 June 1998) (accessed in November 2000, www.mmbank.ru).
73. Statement of Bank of Moscow's press service, 5 June 1998 (accessed in November 2000, www.mmbank.ru).
74. Statement of Bank of Moscow's press service, 30 June 1999 (accessed in November 2000, www.mmbank.ru).
75. Interview with A. Borodin on website of Novgorod region (accessed in November 2000).
76. Ibid.
77. Interview with A. Borodin, *Ekspert*, No. 34 (8 September 1997).

78. Ibid.
79. According to *Profil'*, No. 31 (28 August 1998).
80. According to *Profil'*, No. 26 (13 July 1998).
81. *Profil'*, No. 27 (149) (19 July 1999); *Profil'*, No. 41 (213) (30 October 2000).
82. *Vechernyaya Moskva* (7 March 2000).
83. Rosvooruzhenie's 1998 financial operations were estimated at \$2.3 billion, according to a Bank of Moscow press service statement of 5 May 1999. This information (as of November 2000) is available at the Bank of Moscow's web-site at www.mmbank.ru.
84. Statement of Bank of Moscow press service, 5 May 1999 (accessed in November 2000, www.mmbank.ru).
85. Interview with A. Borodin, *Vedomosti* (3 August 2000).
86. Interview with A. Borodin, *Economika i zhizn'*, Moscow edition, No. 14 (22 September 2000).

PART II

Governance Issues

5. Banks and illegal activities[1]

Heiko Pleines

Capital flight, tax evasion and money laundering are often seen as major problems of post-Soviet Russia, indicating economic breakdown, the government's failure to create a functioning state and the criminalization of society. At the same time, it is often assumed that banks – and especially those banks belonging to influential businessmen, so-called 'oligarchs' – are at the centre of these problems. Illegal capital flight, tax evasion and money laundering are indeed all based on schemes which are intended to hide certain financial flows from state authorities. However, this does not necessarily imply that banks are the main culprits.

This paper will examine the role of Russian banks in these three illegal activities. In the first three parts the main characteristics of illegal capital flight, tax evasion and money laundering will be depicted, devoting particular attention to schemes requiring the involvement of banks. In the following part the findings will be summarized, concentrating first on the importance of Russian banks for the realization of these illegal activities and second on the degree to which the Russian banking sector has been criminalized because of its involvement. The conclusion presents the general policy options available to tackle related problems.

ILLEGAL CAPITAL FLIGHT

Capital exports are used to finance imports of goods and services or investments abroad. They are a result of international economic integration. Over recent decades a general tendency of capital exports from developing countries to the main industrialized economies can be observed. Capital flight is usually defined to include all outflows that occur in excess of those that would normally be expected as part of an international portfolio diversification strategy. This definition covers legal outflows of funds that comply with existing regulations as well as exports of legally owned funds under violation of capital controls or taxation rules and outflows of funds from truly criminal activities (Loungani and Mauro, 2000, pp. 3–4).

The main reason for capital flight is distrust in the domestic economy. In the Russian case residents saw their assets depreciated in the early 1990s due to a high rate of inflation and frequent devaluation of the home currency. In addition income earned in the country has been subject to a tax system often described as prohibitive and chaotic. Moreover, the volatility of domestic financial markets and their unregulated state strengthens residents' unwillingness to invest money at home. Altogether that means residents regard the after-tax rate of return on domestic investment to be below the world rate of return.[2] In addition, capital flight can be used as a means of money laundering.[3]

Extensive capital flight causes instability in the exchange markets and in the long run hampers domestic capital formation, thus deepening a recession or slowing down economic growth. Moreover, it deprives the home government of tax yields. Accordingly, many countries affected by extensive capital flight have reacted with legal restrictions in order to reduce capital exports. In Russia the export of domestic currency is generally banned. Exports of foreign currency are subject to foreign exchange regulations, which make the export of sums of money above a certain limit subject to state approval.[4] Earnings from exports have to be returned to Russia, generally. The relevant conditions are first of all set by legislation and by Central Bank regulation and have been changed regularly.[5] As a result of this regulation the possibilities for legal capital exports from Russia are very limited: that is, most capital that leaves Russia does so by violating at least foreign exchange regulations.

Estimates of illegal capital flight from post-Soviet Russia range between USD 10 and 25 billion per year.[6] The Central Bank of Russia has calculated that illegal capital transfers abroad amounted to USD 25 billion in 1998, declined to USD 15 billion in 1999 and rose again to USD 23 billion in 2000 (http://www.cbr.ru). According to Tikhomirov,

> the major part of Russian capital is transferred to (a) Western countries which have established and stable banking systems; (b) countries with large local Russian-speaking communities; (c) countries that have a liberal off-shore legislation; and (d) countries which offer high returns on investments. The latter has become a feature of capital flight from Russia only in the last 1–2 years.

Typical countries belonging to group (a) are the USA, Switzerland, Great Britain, Germany or Luxembourg. Representatives of group (b) are Latvia or Israel. Classical off-shore centres for Russian flight capital (group c) are Cyprus, the British Channel Islands, Nauru and the Bahamas. The most important countries in group (d) are Malaysia and the People's Republic of China (Tikhomirov, 2001, p. 272).

Mainly, three different ways are used to export capital illegally. The first way is the outright smuggling of foreign currency or of goods which are then sold abroad with the payment remaining in a foreign bank account. The second way is based on false import–export contracts, the third uses financial transactions conducted by domestic banks.

The basic idea of false import–export contracts is to undervalue exported goods and services or to overvalue imported ones. If exports are undervalued, the payment made officially and checked by the Central Bank is less than the real value of the exported goods. The difference between the world market price and the price given in the contract is paid into a foreign bank account, controlled by the Russian company (Sotnik, 1999, p. 12). According to an estimate by the German Institute for Economic Research (DIW), Russian exports to Germany were on average undervalued by a capital flight factor of 43 per cent in the period 1994–96 (DIW, 1997, p. 998). If imports to Russia are overvalued, the difference between the amount officially stated in the contract and the real value of the imported goods is again paid into a foreign bank account, controlled by the Russian company. The Russian company can also declare that the foreign company has failed to deliver goods already paid for or, vice versa, has failed to pay for exports already made. If it is in collusion with its foreign counterpart the Russian company can in both cases ask the foreign company to transfer payment to a foreign bank account controlled by the Russian company. Tikhomirov has estimated that under false import–export contracts altogether about USD 83 billion left Russia illegally in the period 1992–97 (Tikhomirov, 2001, p. 263).

In order to fight such schemes Russia has introduced controls aimed at clarifying the real value of exported and imported goods. In reaction Russian companies have created more complicated schemes by trading services, the real value of which is harder to estimate, by including a number of foreign partners in the transaction or by founding their own subsidiaries abroad.

Since the mid-1990s, when electronic banking became common practice in Russia and business ties between Russian and foreign banks were well established,[7] domestic banks have been increasingly used for illegal capital flight. Banks involved in illegal capital transfers often work from offshore centres. The official advantage of offshore banks is that they are set up in regions with extremely low tax rates. Completely legal investments are therefore attracted (for example, Gorbunov 1995). But offshore zones also have laws which give banking secrecy the highest priority. Registered companies can very often do business without any state supervision. That is why offshore centres are especially interesting for companies trying to invest illegal money. In the late 1990s Russian individuals and companies operated an estimated 60 000 offshore companies (*Segodnya*, 17 January 1997, p. 3).

Flight capital can be transferred from a Russian branch of the bank to the offshore zone by telegraphic money transfer or in the form of cheques. If the value of the transaction remains below a certain limit, which in 2001 stood at about USD 10 000,[8] the bank is not obliged to notify the Russian authorities. Conducting several transactions a day over a longer period of time can be used to transfer considerable amounts of money abroad without notifying the Russian authorities. However, in many cases Russian banks collaborate with their clients and transfer larger amounts abroad, either declaring the money to be their own or that of several fictitious clients or simply ignoring their duty of notification (Pleines, 1998, pp. 26–7).

Insurance companies also engage in capital flight. In such a case a Russian company founds an insurance company, which then sets up an offshore reinsurance company. The Russian company insures its whole property for the highest premium with the insurance company. The contract is made on a ruble basis. The Russian company, therefore, does not even need a license for a foreign currency account. The insurance company reinsures the fixed risks with the offshore reinsurance company on a dollar basis. Thus the Russian company transfers large amounts of capital abroad, is able to hold them in an offshore centre and at the same time reduces its tax payments since it does not have to pay taxes for its payments to the insurance company (*Segodnya*, 27 September 1995, p. 7).

The amount of illegal capital exports organized by Russia's financial sector is hard to estimate. The only indicator available is the number of detected cases and the amount of flight capital involved. Investigations of the business activities of Russian banks conducted by Western audit companies on behalf of foreign creditors after the financial crisis of August 1998 revealed, for example, that USD 1.5 billion had disappeared out of Inkombank between August and November 1998 (*Kommersant-Daily*, 3 November 1998). Between October 1998 and autumn 1999 more than USD 7 billion were transferred illegally from Russia to the Bank of New York in altogether about 10000 financial transactions, according to reports by US authorities.[9]

Drawing from a number of expert estimates based on data from the Central Bank of Russia, the State Customs Committee and the Federal Service for Export Control, Senchagov comes to the conclusion that in the period 1992–95 about 77 per cent of the illegal capital flight (equal to USD 75 billion) was arranged with the help of false import–export contracts, a further 15 per cent (equal to USD 15 billion) was directly smuggled out of the country,[10] and the remaining 7 per cent (equal to USD 7 billion) left the country as the result of international financial transactions. Since measures to fight false import–export contracts have been tightened and the domestic banking sector has gained in importance and professionality, the share of financial transactions in illegal capital flight is assumed to have increased considerably in the second half of the 1990s. However, it seems to have remained well below 20 per cent of the total amount.[11]

TAX EVASION

Tax evasion means the illegal manipulation of information by tax payers in order to deceive the tax authorities with the aim of reducing the officially demanded tax burden or avoiding taxation completely. Enterprises have mainly two possibilities for tax evasion. First, they can hide parts or all of their business activities, thus operating untaxed as part of the shadow economy. Secondly, they can manipulate their accounts of official business activities, thus reducing the tax base, for example, for VAT or profit tax.

In a survey – which was, however, not representative – Russian managers declared in 1997 that a 'typical' Russian enterprise tends to underreport sales by about one-third. Only 30 per cent of the enterprises claimed that they were not hiding any sales (Shleifer and Treisman, 1996, p. 96). In another – again not wholly representative – survey only one-quarter of small enterprises polled in early 2001 stated that they were declaring their taxes honestly (Fruchtmann and Pleines, 2001, p. 48). In general it is estimated that the Russian shadow economy amounts to 30–50 per cent of the country's GDP. The value of taxes evaded is on average estimated to equal 15–20 per cent of GDP (that would have been USD 30–40 billion in 2000).[12]

There is a number of different approaches which try to explain the high degree of tax evasion and shadow activity in Russia. The neo-institutional line of arguments concentrates on the actual benefits and costs a person thinking about tax evasion is facing. As result of a rational choice the person opts for the behaviour that promises the best outcomes. The tax burden in Russia is very high – often called prohibitive, tax regulations are complicated and tax declarations time consuming.[13] In 1998 due tax payments equalled on average nearly 80 per cent of a Russian company's cash earnings (Busse, 2000, p. 132). According to different calculations the tax burden foreseen by the tax code amounted to 55–60 per cent of the country's GDP in that year (Spravochnik, 1999, p. 96), whereas the corresponding figure for OECD countries averaged 37 per cent, and for the EU 41 per cent (*Economist*, 4 November 2000, p. 150). Russia's tax reform 2000, though simplifying legislation considerably, has not led to a significant reduction in the overall tax burden.[14]

While the costs of being an honest tax payer are relatively high for Russian entrepreneurs, the risk attached to tax evasion is relatively low. Two main reasons for this are the inefficiency of the tax administration and widespread corruption among tax authorities, which allows tax payers to hide offences with the help of bribes.[15] In addition specifics of the Russian economic system, like the considerable amount of barter deals and inappropriate accounting standards, make it more difficult to prove tax evasion.[16]

Whereas neo-institutionalist arguments are based on costs and benefits of tax evasion as perceived by rational actors, the 'legacy' approach stresses the role of patterns of behaviour inherited first of all from the Soviet planned economy. In a systematic analysis of her empirical study Eva Busse comes to the conclusion:

> Systemic shortcomings of Russian taxation provide opportunities to engage in informal evasion practices. It is important to note, however, that the incentive function of these opportunities is greatly enhanced in the Russian context by people's dispositions to act in corresponding ways. This social disposition is rooted in a) people's expectations and skills inherited from the Soviet past and b) their willingness to evade due to the tax system's fundamental lack of legitimacy. (Busse, 2000, pp. 139–40)

In this context it is argued that the traditional personalization of relations between state actors and entrepreneurs leads to a situation where tax payments (and tax regulations) are not only subject to bargaining, but also tax payers are encouraged to evade taxes either with the help of corruption or as the anticipated result of a bargaining process.[17] The impression, derived from personal experience as well as from mass media reporting, that the amount of taxes to be paid is subject to bargaining erodes the legitimacy of the tax code and thus the willingness of tax payers to accept the rule of the tax law (see, for example, Busse, 2000 or Easter, 2000).

In order to evade taxes enterprises can either decide not to report business activities to the state authorities, thus operating in the shadow economy, or they can manipulate their accounts of reported business activities. Illegal ways to reduce due tax payments on reported business activities can be grouped into three categories:[18]

1. Underestimating the value of barter deals. This is for the mutual benefit of all enterprises involved since VAT payments are reduced. In addition the enterprises' earnings (and – in case the enterprise is not officially loss-making – taxes on profits as well) are reduced leading to a reduction in earnings- and profit-based tax payments.[19]

2. Overstating operating costs or declaring fictitious costs. Increasing reported costs reduces reported profits and with that profit-based tax payments.
3. Understating earnings (thus accumulating black cash). In the standard scheme the business contract indicates a lower payment than the one actually made. The difference between the sum stated in the contract and the sum actually paid remains with the supplier as black cash. In Russia two more complicated schemes are applied regularly. In the 'encashment scheme' an enterprise officially receives cashless payment for services. However, these services were performed only on paper. In reality the enterprise returns the monetary equivalent of the payment (minus a fee) to the customer, who does not have to report the cash to the tax authorities. In the reverse encashment scheme goods are delivered to a customer, who does not pay to the supplier but to a sham firm unofficially controlled by the supplier. Both transactions are not recorded. Instead the supplier pretends to have delivered the goods to the sham firm, receiving either non-cash payment or no payment at all, because the sham firm (often called a one-day firm) has already disappeared, leaving the cash received from the customer as black cash at the disposal of the supplier.

The main problem faced by all enterprises engaging either in the shadow economy or in black cash tax evasion is how to spend the unrecorded money without arousing the suspicions of the tax authorities or law enforcement agencies. Owners of small enterprises tend to use black cash to pay their workers (thus in addition avoiding social security taxes) or to spend it on private consumption. Black cash can also be used to finance bribe payments.[20] Bigger enterprises often transfer black cash to bank accounts abroad.[21]

Apart from the transfer of black cash abroad, all transactions related to tax evasion can be conducted without using banks.[22] Accordingly, only 10 per cent of the tax code violations detected by the tax police in 1999 were conducted by companies in the financial and credit sector (Soltaganov, 2000, p. 31). This is no coincidence since Russian banks are often seen as the prolonged arm of the tax authorities. Enterprises can open bank accounts only with the consent of the tax authorities and the banks are obliged to provide the tax authorities with all information 'necessary for monitoring the completeness and accuracy of the payment of taxes and other mandatory charges by those enterprises'. A number of state bodies are entitled to withdraw funds from bank accounts of legal and physical persons without their consent, and often they do not even need to get judicial approval of the action.[23]

The only problem faced by enterprises engaging in black cash evasion is that the state heavily restricts the ability of non-financial enterprises to hold cash legally. Accordingly some smaller banks are affiliated with financial agents running the sham firms involved in black cash tax evasion schemes. These financial agents provide most of the cash needed in such schemes, for example by officially trading junk bonds which they have in fact bought at a fraction of the nominal value, at prices close to the nominal value (Yakovlev, 2001, p. 42).

MONEY LAUNDERING

Money gained through crimes cannot be explained to the tax authorities and therefore cannot be used in the legal economy in larger amounts without raising suspicion.[24] Money laundering is the processing of these criminal proceeds to disguise their illegal origin in order to allow its owner to use the money without specific restriction (FATF, 1999). In Russia the sources of illegal income, which has to be laundered, are first of all the illegal sale of natural resources, the smuggling of drugs, arms, alcohol and tobacco, traditional organized crime activities like racketeering, prostitution or theft and white-collar crimes like tax evasion or embezzlement.[25]

Though money laundering on a massive scale has some negative macroeconomic consequences,[26] it is first of all being prosecuted as part of the fight against organized crime. In Russia money laundering was introduced as a criminal offence with the new criminal code in January 1997.[27] However, the corresponding bill on 'Measures against the legalization (laundering) of illegally gained incomes' was not passed into law.[28] Though a number of cases of supposed money laundering have been investigated, only a handful has reached the courts and there were no convictions at all until 1999. As a result the Paris-based Financial Action Task Force (FATF), set up by the Group of Seven leading economic powers (G-7), included Russia in its blacklist of banking centres with insufficient methods of fighting money laundering. However, in 2001 the Russian government started another effort to tackle the problem. In February 2001 the Russian Central Bank embraced the Wolfsberg principles for the fight against money laundering.[29] In April Russia's parliament finally ratified the international convention against money laundering,[30] which had been created in 1990 and signed by Russia in 1999. In August 2001 the President signed the new anti-money laundering law, which is to enter into force in February 2002.

Drawing conclusions concerning the extent of money laundering in Russia by using the estimated number of unknown cases hardly makes sense with no proven case at all until 1999. Accordingly, figures for the amount of money laundering in Russia are based on estimates of illegal income generated in Russia. It is then assumed that most of the income is being laundered.[31] The Russian Interpol office has come to the conclusion that in the mid-1990s the drug mafia alone laundered up to USD 35 billion a year in Russia (Interfax, 16 April 1997). According to an estimate by the Russian Ministry of the Interior at the time more than USD 300 billion were being laundered annually in Russia (Aminov and Revin, 1997, p. 51). However, taking into consideration that total nominal Russian GDP stood at a mere USD 400–500 billion in these years, this seems to be much too high an estimate.

One of the most widespread ways of money laundering is the illegal transfer of 'dirty' money abroad.[32] However, money can also be laundered domestically. For this purpose organized criminal gangs run completely legal businesses, which – as a result of manipulations in accounting – report profits far above those really achieved. Russian accounting standards make this relatively easy.[33] The gap between real and reported profit is filled with money from illegal activities. Accordingly the money appears as legally gained profit in the books of the company. The main disadvantage of this method is that profit tax has to be paid for the laundered money. Moreover, in order to be able to make credible-looking tax declarations only limited amounts of money can be laundered in one and the same company.

If instead a bank is used as cover-up for money laundering these disadvantages can be avoided. Even small banks can launder money in large amounts by claiming profits from dealings on financial markets, which are difficult to control and can be immensely profitable, by paying money to the accounts of fictitious customers or by transferring money to offshore zones.

Since a lot of private banks were newly founded after the end of the Soviet Union with legal requirements and state controls at a low level, organized criminal groups could easily develop close contacts with banks and could even found their own banks. However, since Russia's banking sector was underdeveloped in the first half of the 1990s, many Russian criminal groups engaged in the Baltic banking sector. In the Baltic states the banking sector had already established international business ties. The Baltic currencies were more stable than the Russian ruble and foreign currency operations were subject to rather limited controls.

The Russian mafia therefore used banks in the Baltics for illegal money transfers to Western bank accounts and for money laundering activities. The biggest scandal arose around the Latvian Banka Baltija. It was the country's number one bank with capital more than four times as high as that of the bank ranking second (*Baltic News*, 1 April 1995, p. 25). Nearly

50 per cent of all Latvian companies had an account with the bank, as well as 19 out of the 26 district administrations. The bank also improved its connections by making illegal donations to members of the Latvian parliament (*Baltic Independent*, 30 June 1995, p. B1).

The bank's connections ensured that control by the Latvian National Bank did not take place. Thus the bank could engage in criminal activities such as shady deals with foreign currencies, money laundering and financing of the illegal arms trade. One of the leading persons in the bank, Aleksandr Laventa, was accused of being personally involved in operations by the Russian and Ukrainian mafia. However, since many documents concerning the bank's business were destroyed, it is very hard to reconstruct the bank's illegal activities (RFE/RL Newsline, 27 October 1997). However, the Latvian Parliament's investigation panel into the case concluded in its final report, issued in October 1996, that the bankruptcy of Banka Baltiya had been caused by its leadership's 'continuous and systematic violation of the law' (OMRI Daily Digest, 30 October 1996).

Moisjeh Gurevich, a member of the board and co-founder of the bank, was killed in May 1995. The former security chief of the bank was shot in 1997. Laventa was brought to trial in October 1997. His case was halted in September 2000 for health reasons (RFE/RL Newsline, 6 September 2000).

With the establishment of the Russian banking sector the Baltic banks lost their importance in the mid-1990s.[34] Their position received a further blow when the discovery of links between banks and organized crime led to a number of bank closures and collapses (*Economist*, 20 January 1996, p. 93). In late 1996 all three Baltic states signed a declaration pledging that they would implement legislation complying with EU and international directives on money laundering (OMRI Daily Digest, 15 November 1996). But at that time the mafia had already turned its back on the Baltic states, since the Russian banking sector was now offering much better opportunities. In November 1995 the acting chairman of the Russian Central Bank admitted that 'there is a small group of banks which deal actively with illegal structures and launder money. The so-called mafia works actively in this area.' (*Financial Times*, 13 November 1995, p. 3).

The best known example of this was the Moscow-based Solntsevo gang, which had established a whole network of companies. The gang was said to be the largest of its kind in Moscow with over 2000 active members. It allegedly controlled several banks and financial organizations and about 100 smaller commercial enterprises. The gang was investigated in 1995 by the largest police action of its kind, with about 500 policemen taking part. But the operation was only partly successful, probably due to leaked information. The organization of commercial structures for money laundering was one of the major activities of the gang.[35]

THE ROLE OF RUSSIAN BANKS

It has been shown that Russian banks play only a minor role in illegal capital flight and tax evasion. Schemes for illegal capital flight are first of all based on false import–export contracts and if banks provide financial services in connection with such contracts, there is no need to inform them of the true nature of the business. The same applies to tax evasion. Again, many schemes are based on false contracts, often involving barter deals, which do not require the participation of banks at all. The minor role banks have in illegal capital flight and tax evasion is due to two reasons. First, banks are often considered to be the prolonged arm of the state authorities, especially the tax authorities. Secondly, many enterprises engage in transactions which can be used for capital flight (import–export business) or tax evasion (for example, barter deals) without the need to let a bank know the illegal nature of the transaction.

Based on the estimate presented above that only 10–15 per cent of illegal capital flight seems to be organized by banks, banks were responsible for an illegal capital flight of USD 2–3 billion in 2000. Their share in the organization of tax evasion should stand at roughly the same level. This would mean that banks knowingly participated in tax evasion schemes involving USD 3–6 billion in 2000. Accordingly, we can estimate that through the organization of illegal capital flight and tax evasion Russian banks ensured a turnover of about USD 4–8 billion in 2000.[36] For comparison, total assets of Russian banks stood at USD 77 billion in mid-2000.[37]

Whereas banks play only a minor role in capital flight and tax evasion the situation is different with the laundering of money from organized crime. In principle, money laundering too can be organized without the participation of banks. However, bigger mafia gangs need to launder huge amounts of money regularly and the risk attached to the laundering of mafia income is higher than the one connected with illegal flight capital or black cash from tax evasion. Accordingly, organized crime often prefers to control the enterprises involved in money laundering. Moreover, because of the illegal nature of organized crime, criminal gangs do not have the possibility to organize capital flight or tax evasion as part of their normal business activities. That means independently of whether they use import–export companies, industrial enterprises or banks, in all cases they have to gain control over or set up new companies. And organized crime is influential enough to gain control over smaller Russian banks. If a bank is controlled by the organizer of illegal schemes to launder money, the risk that the bank will inform relevant state authorities is considerably reduced.

As a result a certain part of the Russian banking sector has been taken over by organized crime.[38] This part mainly consists of smaller banks, which can be more easily controlled by criminal gangs and sometimes have even been founded by them. Bigger banks have been concentrating on rent-seeking often in combination with corruption. In the Russian context contacts between bankers and state officials were in many cases transformed into corruption networks. When making decisions on licenses, credits, the sale of government bonds, the authorization of banks to deal with state funds or – after the financial crisis of 1998 – the distribution of state funds for bank restructuring, state employees had considerable latitude which allowed them to open 'negotiations' with individual banks in order to obtain bribes. For the banks rent seeking was a much bigger game than organizing capital flight. For commercial banks the managing of state budget funds alone meant an annual turnover of up to USD 25 billion in the mid-1990s (see Pleines 2000 and Tompson 2000) compared to a turnover of USD 2–3 billion from the organization of illegal capital flight. If bigger banks got involved in capital flight, they were normally operating on their own account. Especially when the financial crisis of August 1998 threatened many of the big banks with bankruptcy, they used capital flight as a secure way to hide their assets from debtors. However, even these bigger banks have often used smaller banks as front companies, in order to avoid direct involvement in illegal schemes.[39]

Though many Russian banks have obviously been engaged in criminal activities of one sort or another, there are no grounds for the claim, often made by journalists and certain representatives of Russian law enforcement agencies, that organized crime controls a large part of the Russian banking sector. Organized crime has contacts with many banks, but only in a limited number of cases, first of all concerning smaller banks, does this entail outright control.

CONCLUSION

Since all the evidence available suggests that the role of banks in tax evasion and illegal capital flight is rather limited, efforts to tackle these problems should concentrate on other aspects. Important factors explaining tax evasion are not criminal banks but rather a relatively high tax burden, an inefficient and corrupt tax administration, inappropriate accounting standards, the widespread barter economy, racketeering, lack of experience with direct taxes and, last but not least, a personalized relationship between tax inspectors and tax payers. Capital flight is caused not by the conspiracies of Russian banks, but by a highly unattractive environment for domestic investments.

Moreover, if we accept that illegal capital flight and tax evasion are not a problem of banking regulation but rather a consequence of Russia's general economic environment, it makes sense to limit the legal definition of money laundering, as given in the Criminal Code, to money originating from activities of organized crime. Thus it becomes possible to increase the risk attached to transactions with organized crime money and there might be a chance of fighting organized crime more efficiently.[40] After a long discussion this view finally made it into the anti-money laundering law of 2001.

If the primary aim is not to fight illegal capital flight, tax evasion and money laundering, but to clean up the banking sector, money laundering, tax evasion and capital flight are important problems which can only be fought with the help of tight controls. However, in the Russian case this should not mean increasing state control over banks, but rather shifting from attempts by the tax authorities to get information about individual tax dodgers and the liquidity of companies with tax arrears towards the monitoring of business practices of suspicious banks, conducted first of all by law enforcement agencies. However, in order to secure real control it would be vital to cut the corrupt connections most banks have established with state officials and politicians. At the same time, incentives should be created to induce banks to engage in 'normal' banking activities, that is, to function first of all as financial intermediaries crediting investments, instead of building their business around contacts with state officials or criminal groups.

NOTES

1. This text has been prepared as part of the project 'The Role of Economic Culture in Russia's Tax System', which is being sponsored by the Otto Wolff-Foundation and the Alfred + Cläre Pott-Foundation. (For further information on the project see: http://www.forschungsstelle.uni-bremen.de/projekte/wirtschaftskultur_Projekt_engl.html).
2. For an elaboration with special reference to Russia see Loungani and Mauro (2000), pp. 10–13. A general overview of reasons for capital flight is given by Hallwood and MacDonald (1994), pp. 371–2 and Kim (1993), pp. 19–22.
3. According to the Russian Tax Police 30–40 per cent of illegal capital flight from Russia consists of dirty money (Soltaganov, 2000, p. 85). However, it is not clear how the figure was calculated. See the section on money laundering.
4. The limit was raised to USD 75 000 per year in March 2001.
5. An overview of relevant legislation and regulation is given in Loungani and Mauro (2000), pp. 13–18; Tikhomirov (2001), pp. 266–71; Westin (2000); Mel'nikov (2000); Volzhenkin (1999), pp. 218–22.
6. On different estimates and methods used for the Russian case see Petrov (2000); Kosarev (2000); Westin (2000); Bulatov (1999); Senchagov (1999); Albakin (1998); Tikhomirov (1997). For a general discussion of different methods to measure capital flight see Sheets (1996) and Claessens (1997).
7. By the end of 2000 nearly 1 000 Russian banks had correspondent accounts in German banks and more than 600 in American banks (*Russian Banking News – NewsBase*, 2 May 2001, p. 4).

8. Defined as 4000 times the legally defined minimum monthly wage. With the new Law on Money Laundering the limit will amount to about USD 20 000 from February 2002.
9. There is a huge number of journalistic accounts of the affair. Good overviews are provided by Arsen'ev (1999); Albats (2000); Reuters (15 September 2000).
10. About half in the form of goods and the other half in the form of cash.
11. Tikhomirov (2001), pp. 262–3 and Kuchkin (2000), p. 233. See also Loungani and Mauro (2000), footnote 12.
12. On estimates and methods used in the Russian case see Iakovlev and Vorontsova (1998); Yakovlev (1998); Dolgopyatova (1998); Orekhovskii (1996). See also the chapter on 'Measurement issues' in Feige and Ott (1999), pp. 141–306. A general overview of measures to estimate tax evasion is given by Tanzi and Shome (1993).
13. A good example of this kind of argument is Commander and Tolstopiatenko (1997). An empirical study showing a positive correlation between the amount of the shadow economy on the one hand and tax burden, degree of corruption, racketeering and trust in courts on the other hand is presented by Johnson, McMillan and Woodruff (1999).
14. The Russian government officially predicted a reduction of the tax burden equal to 2 per cent of GDP.
15. On this see, for example, OECD (2000), p. 103. A formal model of tax evasion in cases of corruptible tax authorities is developed by Bowles (1999).
16. A more detailed discussion of these aspects can be found in Pirtillä (1999). Related empirical data for the Russian case is provided by Yakovlev (2000).
17. That is, if a tax payer is sure that after having bargained with the tax authorities he will not have to pay all taxes, he is highly unlikely to feel obliged to keep to the letter of the tax code.
18. For a description of different methods of tax evasion see Yakovlev (2001; in an earlier version published as Yakovlev [1999]); Il'in (2001), pp. 84–107; Dolgopjatova (1999); Murzov (1997), pp. 89–130. An overview of related legislation is given by Mikhalev, Danikov and Kasyatina (2000).
19. Detailed documentation of state regulation of barter deals and control by tax authorities is given in Dan and Valeksa (1998) and Kalinina (1998). On the tax authorities' efforts to fight price manipulation through barter deals see Ganeles (2000).
20. In his empirical study Yakovlev has found no evidence for this. However, with only 10 respondents his panel cannot be seen as representative.
21. Since the black cash transferred abroad has been accumulated in violation of the tax law, this is illegal capital flight (see the part on illegal capital flight above).
22. A formal exception is the case of black cash tax evasion, since according to Russian regulations inter-firm cash payments above a certain sum have to be conducted through bank transfers. (Since the end of 1999 the limit stands at 10000 rubles – at present equal to USD 350. Earlier it was set at 2000 rubles.) However, the only practical problem is that for those transactions which are illegal the cash has to be transferred physically.
23. Tompson (1997), pp. 1162–70. The Russian Constitutional Court has ruled that tax authorities have the right to confiscate overdue tax payments – but not fines and hidden profits – from the bank accounts of judicial persons without prior consent of the account holder. (Constitutional Court decision 20-P, 17 December 1996. A discussion of the decision can be found by Kutter and Schröder (2000), pp. 30–32.)
24. In this article – as well as in Russian legislation until 2001 – the definition of money laundering is not restricted to the income of organized crime, but includes all income obtained illegally.
25. Dahan (2000), p. 239. According to the Russian Tax Police organized crime accounts for only 10 per cent of the money being laundered in Russia (Soltaganov, 2000, p. 55). However, it is not clear how the figure was calculated.
26. First of all redirecting investment into speculative businesses and distorting macroeconomic statistics.
27. Art.174 UK RF [=Criminal Code of the Russian Federation]. For a discussion of the new regulation see Bolotskii (1996).
28. Dahan (2000), pp. 242–3. A summary of the bill's draft version as of 1999 is given: ibid.,

pp. 246–52. For a discussion see also Aliev and Bolotskii (1999). The bill was rewritten again in early 2001. See Rubchenko and Shokhina (2001).

29. *Central Bank of Russia letter N 24–T* (15 February 2001). The Wolfsberg principles had been set up by leading Western commercial banks in October 2000. The general idea of the principles is that banks should not deal with money of unknown origin.
30. The so-called Strasbourg convention developed by the Council of Europe. The convention concentrates on measures to improve international cooperation in the fight against money laundering.
31. At the same time the possibility is being ignored that illegal income generated abroad is being laundered in Russia.
32. The money then becomes part of flight capital, being first of all directed to offshore banks (see the relevant part above). According to the Russian Tax Police 30–40 per cent of illegal capital flight from Russia consists of dirty money (Soltaganov, 2000, p. 85). However, it is not clear how the figure was calculated. Specifically on money laundering through capital flight see also Dikanova and Osipov (2000), pp. 160–209; Fituni (2000), pp. 214–16.
33. Russian Accounting Standards 'tend to overstate real profitability and the value of the business' (Ivanov 2000, p. 13).
34. In 1994 there were 55 banks in Latvia, 21 in Lithuania and 20 in Estonia, but already about 2 000 in Russia.
35. *Kommersant-Daily* (25 August 1995), p. 14. The alleged boss of the gang was arrested on money laundering charges in Switzerland in 1996. However, he was released after a trial which failed due to lack of evidence that Swiss legislation had been violated. (For details see the documentation of the trial: Yakubov 1999).
36. Since tax evasion sometimes takes the form of capital flight, the amount for tax evasion plus illegal capital flight is lower than the sum of the separate estimates.
37. *Bulletin of Banking Statistics (Central Bank of the Russian Federation),* September 2000, p. 69. The figure for total turnover of Russian banks, which would be the best comparison, is not available.
38. Russian state officials often declare that one-third of Russian banks are controlled by criminal groups (see for example *ITAR-TASS*, 23 March 2001). However, how this figure has been calculated remains unclear. One should expect the state to close down these banks if there exists proof of their connection to organized crime.
39. In the Bank of New York affair, allegedly involving illegal capital flight and money laundering of at least US$ 7 billion, the Russian banks MDM and Sobinbank, at that time medium-size banks, conducted most of the operations under investigation, according to newspaper reports on the order of bigger banks and influential Russian businessmen. (A brief summary of these allegations is given by Albats 2000.)
40. A similar argument is made by Tosunyan and Ivanov (2000).

REFERENCES

Albakin, Leonid (1998), 'Begstvo kapitala. Priroda, formy, metody bor'by', *Voprosy ekonomiki*, No. 7, pp. 33–41.

Albats, Yevgenia (2000), 'Power play. BONY scam to test Putin as reformer', *Moscow Times,* 24 February.

Aliev, V. M. and B. S. Bolotskii (1999), 'Razrabotka rossiiskogo zakonodatel'stva o protivodeistvii legalizatsii (otmivaniyu) dokhodov, poluchennykh nezakonnym putem', *Gosudarstvo i pravo*, No. 6, pp. 44–50.

Aminov, D. I. and V. P. Revin (1997), *Prestupnost' v kreditno-bankovskoi sfere*, Moscow.

Arsen'ev, Vadim (1999), 'Groza Ameriki', *Kommersant' Dengi*, 25 August, pp. 11–13.

Bolotskii, B. S. (1996), 'Problemy protivodeistviya legalizatsii (otmivaniyu) dokhodov ot nelegal'noi ekonomicheskoi deyatel'nosti', *Sotsial'no-politicheskii zhurnal*, No. 6, pp. 15–25.

Bowles, Roger A. (1999), 'Tax policy, tax evasion and corruption in economies in transition', in E. L. Feige and K. Ott (eds), *Underground economies in transition*, Aldershot, UK: Ashgate, pp. 67–86.

Bulatov, A. S. (1999), 'Parametry i otsenka masshtabov utechki kapitala iz Rossii', *Dengi i kredit*, No. 12, pp. 68–72.

Busse, Eva (2000), 'The embeddedness of tax evasion in Russia', in A. V. Ledeneva and M. Kurkchiyan (eds), *Economic crime in Russia*, The Hague: Kluwer Law International, pp. 129–43.

Claessens, Stijn (1997), 'Estimates of capital flight and its behavior', *Revista de Analisis Economico*, No. 1, pp. 3–34.

Commander, Simon and Andrei Tolstopiatenko (1997), 'A model of the informal economy in transition economies', *William Davidson Institute Working Paper*, No. 122.

Dahan, Frédérique (2000), 'Money-laundering control and the rule of law in Russia', in A. V. Ledeneva and M. Kurkchiyan (eds), *Economic crime in Russia*, The Hague: Kluwer Law International, pp. 237–56.

Dan, S. and A. Valeksa (1998), *Barter*, Moscow.

Dikanova, T. A. and V. E. Osipov (2000), *Bor'ba s tamozhennymi prestupleniyami i otmyvaniem 'gryaznykh' deneg*, Moscow.

DIW (1997), 'Die wirtschaftliche Lage Rußlands', *Wochenbericht*, No. 51–2, pp. 965–1009.

Dolgopyatova, Tat'yana (1998), *Neformal'nyi sektor v rossiiskoi ekonomike*, Moscow.

Dolgopyatova, Tat'yana et al. (1999), 'Schattenwirtschaft in Russland. Aktivitäten legaler russischer Unternehmen', *Bericht des BIOst*, No. 37.

Easter, Gerald (2000), 'Institutional legacy of the old regime as a constraint to reform. The case of fiscal policy', in Stefanie Harter and Gerald Easter (eds), *Shaping the economic space in Russia*, Aldershot: Ashgate, pp. 296–319.

Feige, Edgar L. and Katarina Ott (eds) (1999), *Underground economies in transition*, Aldershot, UK: Ashgate.

Financial Action Task Force (1999), 'Money laundering', *OECD Policy Brief*, July.

Fituni, Leonid (2000), 'Illegal aspects of trans-border capital flows from the former Soviet Union', in A. V. Ledeneva and M. Kurkchiyan (eds), *Economic crime in Russia*, The Hague: Kluwer Law International, pp. 209–21.

Fruchtmann, Jakob and Heiko Pleines (2001), 'Das russische Steuersystem', *Arbeitspapiere und Materialien der Forschungsstelle Osteuropa*, No. 25.

Ganeles, O. (2000), 'Kontrol' tsen nalogovymi organami. Otechestvennyi i zarubezhnyi opyt', *Ekonomist*, No. 10, pp. 66–9.

Gorbunov, A. R. (1995), *Offshorny biznes*, Moscow.

Hallwood, Paul and Ronald MacDonald (1994), *International money and finance*, Oxford, UK and Cambridge, US, 2nd ed.

Iakovlev, A. and O. Vorontsova (1998), 'Methodological approaches to estimating the size of unreported cash turnover', *Problems of Economic Transition*, No. 10, pp. 77–92.

Il'in, Anton (2001), *Kriminal'naya matrica. Nalogovaya prestupnost' v Rossii*, St Petersburg and Moscow.

Ivanov, Andrei (2000), 'Accounting', *Russia Market Weekly*, 29 May, pp. 13–14.

Johnson, Simon, John McMillan and Christopher Woodruff (1999), 'Why do firms hide? Bribes and unofficial activity after communism', *CEPR Discussion Paper*, No. 2105.

Kalinina, E. M. (1998), *Barter*, Moscow.

Kim, Taeho (1993), *International money and banking*, London, UK und New York, US.

Kosarev, A. E. (2000), 'Voprosy makroekonomicheskoi otsenki begstva kapitala iz Rossii', *Voprosy statistiki*, No. 2, pp. 9–12.

Kuchkin, S. V. (2000), 'Begstva kapitala. Prichiny, masshtaby, metody preodoleniya', in A. I. Arkhipov (ed.), *Problemy usileniya roli gosudarstva v stabilizatsii i pod'eme ekonomiki*, Moscow, pp. 232–41.

Kutter, J. Vivika and Tim Schröder (2000), *Die Rechtsprechung des russischen Verfassungsgerichts 1995–1999*, Berlin.

Loungani, Prakash and Paolo Mauro (2000), *Capital flight from Russia* (IMF Policy Discussion Paper PDP/00/6), Washington, US: IMF.

Mel'nikov, V. N. (2000), 'Sistema valyutnogo regulirovaniya i valyutnogo kontrolya v Rossii – etapy razvitiya i perspektivy', *Dengi i kredit*, No. 1, pp. 11–17.

Mikhalev, V. V., P. Danikov and R. V. Kasyatina (2000), 'O kvalifikatsii nalogovikh prestuplenii i pravonarushenii', *Nalogovyi vestnik*, No. 9.

Murzov, I. A. (1997), *Transformatsiya nalogovoi sistemy v ekonomike perekhodnogo perioda*, Novosibirsk.

OECD (2000), *Economic Surveys 1999–2000. Russian Federation*, Paris.

Orekhovskii, P. (1996), 'Statisticheskie pokazateli i tenevaya ekonomika', *Rossiiskii ekonomicheskii zhurnal*, No. 4.

Petrov, Yu. (2000), 'Vyvoz kapitala i nalogovyj potentsial rossiiskoi ekonomiki', *Rossiiskii ekonomicheskii zhurnal*, No. 10.

Pirtillä, Jukka (1999), 'Tax evasion and economies in transition. Lessons from tax theory', *BOFIT Discussion Paper*, No. 2.

Pleines, Heiko (1998), 'Korruption und Kriminalität im russischen Bankensektor', *Bericht des BIOst*, No. 28.

Pleines, Heiko (2000), 'Large-scale corruption and rent-seeking in the Russian banking sector', in A. V. Ledeneva and M. Kurchiyan (eds), *Economic crime in Russia*, The Hague: Kluwer Law International, pp. 191–209.

Rubchenko, Maksim and Ekaterina Shokhina (2001), 'Prizrak finansovogo kontrolya', *Ekspert*, No. 11, pp. 40–42.

Senchagov, V. K. (1999), 'Begstvo kapitala. Priroda, masshtaby i usloviya predotvrashcheniya', *Eko*, No. 3, pp. 3–9.

Sheets, Nathan (1996), 'Capital flight from the countries in transition. Some empirical evidence', *Journal of Policy Reform*, pp. 259–77.

Shleifer, Andrei and Daniel Treisman (2000), *Without a map*, Cambridge, US and London, UK: MIT Press.

Soltaganov, V. F. (2000), *Nalogovaya politsiya*, Moscow.

Sotnik, Andrei (1999), 'Za kogo dolzhen rasplatit'sya "Norsi-oil"', *Moskovskie Novosti*, 13 April, p. 12.

Tanzi, V. and P. Shome (1993), *A primer on tax evasion* (IMF Working Paper WP/93/21), Washington, US: IMF.

Tikhomirov, Vladimir (1997), 'Capital flight from post-Soviet Russia', *Europe–Asia Studies*, No. 4, pp. 591–615.

Tikhomirov, Vladimir (2001), 'Capital flight. Causes, consequences and counter-measures', in Klaus Segbers (ed.), *Explaining post-Soviet patchworks.*

Vol. 2, Pathways from the past to the global, Aldershot, UK: Ashgate, pp. 251–80.
Tompson, William (1997), 'Old habits die hard. Fiscal imperatives, state regulation and the role of Russia's banks', *Europe–Asia Studies*, No. 7, pp. 1159–85.
Tompson, William (2000), 'Nothing learned, nothing forgotten. Restructuring without reform in Russia's banking sector', in Stefanie Harter and Gerald Easter (eds), *Shaping the economic space in Russia*, Aldershot, UK: Ashgate, pp. 65–101.
Tosunyan, G. A. and E. A. Ivanov (2000), 'Vliyanie zakonodatel'stva na tenevoi i kriminal'yi oborot kapitala v Rossii', *Gosudarstvo i pravo*, No. 1, pp. 40–47.
Volzhenkin, B. V. (1999), *Ekonomicheskie prestupleniya*, St Petersburg.
Westin, Peter (2000), 'Export revenues. Repatriation or expropriation', *Russian Economic Trends*, February, pp. 3–10.
Yakovlev, A. (1998), *Neformal'nyi sektor v rossiiskoi ekonomike. Formy sushchestvovaniya, rol' i masshtaby*, Moscow.
Yakovlev, Andrei (1999), 'Black cash tax evasion in Russia', *BOFIT Discussion Papers*, No. 3.
Yakovlev, Andrei (2000), 'Pochemu v Rossii vozmozhen bezriskovyj ukhod ot nalogov?', *Voprosy ekonomiki*, No. 11, pp. 134–52.
Yakovlev, Andrei (2001), 'Black cash tax evasion in Russia. Its forms, incentives and consequences at firm level', *Europe–Asia Studies*, No. 1, pp. 33–55.
Yakubov, Oleg (1999), *Mikhailov ili Mikhas. Tainy zhenevskogo protsessa*, Moscow.

6. Banks and the loans-for-shares auctions

Duncan Allan[1]

The 'loans-for-shares' auctions in November and December 1995 involved the quasi-privatization of some of Russia's most prized state-owned firms to well-connected business groups, primarily banks, amid accusations of corruption and insider-dealing. The most widely-accepted explanation for this saga, one of the biggest public scandals of the Yeltsin era, has been presented to greatest effect by Chrystia Freeland:

> At heart, the loans-for-shares deal was a crude trade of property for political support. In exchange for some of Russia's most valuable companies, a group of businessmen – the oligarchs – threw their political muscle behind the Kremlin. What made that bargain a Big Idea and not just run-of-the-mill corruption was its scale. Over the course of four months [*sic*], the government privatised the behemoths of the Russian economy – a half-dozen huge enterprises, including the world's dominant producer of nickel and several reserve-rich oil companies – selling them for a fraction of their potential value. It was the sale of the century.

The motivation for the carve-up, according to Freeland, was straightforward:

> [L]oans-for-shares was implemented for one central reason – because the government in general and the young reformers (who still controlled the privatisation process) in particular took the calculated gamble that this was the Big Idea which could save Russia's capitalist revolution. Loans-for-shares bought Yeltsin the political, financial and strategic support of the future oligarchs in the upcoming presidential elections. It meant pawning Russia's crown jewels, but if that was the price of keeping the communists out of the Kremlin, the young reformers were willing to pay up.

Freeland concludes by arguing that the auctions were a watershed in the development of Russia's post-communist politico-economic system:

> That 'necessary pact' turned out to be a Faustian bargain. The young reformers defeated the communists, but they lost their souls in the process. They had come to power as democrats; to stay there, they created a shadowy, unelected cabal.

> They had come to power to create a fair, equitable law-abiding market economy; to keep it, they sponsored one of the world's sleaziest insider deals. Ultimately, loans-for-shares destroyed the young reformers: it cost them their ideals, their reputations and eventually their jobs. Worse yet, ultimately it scotched any remaining short-term hopes for the emergence of a healthy, prosperous Russian capitalism. Instead, Russia's market economy is now corrupt, distorted and inefficient, and loans-for-shares is both the cause and the symbol of its malaise. (Freeland, 2000, pp. 162–3)

This paper puts forward a different interpretation. It argues that the provenance of the loans-for-shares auctions lay not in an attempt by the 'young reformers' to buy the support of leading banks in anticipation of the 1996 presidential election, but in issues whose roots date back to mid-1994. In brief, the Government was without a privatization policy worth the name by the summer of 1995, yet was faced by a pressing need to raise revenues for the federal budget. This confluence of circumstances created an opportunity for a group of banks to lobby the state for material gain. The episode demonstrated too that the banks were not the omnipotent organizations which many observers took them to be. To understand the nature of the opportunity and how the banks (and others) exploited it, we need to look briefly at the background to the story.

PROBLEMS OF POST-VOUCHER PRIVATIZATION

The Russian Government's programme of mass privatization concluded at the end of July 1994. The successor programme aimed to consolidate the results of voucher privatization, the main goal of which had been political – creating a large private sector as quickly as possible – by shifting policy towards the privatization of state property in ways which facilitated investment, efficiency and enterprise restructuring. Despite lengthy negotiations, however, Anatoly Chubais (Deputy Prime Minister and Chairman of the State Property Committee: GKI) was unable to persuade the State Duma (lower chamber of parliament) to support the Government's proposals. These were therefore issued in the form of a presidential decree, signed on 22 July ('Ob osnovykh napravleniyakh', 1994). The Government had anticipated the start of 'monetary' privatization with a good deal of confidence, yet its hopes were misplaced. In short, the privatization of state property ground to a halt. There were three sets of reasons why.

Technical and administrative factors were one. In particular, the GKI as an administrative institution was unprepared for the new phase. Key tasks (like carrying out pre-sale audits and valuations of property, and then organizing auctions according to reliable legal and procedural criteria and assessments of market demand) were for a long time beyond the department. The GKI was also constrained by the likelihood that selling a large volume of shares at once would drive down prices and collapse Russia's fledgling equity market. Finally, it was diverted by a rash of pyramid schemes which failed in the summer of 1994 and required remedial action.

A second group of reasons was economic and financial. In particular, it was hoped that foreign investors would play a major role in the restructuring of newly-privatized companies. And there was indeed a boom, at an admittedly low level, on the equity market as a result of the privatization of dozens of blue-chip enterprises during the spring and summer of 1994, the low market valuations of these companies and the perception that Russia was at last close to the goal of financial stabilization. Foreign confidence in the stock market was, however, shattered in the final quarter by 'Black Tuesday' (the first serious exchange-rate crisis to hit post-communist Russia) on 11 October, the outbreak of fighting in Chechnya at the end of November and the financial crisis in Mexico, culminating in the devaluation of the peso on 19 December.

Yet the most destabilizing factor was political and stemmed from the reshuffle of the Government which took place after Black Tuesday. Chubais was promoted to the rank of First Deputy Prime Minister in charge of macroeconomic policy. His position as Chairman of the GKI was, however, filled by Vladimir Polevanov, until then the Governor of Amur *oblast'*. With the support of Chubais's main rival in the Cabinet, First Deputy Prime Minister Oleg Soskovets, Polevanov was within weeks calling for the renationalization of certain branches of industry and a halt to further privatizations. After a bitter struggle lasting several weeks, Prime Minister Viktor Chernomyrdin and Chubais persuaded President Yeltsin to sack Polevanov on 19 January.

The up-shot was that the Government's privatization policy lay in ruins by early 1995. Just 12 privatization auctions and 13 investment tenders were held during the whole of January. Six of the investment tenders had to be cancelled because of a lack of participants (Privalov, 1995, p. 32). Foreign investment in the stock market, the authorities' great hope in 1994, came to a derisory \$20–25 million in January, down from \$500–700 million at the height of the boom (Tutshkin, 1995). The GKI at this stage still intended that privatization should be carried out to attract investment and promote enterprise restructuring. Such thinking was, however, being overtaken by events.

Black Tuesday had been a traumatic experience for the authorities, and Chernomyrdin especially. He was finally convinced that the goal of financial stabilization must be placed at the heart of his Government's strategy. Inflation was to be defeated, above all, by using 'non-inflationary' sources of financing for the federal budget deficit, in particular increased sales of Treasury bills (known by their Russian acronym, GKOs). This approach was spelled out in a series of decisions taken in the first quarter of 1995. These were: the 1995 budget, approved by the Duma on 15 March; the conclusion by the Government and the International Monetary Fund (IMF) of a one-year Stand-By Arrangement (SBA) worth $6.8 billion (approved by the Fund's Executive Board on 11 April); and a ban on the crediting of the federal budget deficit by the Central Bank (CBR). Raising revenue for the budget, hitherto a secondary goal, now became the driving force behind privatization policy. Under the terms of the 1995 budget, the treasury was to receive 9.1 trillion rubles out of total privatization receipts of 24 trillion rubles. Just 13 billion rubles were collected in January (Lantsman, 1995).

The new Chairman of the GKI, Sergei Belyaev, was unprepared for the change in priorities, and he and his colleagues were unable quickly to prepare a workable package of proposals. Lack of time was not their only headache. The importance attached to maximizing revenues placed renewed emphasis on speed, and this rekindled the opposition of the sectoral ministries. Powerful opponents of the GKI between 1992 and 1994, they had been quiescent while privatization policy drifted, but they now went into action to prevent any diminution in the size of their empires.

Despite these difficulties, a decree signed by Yeltsin on 11 May confirmed that budgetary imperatives now underpinned the privatization effort. Among other things, the decree: gave the Government a month to draw up a list of 'strategic' enterprises which would remain in state hands; cancelled restrictions on the sale of federal property not on this list; formed a government commission to monitor the generation of privatization revenues; and gave the green light to the sale of land under privatized enterprises ('O merakh po obespecheniyu', 1995). These were the circumstances in which a group of Russian banks approached the authorities with an unusual proposal.

LOANS-FOR-SHARES: THE PROPOSAL

Present at a meeting of the Government on 30 March were the representatives of three banks. One, Vladimir Potanin (President of Oneksimbank),[2] addressed the session, offering on behalf of a consortium – the Inter-Bank Credit Alliance (MKS) – to lend the Government money to cover at least some of the projected privatization revenues specified in the 1995 budget. The authorities would put up shares in state enterprises as collateral for the loan. The consortium would manage the assets for an unspecified period and prepare them for sale to strategic investors. It would be paid interest for its loan. If the Government did not repay the loan on time, the assets would become the property of the banks. Potanin communicated the banks' proposal to the Government not through Chubais and the Cabinet's 'young reformers', as is often supposed, but via Soskovets (Borodulin, 1995a; and Skvortsov and Loginov, 1995). Other members of the Cabinet, including Chernomyrdin and Chubais, quickly learned about it, however ('Kommercheskie banki', 1995 and Kirpichenko et al., 1995, p. 14). According to Al'fred Kokh (First Deputy Chairman of the GKI), the proposal was a 'well-prepared improvisation' which senior policy-makers had discussed with the bankers before the meeting on the 30 March (Kokh, 1999, p. 263). The Government backed the offer in principle, although it was agreed that more information was needed before a final decision could be taken. Chernomyrdin gave the banks two weeks to formulate an in-depth proposal (Borodulin, 1995a). The initiative was attractive to the authorities because it offered a ready source of budgetary revenues in a way which did not soak the markets. But why did the banks make the offer when they did?

Part of the answer lies in Russia's changing economic circumstances. The development of the country's financial sector during the late 1980s and the first half of the 1990s did not encourage the emergence of real banks, if we take the term to refer to institutions engaged in financial intermediation between creditors and borrowers. Banks grew instead because of three factors. The first was their involvement in the importing of scarce goods, especially foodstuffs and consumer durables, in the shortage-ridden early 1990s. The second was the unstable financial conditions of the time. Banks could reap handsome profits by speculating on exchange-rate fluctuations, while their balance sheets were cushioned by loose monetary policies and high levels of inflation, which eroded the real value of their liabilities. Yet the most important reason for the development of the banking sector was its parasitical dependence on the state. This enabled banks to enrich themselves as conduits, channelling credits to enterprises and budgetary flows to state-funded organizations, or as tax-collecting agencies, or as licensed 'special exporters' of certain commodities. It was apparent by early 1995, however, that the banks would have to rethink some of their strategies. Material shortages had by then almost entirely disappeared. Black Tuesday had galvanized the authorities to squeeze inflation out of the economy, as demonstrated by repeated statements by policy-makers and a tightening of monetary policy at the end of 1994 (which was feeding through into falling inflation by February 1995). Access to the state consequently became even more important.

One way of building additional ties to the state would be for the banks to participate in official investment programmes, which might unlock new financial flows. An illustration of interest in this was the formation in December 1994 of Nadezhnost', a club made up largely of former *spetsbanki*[3] (Agroprombank, Sberbank, Vneshtorgbank, Vozrozhdenie, Mosbiznesbank, Promstroibank and Tokobank). The group aimed to pool the financial resources of the members with those of the state, ostensibly at least to promote investment in industry (Loginov, 1995; Kirpichenko et al., 1995, p. 16). Another possibility would be if the banks coordinated their activities with those of the authorities in the fields of privatization and the management of the securities market. These were the objectives of MKS, created in early 1995, which comprised six 'new' banks (Inkombank, Imperial, International Finance Company (MFK), Oneksimbank, Menatep and Stolichnyi) and three members of Nadezhnost' (Tokobank, Mosbiznesbank and Vozrozhdenie) (Zasursky, 1995). These banks were the leading domestic operators in Russian equities, and they had as much interest as the Government in avoiding anything like the release of large volumes of shares in privatized enterprises all at once, which might destabilize the stock market.

A related motivation for the loans-for-shares proposal was the interest shown by Western financial institutions in Russian stocks the previous year. This had quickly waned since the autumn, but the banks knew that some of the large state-owned companies the authorities were looking to sell in part or in whole were still of potential interest to overseas investors. Indeed, the authorities had for some time been looking at an alternative scheme. According to this idea, the Government would contract foreign banks to place corporate bonds in Russian firms on the international capital markets. The proposal, backed in 1994 by Deputy Prime Minister Aleksandr Shokhin, was subsequently taken up by officials close to Chernomyrdin ('Mezhdu Konsortsiumom', 1995). Their objection to loans-for-shares was that it would exclude foreign input and drive down prices for the assets involved. They did not rule out participation by domestic banks, but their preference was to work with the Nadezhnost' group, and the thrust of their thinking in any case was that Western institutions should play the leading role. Talks between the Government and Western institutions had reached an advanced stage by the spring of 1995 ('Konsortsium prodolzhaet', 1995). Russian financial institutions were in no position to compete with their Western counterparts in terms of their resources, or experience of equity transactions, or expertise in industrial restructuring. This was one of the concerns addressed in a revised version of the MKS proposal, sent by Potanin to the Government on 5 April, which warned that the Russian stock market might fall under the sway of foreign banks (Kirpichenko et al., 1995, p. 14). Loans-for-shares was in this sense, according to one contemporary analysis, 'a strategic offensive by major financial structures in their struggle with foreign investors for Russian property' ('Usloviya kredita', 1995).

A final reason why the MKS banks tabled the loans-for-shares proposal when they did was opportunism. It was clear by the spring of 1995 that the authorities had got themselves into a mess as regards privatization and that they had little idea about how to extricate themselves from it. The fact that they felt unable to reject out of hand an idea as convoluted as loans-for-shares in itself was proof of how superficial their thinking about monetary privatization had been. The overriding priority attached to budgetary policy meant that the authorities were increasingly inclined to take seriously any suggestion, even one as flawed as Potanin's, which might raise revenues for the treasury. As Potanin would later remark, '[i]t was the government which had a hole in its budget. They were the ones who were worried' (Freeland, 2000, p. 168).

It is worth noting that the term 'consortium' was a misnomer. MKS was recognized as a group by the CBR, which had granted it a banking licence on 22 March, but membership of it was never clear and stable. Such fluidity reflected the volatility of relations between the banks which were driven by relations between their leading personalities and by the logic of a business environment founded on short-term considerations. There was within MKS a core group of Oneksimbank and Menatep (and possibly Solichnyi). Other banks (including Inkombank, MFK, Imperial, Vozrozhdenie, Tokobank and Mosbiznesbank) were involved in discussions about the initial loans-for-shares proposal. Still others (like Alfa, Sberbank and Vneshtorgbank) expressed an interest in joining the consortium, or (like Rossiisky kredit) voiced support for its objectives without getting involved. The point is that the consortium was not a unit. Besides reducing its ability to influence the authorities, this lack of cohesion contained potential for a split if circumstances changed – as they did a few months later.

Although the Government had backed the loans-for-shares proposal in principle on 30 March, several departments, not least the GKI, harboured serious reservations about it. To begin with, the banks had not offered to lend the full amount of privatization revenues in the budget, but only 'several trillion' rubles, as one member of the consortium revealed a few days later (Zasursky, 1995). A second problem centred on doubts about whether the banks had the resources and the expertise to manage such an ambitious operation. Least attractive of all, however, was the way the offer made no provision for competitive tendering. In the form sketched by Potanin, it seemed to suggest that a bundle of very big enterprises would be handed to the banks, as a group, on a plate. This raised the possibility that, as one observer presciently put it, 'the Government [would] . . . be accused of corruption and protectionism'. If accepted, the proposal in its current shape could trigger 'a scandal bigger than all previous privatization mistakes' (Zhagel', 1995a). The authorities were therefore in no hurry to embrace loans-for-shares. Yeltsin's decree of 11 May referred to the idea, but gave the Government two months to devise a framework for implementation. It also stated that state-owned property in any loans-for-shares scheme could be transferred to private creditors only via competitive tenders. This provision represented a major dilution of the original proposal and featured in a memorandum of understanding signed on 12 May by the GKI and the MKS consortium (Stanova and Trosnikov, 1995). Nor did the decree choose between loans-for-shares and the scheme advocated by Chernomyrdin's advisers: it also instructed the GKI and the Federal Securities Commission to come up with a way of selling shares in major companies on Western capital markets ('O merakh po obespecheniyu', 1995). The authorities were keeping their options open.

Their relaxed position reflected a growing confidence about the country's economic prospects. The turmoil unleashed by Black Tuesday now seemed to have been consigned to the past. The federal deficit for the first five months of 1995 was easily within the SBA ceiling. Demand for GKOs was buoyant, and the Finance Ministry professed optimism that the budgetary target for government paper would be met. The IMF's first monthly appraisal of economic performance under the SBA, carried out in May, went smoothly. Besides unlocking a first disbursement of $500 million in budgetary support, this seal of approval strengthened market confidence and raised demand for GKOs still further. The authorities therefore believed at this juncture that they could meet the revenue targets in the federal budget without resorting to the loans-for-shares proposal.

They also put the scheme on ice because of the hostility of the managers of some of the enterprises in which the banks were interested. These included some of the most influential figures in Russian industry, whose political connections were as formidable as those of the banks. Managers at LUKoil, Russia's largest oil producer, expressed deep scepticism about the scheme, questioning the commitment or the wherewithal of the banks to invest in industry in general and the oil sector in particular. Equally, Rem Vyakhirev (Chairman of the Board of Management at Gazprom) pledged that he would never allow shares in his company to be managed by Russian banks, not least because he was in talks with Western institutions about plans to float Gazprom equities on foreign markets. Vyakhirev said that he had voiced his opinion 'to the people who are running privatization', adding that 'they agreed with us' (Borodulin, 1995b).

The GKI meanwhile struggled to implement Yeltsin's decree of 11 May. The most pressing deadline was the completion by mid-June of a list of enterprises exempt from privatization. This entailed tackling the branch ministries, whose officials demanded a significantly longer list than the one the GKI had in mind. The GKI began with a draft of about 2000 enterprises which it circulated to interested departments for comments. As a result, the size of the list swelled by over 40 per cent to 2 809 by mid-June (BBC, 1995a). Still this did not satisfy the ministries, led by the Ministry of Transport and the State Committee for the Defence Industries, which pushed for an even higher number. A list of 3054 enterprises was approved provisionally by the Government on 13 July (Borodulin, 1995c). With this agreed, the GKI could at last turn to privatization. The idea was to begin with blue-chip companies, including assets in the oil, electricity and telecommunications sectors (BBC, 1995b). Still, however, the GKI could not make progress. Symptomatic of the department's inability to take control of matters was a draft timetable of auctions, scheduled for the second half of the year, which was leaked to the press in mid-June. Compiled in haste, it was riddled with mistakes. The most egregious were the inclusion of enterprises which had already been privatized, incorrect data about the size of state-owned stakes in others and enterprises which had not even been corporatized (Lysak, 1995). As Belyaev reported to the Collegium of the GKI at the end of July, 'the process of selling state-owned packets of shares has not been proceeding as intensively as required' ('Rasshirennaya Kollegiya', 1995).

LOANS-FOR-SHARES: THE POLICY

In other words, privatization policy was still floundering with less than five months of the year left. And it was now that the events occurred which pushed the authorities into adopting the loans-for-shares scheme. Mindful of the surge in inflation caused each autumn by the disbursement of credits for agriculture and supplies for the northern regions (and which in 1994 had led to Black Tuesday), the Government and the CBR announced the introduction of an exchange-rate band, the 'ruble corridor', on 5 July. The movement of the ruble against the dollar would be confined during the third quarter (later extended to the end of the year) to a band ranging from \$1/4 300 rubles to \$1/4 900 rubles. The aim was to promote exchange-rate stability, thereby smothering inflationary expectations, which were expected to be strong in the run-up to the Duma elections in December. The CBR was confident that a combination of larger hard-currency reserves and falling inflation would enable it to regulate the market.

This strengthened commitment to financial stabilization still lacked credibility in the eyes of some, however. A number of banks discounted the new policy and continued to operate on the assumption that inflation would again take off in the autumn. This assessment caused them to form forward hard-currency positions on the markets during the summer founded on the expectation that renewed inflation and the consequent depreciation of the ruble would again bring them large profits. It was clear by early August that the ruble was not depreciating, but was continuing to appreciate in real terms, and they began to incur substantial losses. This led to a shortage of liquidity on the inter-bank market, on which many banks relied to meet short-term obligations, where the annual interest rate for one-day credits had soared to over 2 000 per cent by the final week of August. The CBR contained the crisis by easing reserve requirements, but the banking sector was badly shaken. The episode was almost certainly inevitable: movement towards financial stabilization entailed problems for many banks, which still owed their existence in large part to high inflation. Yet if it was the first stage of a necessary shake-out, it still had serious short-term implications for the GKO market. Many banks which had eagerly bought GKOs now found that they lacked the money to feed their habit, and this undermined the authorities' hopes of financing the deficit. This was why the Government now decided to dust down the loans-for-shares proposal.

Kokh (now the Acting Chairman of the GKI)[4] announced on 16 August that a presidential decree launching the programme would be signed presently. The headline in one newspaper captured the desperate situation in which the GKI found itself: 'State Property Committee: Everything Will Be Resolved at Five Minutes to Twelve' (Serov, 1995). According to the decree, signed on 31 August, the Government would borrow from private companies during the last quarter of 1995, offering stakes in state companies as security. Rights to manage shares would be awarded to the winners of public auctions who would sign 'credit agreements' of an as yet unspecified length with the Finance Ministry.[5] Creditors would have a say in the running of the enterprises, but their managerial rights would be limited (they would have no powers to alter the legal status of the company, or to increase its charter capital, or to issue securities). Nor would they receive dividends. If the Government failed to repay the loans on time, ownership of the assets would pass to the creditors, who could sell them at auction ('O poryadke peredachi', 1995). The decision to implement loans-for-shares was not taken with enthusiasm. This was partly because the liquidity crisis had renewed concerns that the banks would be unable to find the necessary sums. Two members of the MKS consortium, Inkombank and Imperial, announced in late August that they were pulling out because of the beating they had taken on the currency markets. An anonymous Deputy Prime Minister, quoted in the press, summed up the official mood, remarking that '[b]anks are joining and leaving the consortium, and it's unclear what will happen next' (Pelekhova et al., 1995). Yeltsin echoed these uncertainties when he met representatives of the banks before signing his decree, seeking assurances that they could take part in the scheme. ('Sil'nye banki', 1995). But judging by Kokh's remarks at a press conference on 5 September, at which he emphasized the link between the decree and the Government's budgetary objectives, such worries were now outweighed by fiscal considerations (Samoilova, 1995b).

The loans-for-shares scheme was intended at this late stage to be just one part of a bigger privatization campaign in the final quarter of 1995. The others included the sales of over 6000 stakes in small and medium-size companies and shares in 136 large enterprises (the GKI had been wrestling with both initiatives since the spring). There was additionally talk of selling 9 per cent of EES Rossii (Russia's electricity monopoly), as well as a jumble of other transactions (including the sales of: a piece of the telecoms holding company Svyaz'invest; convertible bonds in LUKoil; and plots of land). Kokh claimed that this package could raise as much as 19 trillion rubles and that the target for budget revenues would be met (Karpenko, 1995). Yet it was quixotic to expect the GKI to sell so much property in so brief a period, given its performance during the previous eighteen months and the repercussions for the equity market, and this announcement was quickly exposed as a wish-list. Most of it had been ditched by early November, leaving loans-for-shares as virtually the only element standing (Bekker, 1995).[6]

With little time left, preparations were so rushed that they bordered on the farcical; as one commentator noted, the loans-for-shares scheme emerged full of 'black holes' (Zhagel', 1995b). Such chaotic and opaque conditions were tailor-made for lobbyists intent on manipulating official policy for their own ends. For starters, no list of enterprises to be included in the scheme existed when Yeltsin signed his decree of 31 August, despite the deadline imposed by his earlier decree of 11 May. The initial draft list comprised 64 enterprises from sectors such as oil, gas, electricity, cement, shipping, metals, timber and paper ('Perechen' predpriyatsii', 1995; Samoilova, 1995c). This had been cobbled together with no consultation with the enterprises concerned, most of whom were vehemently opposed.[7] During subsequent weeks an alliance of managers, ministries and regional administrations lobbied to reduce the number of companies on the list, which was hacked to pieces, initially to 43 enterprises and then lower still (Kokh, 1998, p. 107; Arsen'ev, 1995). Revealingly, the banks were powerless to prevent the cuts from taking place. The final rag-bag collection of 29 enterprises, less than half the original number, was published on 25 September ('Spisok predpriyatii', 1995). Only 17 were auctioned, five attracting no bids at all.[8] The other transactions were cancelled by a decree of 7 December after more lobbying by officials and managers,[9] or postponed on the twenty-fifth pending court hearings on the legality of plans to include the enterprises concerned in the scheme,[10] or shelved by the GKI.[11] The procedural details were not published until November, after the auctions had begun. Nor was there time to carry out proper pre-sale preparations. Key decisions about the stakes to be mortgaged, the starting prices and the special criteria added to the terms of some auctions were taken by a commission chaired by Kokh (Kokh, 1998, p. 108).

It had long been suspected that the members of MKS had their eyes on certain enterprises, and at some point in the autumn – exactly when is impossible to say – the principal movers behind the loans-for-shares proposal, Oneksimbank and Menatep, broke away from their partners and agreed to divide the choicest assets on the GKI's shrinking list between themselves. Vitaly Malkin (President of Rossiisky kredit), who was not party to the stitch-up and would be frozen out of the auctions, revealed in late November that 'some lists [of enterprises] were being circulated' among his competitors ('Bank nameren appelirovat'', 1995). Leonid Nevzlin (then First Deputy Chairman of Menatep) would confirm Malkin's claim more bluntly, remarking that '[w]e reached an agreement on who would take what. We agreed not to get in each other's way . . . In this respect there was an element of insider dealing' (Freeland, 2000, p. 166). As one observer noted after the auctions were under way, 'the impression has formed that all the lots were divided up earlier' (Maksimov, 1995).

It is important that we are clear about the nature of the carve-up. The most enduring myth is the belief that a few mighty banks imposed the loans-for-shares scheme on a large group of reluctant enterprises. Nothing could be further from the truth. As we have already seen, most of the enterprises on the banks' initial list succeeded in lobbying their way off it. As for the others, the banks never stood a chance of gaining control of two of the oil majors, LUKoil and Surgutneftegaz. The extensive political connections, closed corporate structures and relatively healthy financial positions of these two companies rendered them largely impenetrable to outsiders and enabled them to take advantage of this unexpected opportunity to acquire control of their own shares. What otherwise took place was a series of mergers agreed in advance by the banks and the enterprises concerned. With one exception, the banks only took over those companies which, in effect, allowed themselves to be taken over.

The banks and the enterprises involved were able to get their way because the authorities loaded the dice in their favour. Foreigners were barred from taking part in the auctions of the most desirable enterprises on grounds of national security. This was no surprise, but the decision curtailed competition and slashed the revenues which the state could expect to raise. The starting prices were ludicrously low as a result.[12] A second decision with major implications was the selection of Oneksimbank as the GKI's agent, charged with receiving every bid made in every auction, thus conferring on it the powers of gate-keeper and creating obvious scope for a conflict of interest. The GKI also hived off responsibility for running the auctions to private organizations (usually to Oneksimbank and Menatep), which – in a final and astonishing twist – were allowed to participate in those auctions they were organizing.

Why did the authorities agree to such patently unfair arrangements? We can only speculate about the reasons. Perhaps they chose what was by this late stage the easiest way of raising at least some revenues for the budget. One observer – and certainly not the only one who reached this conclusion – alluded to another explanation: 'the banks which succeeded are not only rich by Russian standards, but are the ones with the closest ties to the government-presidential structure' (Narzikulov, 1995a).

As for the 12 auctions which produced results,[13] several patterns stand out. The main one is that Oneksimbank, Menatep and their affiliates dominated proceedings, winning eight and playing influential back-stage roles in three of the other four.[14] With the exception of the auction for 15 per cent of the Chelyabinsk Metallurgical Combine (Mechel), the winners were either the auction organizers, or structures fronting for them, or companies colluding with them. A thin and unconvincing façade of competition was maintained by means of phantom bids marginally lower than the bids deposited by the winners,[15] or in some cases equal to the asking price. The key banks and their affiliates took it in turns to underwrite each others' bids. The result was that, revealingly, the winning bids in all bar two cases (Mechel and the Novorossiisk Shipping Company) were only fractionally above the starting prices. One observer compared the auctions to 'agreed matches', pointing out how '[b]ank-guarantors and direct participants cunningly change places, while firms with different names, but which essentially represent the same interests, are declared the winners. Moreover', he continued sarcastically, 'the winner in most cases turns out to be the bank (or the representative of its interests) which played a blemish-free and utterly insignificant role as the receiver of bids.' Remarking that winning bids were nearly always only just above the asking prices, he noted how 'the impression has been created that all the results were predetermined in advance through the will of some invisible factor' (Leskov, 1995).

Yet even these elaborate charades did not always work. To the annoyance of the auction organizers, businesses not party to the carve-up declared their hands late in the day and competed for six of the most prized enterprises. The outcomes of these auctions were therefore decided by even more brazen methods. It is helpful to look at them briefly because they exposed the insider deal at the heart of the loans-for-shares scheme. Given the subject of this paper, we will concentrate on the five auctions which involved banks.[16]

The first two took place on 17 November, when 15 per cent of Nafta-Moskva, one of Russia's leading oil-exporting companies, was auctioned from a starting price of $16 million. The organizer of the auction was Oneksimbank, part of whose charter capital was owned by Nafta-Moskva, which in turn was a client of the bank. Two bids were made by companies linked to Oneksimbank, one for $16.4 million by Nafta-Moskva itself, underwritten by MFK (a bank so close to Oneksimbank as to be almost indistinguishable from it), the other for $16.1 million by Yunibestbank, guaranteed by Nafta-fin (a subsidiary of Nafta-Moskva). Unexpectedly, a larger bid of $35.5 million was made at the last minute by Evroresurs, backed by the Yokoshima Trust Company, a subsidiary of Bank of Tokyo. The move took Oneksimbank by surprise. The auction committee went to work, ruled that the bid by Evroresurs exceeded its charter capital and ordered the auction to be re-run on 28 December. Everything went smoothly this time. Nafta-Moskva won with a bid of $20.01 million ($10000 above the new starting-price of US$20 million), backed by Yunibestbank and Oneksimbank. Nafta-fin meanwhile lodged a dummy bid of $20 million, underwritten by MFK.

The outcome did not attract more publicity because it was overshadowed by the auction of 38 per cent of Noril'sk Nikel', the world's largest producer of rare-earth metals (accounting in global terms for 20 per cent of production of nickel and 40 per cent of output of platinum). This was destined to be a highlight of the loans-for-shares programme, given the company's vast size and its iconic status within the Russian metals industry. Oneksimbank, the organizer of the auction, had long made plain its intention to gain control of the company, another of its high-profile clients and with which it formed the backbone of the Interros Financial-Industrial Group, created the previous year.[17] One commentary suggested at the time that a 'gentleman's agreement' existed between the banks to reserve Noril'sk Nikel' for Potanin (Katsman, 1995, p. 48). Another feature of the auction was the fact that it involved the one hostile takeover of the series: managers at Noril'sk Nikel' were dead against the inclusion of their company in the loans-for-shares scheme. Notwithstanding their opposition, the auction went according to Oneksimbank's plan. Against a starting price of $170 million, Oneksimbank won with a bid of $170.1 million, guaranteed by MFK, beating two phoney bids of $170 million made by MFK and another of its own affiliates, Reola. The auction hall witnessed a furious row, however, when Oneksimbank, backed by Kokh, used its position as auction organizer to dismiss a larger bid of $355 million lodged by Kont, a subsidiary of Rossiisky kredit. After trying unsuccessfully to reject it because it had been submitted after the deadline for applications had passed, the auction committee declared it invalid because Rossiisky kredit's charter capital, at $100 million, was less than the bid itself, thereby breaching CBR regulations. Rossiisky kredit retorted that the same objection could be levelled at Oneksimbank (whose charter capital allegedly was little more than $100 million) and MFK ($50 million), but these counter-claims were rejected ('Vitaly Malkin', 1995). GKI procedures forbade the rejection of a bid during the auction itself. The auction organizers were supposed to notify bidders in writing before the auction if there were any problems with documentation ('"Rossiisky kredit"', 1995).[18]

The next scandal erupted on 7 December, when 51 per cent of SIDANKO, Russia's fourth-largest oil producer, was auctioned. The starting price was $125 million. In terms of shenanigans and outcome, this auction was remarkably similar to the events surrounding Noril'sk Nikel'. Organized again by Oneksimbank, it was won by MFK, which bid $130 million (underwritten by Oneksimbank). The other bid accepted, for $127 million, was lodged by an unknown company, RTD (also underwritten by Oneksimbank). Another, from the hapless Rossiisky kredit, was rejected on the now-familiar grounds that it had been lodged 23 minutes after the deadline for applications had expired (Samoilova et al., 1995). Rossiisky kredit's representatives again complained, but their protests fell on deaf ears.

The biggest controversy of all took place next day, 8 December, and concerned the auction for 45 per cent of YUKOS, Russia's second-largest oil producer and the company with the largest proven oil reserves. Like the Noril'sk Nikel' transaction, this had attracted a great deal of attention in advance, though for the different reason that Menatep and YUKOS had been determined to merge for some time. It became known shortly before the auction that Khodorkovsky had written to Soskovets four months earlier advertising his interest in YUKOS (Romanova, 1995). And Soskovets in August was asked to authorize the transfer of a block of state shares in YUKOS to Menatep, a move designed to bind these companies more tightly together (Berger, 1995).[19] Senior executives of the two companies outlined ambitious investment plans for YUKOS and affirmed their 'psychological compatibility' at a joint press conference just over a month before the auction (Narzikulov, 1995b).

The asking price for the 45 per cent stake in YUKOS was $150 million. A feature was the requirement that bidders take part in an investment tender for another 33 per cent of the company (with a starting price of US$350 million, plus a three-year commitment of $350 million). The minimum exposure therefore came to $850 million, a sum almost certainly beyond any Russian bank. GKI rules barred banks from participating in investment tenders. The auction, run by Menatep, was therefore contested by an unknown company, Laguna (founded 10 days earlier by Menatep, Stolichnyi and Tokobank), which bid $159 million (guaranteed by Menatep), and another dummy, Reagent, also created by Menatep, which bid $150.5 million (underwritten by Menatep as well). The rules of the auction obliged the winner to make its balance sheet available to the organizing committee; its rights to the YUKOS shares would be handed to the guarantor if it did not. Laguna failed to meet the requirement, and the rights therefore passed to Menatep less than 48 hours after the auction.

What transformed the deal into a scandal was the aggressive competition which Menatep encountered from a group of banks comprising Rossiisky kredit, Alfa and Inkombank. They had issued a joint statement in late November, claiming that Menatep could not meet the investment requirements, that it was using state funds to finance its bid and that it was already notorious for not fulfilling obligations arising from investment tenders ('Sovmestnoe zayavlenie', 1995). The three banks turned up the heat at a press conference on 29 November, when they called on the authorities to postpone the auction and to create a commission to audit the investment-tender records of the participants. Claiming that no Russian bank could meet the conditions of the YUKOS auction, they proposed that at least 50 per cent of their bid be paid in the form of GKOs. If this demand was not met, they warned, they might redeem their T-bills, thus blowing a hole in the GKO market (Baranov and Pelekhova, 1995). The authorities were unmoved: Chubais said that the auction conditions would not be altered, the Ministry of Finance denied claims that Menatep was using state funds to finance its bid, and the CBR threatened the three banks with retaliation if they tried to undermine the GKO market (Skvortsov, 1995). Against this backdrop, there was no doubt about the outcome of the auction. Represented by Babaevskoe, a sweet factory owned by Inkombank, the consortium bid $82 million in cash and $307 million in GKOs. The auction committee rejected the bid, ruling that payment had to be in cash.

The final loans-for-shares auction disposed of 51 per cent of the Sibneft' oil company on 28 December. Sibneft' had been established by a presidential decree only four months earlier ('Ob uchrezhdenii', 1995). Carved out of Rosneft', the state-owned oil holding company, it was widely thought to be the creation of lobbying by the tycoon Boris Berezovsky. He had not been involved in the MKS consortium, and Sibneft' was only included in the loans-for-shares programme at the last minute, ostensibly to plug the gap created by the decision to pull four aerospace factories from the original schedule. Kokh has recounted how, at Berezovsky's instigation, he drafted the decree including the company in the scheme (Freeland, 2000, pp. 179–80). Yeltsin signed the decree on 27 November ('Ob upravlenii', 1995). The outcome of the auction was a foregone conclusion. The winner was a consortium headed by Stolichnyi, competing against one fronted by Menatep, which ran the auction and guaranteed the bids. A rival bid of $175 million from SAMEKO (an Inkombank-owned metallurgical enterprise), underwritten by Mosbiznesbank, was thrown out for tried-and-tested reasons: the paperwork had been completed incorrectly, Mosbiznesbank lacked the funds to guarantee the bid, and the bid had been presented late to the organizing committee.

CONCLUSIONS

This paper began with the contention that the loans-for-shares auctions were not part of a 'Faustian bargain' between the 'young reformers' and the banks. The scheme was not envisaged by the Yeltsin entourage as a down-payment on the political support of the 'oligarchs' ahead of the 1996 presidential elections. There was no direct relationship between the two episodes: the controversial division of state property in November and December 1995 was not a precondition for Yeltsin's victory six months later, and it was not seen as such at the time. The scandal did make the 'oligarchs' and the officials who came to be associated with them targets for the propaganda and platforms of the anti-Yeltsin opposition. A Communist victory at the presidential elections in the summer of 1996 would almost certainly have heralded retribution and the prosecution of many of those deemed to be responsible for these quasi-privatizations. The auctions bound the victors even more tightly to the Yeltsin regime, but that was their effect, not the motivation for them. Asked to choose between Yeltsin and the Communist presidential candidate, Gennady Zyuganov, there was never any doubt about whom the banks would pick. They required no new inducements to help them make their choice.[20]

To understand the loans-for-shares auctions – why they took place when they did, and what role the banks played in them – we need to revisit the 18 months which preceded them, in particular the second half of 1994 and the first half of 1995. The starting-point lay in the inability of the Government for various administrative, economic and political reasons to make progress with privatization in the post-voucher era. Privatization as a process had ground to a halt by the beginning of 1995. By the time the authorities belatedly tried to reinvigorate matters in the spring, all aspects of economic policy-making had been subordinated to the objective of financial stabilization and non-inflationary financing of the budget deficit. The goal of privatization now was to raise money for the treasury. Leading banks meanwhile faced harsher conditions produced by falling inflation and were seeking new ways of gaining access to state resources. They were keen too to protect their positions on the equity market, by heading off official attempts to sell lots of state-owned shares in one go and by ensuring that Western banks did not become the Government's partners during the privatization of Russian companies. Out of these conditions arose the loans-for-shares proposal, which on paper gave the Government and the banks what they wanted.

Chubais has claimed that he embraced the idea at once (Chubais, 1999, p. 184). Yet it is striking that five months elapsed between Potanin's presentation to the meeting of the Government on 30 March and the appearance of Yeltsin's decree giving the go-ahead to the loans-for-shares scheme on 31 August. The evidence suggests that the authorities were in fact deeply sceptical about the proposal, which was opaque in the extreme. Given their thirst for revenues, they were in principle interested in any idea which might fill the state's coffers, but they still hoped at this stage to stabilize the budget from other sources. They were therefore in no hurry to commit themselves. It was not until the banking crisis of August 1995, which damaged the domestic market for government paper, that they took the plunge. Yet having stumbled into accepting loans-for-shares so late in the day, they had left themselves insufficient time to prepare a proper framework for implementation. With the GKI in chaos, the banks which had been the most enthusiastic backers of the idea, Oneksimbank and Menatep, saw their chance. They broke away from their partners and divided the assets among themselves and a band of associates. The auctions were held in November and December amid a barrage of claims of insider-dealing.

So extraordinary was the *coup* that it is easy to see with hindsight why the banks at the heart of it came to be seen as omnipotent 'oligarchs' whose influence was routinely deemed to be behind almost any significant event in Russia, a myth which some of them were only too happy to encourage. Not only did they snap up for ridiculously low prices several enormous industrial enterprises, which immediately became the centrepieces of their business empires, but they also managed to persuade senior officials, at least some of whom had never been keen, to back a scheme which, in the opinion of most observers, had virtually nothing to commend it. They did so, moreover, in the teeth of furious political opposition, which they utterly and arrogantly disregarded, acting throughout with a level of cynical calculation which still takes the breath away. The episode was in this sense a striking demonstration of the political influence which commercial organizations could wield in post-communist Russia.

Yet it is vital to view what happened in context. The auctions resulted from a peculiar set of circumstances, which must be understood if we are to avoid exaggerating the influence of the banks. To begin with, it is telling that the banks could not stop most of the enterprises on the original loans-for-shares list lobbying their way off it. So is their inability to mount hostile takeovers once the auctions began; with the exception of Oneksimbank's capture of Noril'sk Nikel', the auctions put the finishing touches to corporate mergers which had been agreed in advance. More fundamentally, the loans-for-shares scheme confirmed an older and well-established pattern, highlighting the degree to which the banks, or any major commercial group for that matter, relied on links to the state for their wealth and power. The Russian state was weak in a number of ways, including its vulnerability to corruption, its shortcomings as an administrator, its insatiable appetite for budgetary revenues and the absence of consensus among and within the organs of power. In 1995 these weaknesses enabled the banks to manipulate officials and politicians to stunning effect, yet they did not alter the central fact that state patronage was the key to business success. Interviewed in 1996, Khodorkovsky said that he had no illusions about the unequal nature of the relationship: 'big business', he remarked, 'cannot exist without the state' (Khodorkovsky, 1996, pp. 18–19). The loans-for-shares auctions showed what political influence the banks could exert in certain circumstances, yet they underlined too the limits of their independence. They demonstrated, in other words, that the banks were lobbyists, not 'oligarchs'.

NOTES

1. The views expressed in this paper are the private views of the author and should not be taken as an expression of the thinking of the UK Government. My thanks to Professors Julian Cooper and Philip Hanson for comments on an earlier draft.
2. The other two were Mikhail Khodorkovsky (President of Menatep) and Aleksandr Smolensky (President of Stolichnyi Savings Bank).
3. The *spetsbanki* were the 'specialized banks' created as a result of the Soviet banking reforms of 1987 and 1988 to take responsibility for certain functions (for example, financing investment in particular sectors of the economy) away from the Soviet Central Bank.
4. Belyaev had been seconded at the end of July to head the team preparing the parliamentary election campaign of 'Nash dom – Rossiya', the political movement fronted by Chernomyrdin.
5. Another presidential decree signed on 2 November set a deadline of 1 September 1996 for repayment of the loans. See 'O srokakh realizatsii' (1995).
6. The only other major component to be implemented was the sale of 25 per cent of Svyaz'invest in December, but this collapsed at the last minute after a buyer, the Italian telecoms group STET, had been found.
7. As Kokh remarked at the time, the proposed sales 'are not causing delight' among the branch ministries and various enterprise managers. See Kokh (1995).
8. These were the Arkhangel'sk Commercial Port, the Tuapse Sea Merchant Port, two timber companies (Kirovlesprom & Bor) and the West Siberian Metallurgical Combine (see note 9).
9. These were the Far Eastern Shipping Company, the Orsk-Khalilovsk Metallurgical Combine, four aerospace plants (AKB Sukhoi, the Irkutsk Aviation Production

Association, the Ulan-Ude Aviation Production Association and the Arsen'ev Aviation Company 'Progress') and the West Siberian Metallurgical Combine, which had been auctioned on 17 December, but did not attract any bids.

10. These were the Bratsk, Arkhangel'sk and Solombala Pulp and Paper Mills.
11. These were the Oskol Electrical Plant and the Beloretsk Metallurgical Combine.
12. The asking price for the 38 per cent controlling stake in Noril'sk Nikel', for example, was a risible $170 million. Managers at the company reckoned that an accurate valuation would have been $8–10 billion, or between 50 and 60 times higher. See 'Noril'sk Nikel'' (1995). This self-valuation may well have been excessive once factors like political risk and the notorious lack of financial openness at the company had been folded in, but the auction price was nevertheless a massive undervaluation. According to Kokh, the banks pressed for even lower starting prices. See Kokh (1998), p. 109.
13. These were for: Surgutneftegaz, the North-Western Shipping Company, Nafta-Moskva, AO Mechel, LUKoil, SIDANKO, the Novolipetsk Metallurgical Combine, the Murmansk Shipping Company, YUKOS, the Novorossiisk Shipping Company, and Sibneft'.
14. The three were the auctions for: Surgutneftegaz, at which Oneksimbank guaranteed the winning bid; the Novorossiisk Shipping Company (organized by Oneksimbank, which with Menatep underwrote the two phantom bids); and Sibneft', run by Menatep, which also guaranteed both the bids it, as the auction organizer, accepted. Four other banks played minor roles. Three were from the MKS consortium: Imperial, whose affiliate won the LUKoil auction on behalf of the oil company (which happened to own 35 per cent of the charter capital of Imperial itself) and underwrote the other (dummy) bid; Stolichnyi, whose affiliate won the Sibneft' auction; and Tokobank, which guaranteed the winning bid for the stake in the Novorossiisk Shipping Company (lodged by the company itself). The fourth bank was National Reserve Bank, which mounted the obligatory phantom bid for the stake in LUKoil.
15. Three examples were: the auction for 25.5 per cent of the North-Western Shipping Company (mortgaged for $6.05 million against a starting price of $6 million); the auction for 14.84 per cent of the Novolipetsk Metallurgical Combine (mortgaged for $31 million against an asking price of $30 million); and the auction of 23.5 per cent of the Murmansk Shipping Company (mortgaged for $4.125 million against a starting price of $4 million).
16. The other controversial auction, the one for 40.12 per cent of Surgutneftegaz on 3 November, featured a confrontation between two oil companies, Surgutneftegaz itself and Rosneft'. Oneksimbank (16.6 per cent of whose own share capital was owned by Surgutneftegaz, one of its clients) was involved in the background, guaranteeing the winning bid lodged by Surgutneftegaz's own pension fund.
17. Indeed, Oneksimbank had earlier in the year lobbied the Government to transfer the state's 38 per cent stake in Noril'sk Nikel' to Interros. A government resolution to this effect had reportedly been drafted. See 'Oneksimbank vstal' (1995).
18. Oneksimbank claimed to have written to Rossiisky kredit before the auction took place, alerting it to the alleged problems. Rossiisky kredit denied having received any warning.
19. The federal authorities had taken an equity stake in Menatep the previous December, but had been unable to pay for it in cash given their budgetary problems. The transfer of state-owned shares in YUKOS was ostensibly the payment for this earlier transaction. See Berger (1995).
20. For example, Vladimir Gusinsky and the Most group, whose media interests played such a prominent role in Yeltsin's election campaign, at no point featured in the loans-for-shares story. And Alfa, one of the banks which was shut out of two of the auctions, made an important contribution as well.

REFERENCES

Anichkin, Aleksandr (1995), 'Prodazha krupneishei kompanii po "spetspravlam" mozhet dat' kozyr' oppozitsii', *Izvestiya*, 2 November.

Arsen'ev, Vadim (1995), 'Iskusstvo torgovat'sya s gosudarstvom', *Kommersant'*, 41–2, pp. 64–7.

'Bank nameren appelirovat' k prem'er-ministru' (1995), *Kommersant'-Daily*, 7 December.

Baranov, Gleb (1995), 'Delo konsortsiuma pobedilo', *Kommersant'-Daily*, 30 September.

Baranov and Yul'ya Pelekhova (1995), 'Banki reshili borot'sya za YUKOS vmeste', *Kommersant'-Daily*, 30 November.

Basin, Sergei (1995), 'Bankiry spasayut pravitel'stvo', *Nezavisimaya gazeta*, 1 April.

British Broadcasting Company (BBC) (1995a), 'Russian Sell-Off Exclusion List Awaits Official Endorsement', Interfax, 19 June, reproduced in *Summary of World Broadcasts* (*SWB*), 23 June, SUW/0389 WB/3.

— (1995b), 'Russian Government To Sell Shares Worth R16,000bn This Year', Interfax, 20 June, reproduced in *SWB*, 23 June, SUW/0389 WB/2–3.

Bekker, Aleksandr (1995), 'Porazhenie ili kompromiss?', *Segodnya*, 9 November.

Berger, Mikhail (1995), 'Natural'nyi obmen?', *Izvestiya*, 22 August.

Borodulin, Vladislav (1995a), 'Banki predlozhili kredit pravitel'stvu', *Kommersant'-Daily*, 31 March.

— (1995b), 'Pravitel'stvo nachalo sostavlyat' mozaiku', *Kommersant'-Daily*, 18 April.

— (1995c), 'Pravitel'stvo priznalos' v sobstvennykh oshibkakh', *Kommersant'-Daily*, 14 July.

Chubais, Anatoly (1999), 'Kak dushili privatizatsiyu', in Chubais (ed.), *Privatizatsiya po-rossiiski*, Moscow: Vagrius, pp. 157–85.

Freeland, Chrystia (2000), *Sale of the Century. The Inside Story of the Second Russian Revolution*, London: Little, Brown and Company.

Karpenko, Igor' (1995), 'Al'fred Kokh: Yesli privatizatsiya ne dast byudzhetu 9 trillionov rublei, mozhete kaznit' menya 15 dekabrya', *Izvestiya*, 14 October.

Katsman, Yury (1995), 'Igra s zaraneye izvestnym rezul'tatom', *Kommersant'*, 44, pp. 47–50.

Khodorkovsky, Mikhail (1996), 'Krupnyi biznes ne mozhet sushchestvovat' vne gosudarstva', *Kommersant'*, 13, pp. 18–19.

Kirpichenko, Nikita et al. (1995), 'Novye kluby v vysshei finansovoi lige', *Kommersant'*, 13, pp. 14–18.

Kokh, Al'fred (1995), 'Gosudarstvo prodaet pakety aktsii', *Rossiiskie vesti*, 16 September.

— (1998), *The Selling of the Soviet Empire. Politics and Economics of Russia's Privatization Programme. Revelations of the Principal Insider*, New York: SPI Books.

— (1999), 'Gosudarstvo-prodavets', in Chubais (ed.), *Privatizatsiya po-rossiiski*, Moscow: Vagrius pp. 247–69.

'Kommercheskie banki nashli svoego samogo bol'shogo zaemshchika' (1995), *Kommersant'-Daily*, 1 April.

'Konsortsium prodolzhaet prodvizhenie vpered' (1995), *Kommersant'-Daily*, 1995.

Lantsman, Mikhail (1995), 'Anatoly Chubais poprosil GKI prodavat' imushchestvo bystreye', *Segodnya*, 21 February.

Leskov, Sergei (1995), 'Pervye zalogovye auktsiony: vse yasno zaraneye', *Izvestiya*, 10 December.

Liberman, Ira W. and Rogi Veimetra (1996), 'The Rush for State Shares in the "Klondyke" of Wild East Capitalism: Loans-for-Shares Transactions in Russia', *George Washington Journal of International Law and Economics*, 29, 3, pp. 737–68.

Loginov, Mikhail (1995), 'Drugie banki sdelali pravitel'stvu drugoe predlozhenie', *Kommersant'-Daily*, 6 April.

Lolaeva, Svetlana (1995), 'Plan po dokhodam ot privatizatsii na 1996 god, vozmozhno, budet peresmotren', *Segodnya*, 19 September.

Lysak, Oksana (1995), 'Privatizatsiya poka idet bol'she na bumage', *Kommersant'-Daily*, 14 June.

Makarevich, Lev (1995), 'Konkurentsiya mezhdu bankami narastaet, no ee usloviya diktuet gosudarstvo', *Finansovye izvestiya*, 13 April.

Maksimov, Sergei (1995), 'V uzkom krugu', *Nezavisimaya gazeta*, 10 December.

Mel'nikov,Viktor (1995), 'Reforma dozlhna prinosit' dokhody i gosudarstvu', *Kommersant'-Daily*, 12 May.

'Mezhdu Konsortsiumom i Gruppoi ne okazalis' raznitsy' (1995), *Kommersant'-Daily*, 31 May.

Narzikulov, Rustam (1995a), 'Inkombank, "Rossiisky kredit" i "Al'fa Bank" ob"yavili voine Menatepu', *Segodnya*, 28 November.

— (1995b), '78% aktsii YUKOS pereidet v ruki chastnykh investorov', *Segodnya*, 10 November.

'Noril'sk Nikel' protiv auktsiona' (1995), *Nezavisimaya gazeta*, 16 November.

'Ob osnovnykh napravleniyakh gosudarstvennoi programmy privatizatsii gosudarstvennykh i munitsipal'nykh predpriyatii v Rossiiskoi Federatsii posle 1 iyulya 1994g' (1994), *Rossiiskaya gazeta*, 26 July.

'O merakh po obespecheniyu garantirovannogo postupleniya v federal'nyi byudzhet dokhodov ot privatizatsii' (1995), *Rossiiskaya gazeta*, 17 May.

'O poryadke peredachi v 1995 godu v zalog aktsii, nakhodyashchikhsya v federal'noi sobstvennosti' (1995), *Rossiiskaya gazeta*, 5 September.

'O srokakh realizatsii aktsii, nakhodyashchikhsya v federal'noi sobstvennosti i peredavaemykh v zalog v 1995 godu' (1995), *Rossiiskaya gazeta*, 9 November.

'Ob uchrezhdenii otkrytogo aktsionernogo obshchestva "Sibirskaya neftyanaya kompaniya"' (1995), in *Sobranie zakonodatel'stva Rossiiskoi Federatsii*, 36, doc.3530.

'Ob upravlenii i rasporyazhenii aktsiyami otkrytogo aktsionernogo obshchestva "Sibirskaya neftyanaya kompaniya" nakhodyashchimisya v federal'noi sobstvennosti' (1995), in *Sobranie zakonodatel'stva Rossiiskoi Federatsii*, 49, doc.4768.

'Oneksimbank vstal v ochered' vmeste so vsemi' (1995), *Kommersant'-Daily*, 29 June.

Pelekhova, Yul'ya et al. (1995), 'Konsortsium reshil zadachu-maksimum', *Segodnya*, 7 September.

'Perechen' predpriyatii, aktsii kotorykh mogut ispol'zovat'sya v kachestve zaloga' (1995), *Kommersant'-Daily*, 3 June.

Podlipsky, Nikolai (1995), 'Pravitel'stvo prisposobilo vauchernye auktsiony k denezhnoi privatizatsii' *Kommersant'-Daily*, 7 May.

Potemkin, Aleksandr (1999), 'Krizis obnazhil slabost' bankovskikh balansov', *Finansovye izvestiya*, 19 October.

Privalov, Aleksandr et al. (1995), 'Privatizatsiyu tesnili na vsekh frontakh, no i kontrnastuplenie gotovitsya na vsekh frontakh', *Kommersant'*, 5, pp. 60–65.

'Rasshirennaya Kollegiya GKI' (1995), *Ekonomika i zhizn'*, 27, p. 24.

Romanova, Ol'ga (1995), 'Chertova dyuzhina zalozhnikov bez skandalov ne prodaetsya', *Segodnya*, 28 November.

'"Rossiisky kredit" khochet obzhalovat' rezul'taty auktsiona v sude' (1995), *Kommersant'-Daily*, 23 November.

Samoilova, Natal'ya (1995a), 'Pravitel'stvo ne ostavlyaet nadezhdu', *Kommersant-Daily*, 15 April.

— (1995b), 'Voprosov stalo ne men'she, a bol'she', *Kommersant'-Daily*, 6 September.

— (1995c), 'Gosudarstvo opredelilo predmet zaloga', *Kommersant'-Daily*, 26 September.

Samoilova, Natal'ya et al. (1995), 'Vyigrali te, kto dolzhen byl vyigrat', *Kommersant'-Daily*, 8 December.

Serov, Andrei (1995), 'Goskomimushchestvo: vse reshitsya bez pyati minut dvenadtsat"', *Kommersant'-Daily*, 17 August.

'Sil'nye banki. V nikh zainteresovano gosudarstvo' (1995), *Rossiiskaya gazeta*, 1 September.

Skvortsov, Yaroslav (1995), 'Banki ponyali, chto nemnogo pereborshchili', *Kommersant'-Daily*, 5 December.

Skvortsov, Yaroslav and Mikhail Loginov (1995), 'Skromnoe obayanie Oneksimbanka', *Kommersant'-Daily*, 16 November.

'Sovmestnoe zayavlenie, "O finansovykh problemakh privatizatsii, vzaimootnosheniyakh banka 'Menatep' i nekotorykh pravitel'stvennykh struktur"' (1995), *Kommersant'-Daily*, 28 November.

'Spisok predpriyatii, gospakety aktsii kotorykh mogut ispol'zovat'sya v kachestve zaloga' (1995), *Kommersant'-Daily*, 26 September.

Stanova, Yelena and Igor' Trosnikov (1995), 'Konsortsium i GKI ostalis' dovol'ny drug s drugom', *Kommersant'-Daily*, 13 May.

Tutshkin, Aleksandr (1995), 'Barometer GKI obeshchaet investoram "yasno"', *Kommersant'-Daily*, 28 March.

'Usloviya kredita banki predlagayut v pyatnitsu' (1995), *Kommersant'-Daily*, 5 April.

'Vitaly Malkin, prezident banka "Rossiisky kredit"' (1995), *Kommersant'-Daily*, 23 November.

Zasursky, Ivan (1995), 'Rossiiskie banki predlagayut kreditirovat' pravitel'stvu', *Nezavisimaya gazeta*, 11 April.

Zhagel', Ivan (1995a), 'Kak by ni zakonchilas', novaya sdelka veka', *Izvestiya*, 11 April.

— (1995b), 'Nadezhdy pravitel'stva zanyat' den'gi u krupneishikh rossiiskikh bankov stanovyatsya vse boleye prizrachnymi', *Izvestiya*, 2 September.

7. Comparisons with east-central Europe

Martin Myant[1]

This chapter develops a comparative theme by looking at banking in east-central Europe, with particular emphasis on the Czech Republic. There is no typical 'model' that can cover all the transition countries and certainly no model of success that Russia could, let alone 'should', have followed. Indeed, there are some areas of analogy between Russia and the Czech Republic, with the latter country's attempt to develop a specifically 'Czech' capitalism rather than inviting in foreign banks and companies to modernize the economy. As in Russia, this attempt appears to have failed.

Nevertheless, banking in east-central Europe presents a healthier picture than its Russian counterpart. Moreover, the solution that has been chosen after the problems encountered by the 'Czech road', closely following the philosophy in neighbouring countries, probably offers better long-term prospects than the remedies tried in Russia after the debacle of 1998. Needless to say, a remedy applied in one country is not necessarily applicable elsewhere. As will be indicated, much of the development of banking in the former centrally-planned economies is strongly influenced by their differing pasts. This suggests deeper difficulties in the Russian case: these reflect the nature of society as a whole and cannot be seen as specifically banking problems. Moreover, there are wide variations in what would be politically acceptable, particularly in relation to the role of foreign ownership.

THE COMPARATIVE PERSPECTIVE

One of the lessons of the past is that the importance of banking to economic development, and the behaviour of banks themselves, varies between countries and time periods. The differences have led one economic historian to suggest that 'the label "bank" is used imprecisely to identify a variety of institutions' (Ross, 1996, p. 321). As will be argued, the divergences across the former centrally-planned economies are very substantial.

Although economic historians often refer to the 'role' of banks in development, the term has to be used with care. Banks are typically formed as profit-seeking businesses. Their impact on the economy as a whole is a result of how they seek to fulfil this objective rather than the primary purpose of their founders.

It has been a frequent theme in economic policy debates that banks should behave in a particular way – for example by giving more support to long-term investment in the domestic economy – and that their excessive caution or greed for profit by other means are harmful to economic development. However, as private businesses, their 'primary responsibility, at all times' has to be to their depositors (Ross, 1996, p. 328). The differences in behaviour are therefore generally a result of different perceptions on the part of banks as to how they can make profits. They do not reflect different objectives.

Thus, combining the two elements of banks' role in economic development and banks' means of making a profit, differences across time and space can roughly be summarized around different weightings for four broad functions in economic development, corresponding to different means whereby banks make their profits.

The first is in ensuring smooth operation of the payment system. Banks are a crucial element in the monetary system without which a modern market economy would be an impossibility. In this role they are irreplaceable and regulatory policies have generally developed to ensure that it is performed satisfactorily, even if that may conflict with other possible roles. This is not a major source of banks' profits but, as will be indicated, attempts to develop other roles carry the risk that this crucial function may be impaired.

The second is in mobilizing and allocating savings. Taking in deposits and granting credits provide the most straightforward source of profits and are often presented as the defining activities of a bank. However, this requires substantial expertise and experience in judging the reliability of clients, particularly for long-term loans. Success in this gives banks an important role in the capital market, but other institutions may also play a role here. Following Gerschenkron's (1962) distinction between 'early' and 'late' developers, banks played a larger role in financing long-term investment in the latter where other elements of the capital market had not emerged at the time of industrialization.

The third is as a 'substitute' for entrepreneurship, in developing new businesses, reorganizing and merging existing businesses and exercising corporate governance. Even when not involved in major strategic decisions banks might be expected, either by ownership of shares or by checking on the fate of credits, to impose discipline on enterprise managements. This, however, requires still greater expertise. Moreover, close involvement with industrial enterprises – particularly if both by credits and share ownership – can expose a bank to very substantial risks.

The fourth is a 'parasitic' role whereby banks transfer resources away from productive activities, for example into speculation or capital flight. The aim may still be profit maximization for the bank, but that need not be the case. There may be a divergence between the interests of depositors and those who control the bank's behaviour – be they original founders, owners or managers – with the latter seeking personal enrichment at the expense of the former. Where regulation is underdeveloped and where the legal framework is weak, the scope for fraud may be enormous and the banking system may play a very destructive role.

This 'parasitic' model has naturally not been seen as central in economic history where the study has been of successful development rather than its failure. Successful development inevitably involved overcoming distrust towards financial institutions and this was often a very protracted process. New scope for a parasitic role is opened up in transition economies where the fruits of past accumulation exist without the appropriate accompanying institutional framework.

The main distinction in economic history has related to the second and third functions listed above. This has led to a differentiation between the 'Anglo-Saxon' or, at one time, 'Anglo-French', and the 'German' or 'central European' models.

During early industrialization in Britain, investment was largely financed from internal sources and, later in the nineteenth century, also by new share issues. Commercial banks restricted themselves largely to granting short-term credits. Distinct merchant banks and institutional investors financed long-term investment and became involved in share ownership.

In 'late' developers banks were often the key agent in founding enterprises and then retained an active involvement in ownership and management. Germany fitted with this model for a time, as did Austria before the First World War, and also Austria and Czechoslovakia in the inter-war period (Lacina, 1994, p. 140). Banks arranged share issues, often retaining some within their own portfolios. They held directorships, changed managements and arranged mergers and takeovers. In turn, industrialists sat on bank boards so that it was not always clear who was driving decisions (Lacina, 1994, and Mosser and Teichova, 1991).

Czech banks, like their German counterparts, had been particularly important before 1914 in supporting the development of other businesses. In the words of the leading banker of the time, they alone 'enjoyed a degree of trust, with which they could gain the necessary conditions for founding an enterprise' (Preiss, 1912, p. 6). They alone could put together large sums of capital. Czech banks went further, not only setting up companies and establishing cartels, but even becoming involved in organizing trading and sales and in ensuring other forms of close cooperation between companies.

However, the gap between the two broad models should not be exaggerated. Czech bank leaders made clear that permanent participation in running other businesses was a very infrequent aim. Their primary concern was with the fate of credits and it was this that led them to play a wider role in economic development, substituting for the lack of expertise on the part of newly-emerging Czech managers, as well as the lack of capital (Preiss, 1912). Their motivation – to make a profit – and the preferred means to achieve it (by granting safe credits) were the same as those of British commercial banks.

Indeed, German bankers resisted pressure from government to be more generous in giving credits to industry when they felt the risks were too high, as was the case after the First World War (Feldman, 1991). Evidence has also emerged that British banks too became involved closely with companies to which they had given credits (Collins, 1998). Short-term loans easily became long-term when continually rolled over.

Moreover, history has shown that where banks took on wider activities, the risks of failure were increased, posing a threat to the first of the 'roles' mentioned above. History in a number of European countries therefore saw fluctuations between governments encouraging banks to take on a wider role and rules restricting them from long-term ownership in non-financial enterprises (James, Lindgren and Teichova, 1991, and Collins, 1998). The distinction between an 'Anglo-Saxon' and a 'continental' model should not be exaggerated. Claims that banks play major roles today in directing or controlling enterprise managements – with Germany and Japan among the important countries frequently mentioned – have also been tempered by research on corporate governance (Edwards and Fischer, 1994, and Aoki, 1994).

BANKING IN TRANSITION ECONOMIES

The particular circumstances of economic transition have presented both a distinct set of constraints and a different set of opportunities. The most important constraint stems from the near impossibility of playing a traditional banking role. The standard business of taking in deposits and granting credits depends on stability of relationships and on knowledge built up over a long period of time. The most difficult task is the assessment of risk. This may be possible for established enterprises with secure markets, such as utilities or raw materials exporters, but is almost inconceivable for new enterprises in the rapidly expanding service sector.

This constraint is matched by possibilities that were absent in the early stages of industrial development. An economic structure already exists which had links to an established finance system. Banks need not channel savings into investment: they have more scope for parasitic activities, funneling funds from enterprises that already exist and playing a role that is clearly negative for the prosperity of the economy as a whole. Liberalization of world financial flows opens up new possibilities for this and for other means for banks to make money. The newness of relationships and the ineffectiveness of a legal framework, that is either weak or too new to have established itself, create possibilities for individual enrichment with bank owners and bank managers able to pursue their own private interests at the expense of the interests of the bank as a business.

This leaves scope for a range of types of banking activity. At one extreme are the most cautious banks, involved primarily in taking in deposits and granting short-term, safe credits. Others may become involved in financing long-term investment and even try to substitute for absent entrepreneurship. As will be argued, the ability to play these roles successfully is very limited. At the other extreme are institutions that have found alternative means to make money in the newly liberalized environment, often pursuing relatively narrow purposes and serving the interests of a few individual founders, owners or managers. The balance between the different types and their exact form varies somewhat between individual transition economies.

In the Russian case there has been a very high representation for banks that perform the largely parasitic function, exploiting the easy environment to funnel wealth out of the country. Banks have largely failed in terms of the first three functions set out at the start. They cannot even guarantee a functioning payments system, as indicated by the high level of barter relations, although they are an active agent in finding alternative means of exchange.

They have not financed economic development and financial–industrial groups cannot be seen as analogous to similar groupings in Japan or other Asian countries. As other contributions in this volume indicate, banks and enterprises have sought close links to pursue objectives that relate to a specific situation in which normal processes of a market economy are not functioning adequately. There is no analogy to the links developed as part of long-term programmes of investment and growth.

In east-central Europe the first function is satisfactorily fulfilled. A money-based system operates. Particularly in the Czech Republic banks are also the central element in the capital market, directing savings into investment, and they have in some cases tried to exercise control over enterprise managements. In Poland and Hungary banks are less prominent and closer to the model of cautious orthodoxy, granting mostly safe credits.

In all cases, however, part of the banking sector has followed the 'parasitic' model, appearing as a cover for corrupt or criminal activity. Moreover, the more welcome roles have often not been performed very well: banks inexperienced in market conditions have made a lot of mistakes. In the Czech case this, as will be demonstrated, was exacerbated by government pressure.

WHY DO BANKING SYSTEMS DIFFER?

The differences between Russia and east-central Europe can be understood in terms of three broad explanations.

The first focuses on 'path dependency', with an emphasis on how the old system broke up. Johnson (2000) suggests that this can explain a great deal of the chaos in Russian banking. Lax controls at the end of central planning encouraged the emergence of banks that profited from quite specific features of the disintegrating planning system. The political confusion as the Soviet Union fell apart again gave an opening for new banks to emerge and profit from encroaching economic chaos. There is a clear contrast here with the ordered transitions in east-central Europe where there was never any doubt who was in control of political life and of economic policy. Nevertheless, 'path dependency' is at best a partial explanation, built around an implicit assumption of identical starting points, although this was clearly not the case.

The second focuses on policy choices during the transformation. Nominally there was an emphasis on liberalizing relations as much as possible. Central planning, allegedly based on excessive centralized controls, was to be replaced by an absence of rules with the implicit, and sometimes explicit, assumption that a functioning market economy could emerge spontaneously.

However, in east-central Europe there were two powerful counter-pressures. The first was a greater coherence in policy making and a greater determination to maintain economic stability, meaning considerable continuity in managements and organizational structures. Despite the end of central planning, a central authority kept a grip on policy making. The development of diverse interests and lobbies, such as the banking lobby in Russia, was never such as to lead to even a partial domination of political power by warring business interests.

The second counter-pressure was a quest for acceptance into the European 'mainstream'. Together these meant that there was a consensus around the aim of maintaining a stable and functioning financial system and also an acceptance of the need to accept rules and regulations from mature market economies and especially the EU. These often conflicted with free-market dogma. It gave policy-making a coherent aim that could come before serving sectional interests. It was an aim that fitted with national aspirations and that could be presented as returning to a pre-communist past that had had much in common with that of western Europe.

These two possible explanations for differences between transition economies have areas of overlap: policy possibilities reflected partly the heritage left by the form of transition. They also both beg the further questions of why paths differed and why policy choices diverged. This points to the third explanation, the possibility that countries differed substantially even under central planning.

This is a theme that could hardly be researched in the past. Inside those countries the differences were played down while outside observers were looking largely only for signs of market relations. Comparisons of other aspects of the regulation of relations between economic units were not studied.

The assumption in East and West alike was that credits and the banking systems played very similar roles that left them subordinate to central planners. In the most general sense this was true. Banks gave credits in line with plan decisions and did not bear the risks themselves. Nevertheless, there were always differences. The conception of banking in Czechoslovakia took shape after the currency reform of 1953 which saw the elimination of much of the stock of accumulated savings alongside an end to wartime rationing. The intention was to follow the Soviet example. It was, however, the Soviet example not as it really operated, but an idealized version described in textbooks (Batyrev and Sitnin, 1947, and Myant, 1989). Here central planning worked by firms adhering to strict budget discipline. Finance could then play a role.

Czechoslovak planning, for all its inadequacies, may have been closer to this model. Even laws and contracts played some role in relations between enterprises, justifying 30 pages in a standard 1970s text on economic organization (Řezníček, 1978). It was an imperfect mechanism. Studies of the reality of planning show both how adept lower levels were at distorting the centre's intentions and the importance of interventions from contacts at high levels in overcoming difficulties (Myant, 1989, pp. 209–13). These were familiar too from Soviet experience, but there are no easy Czech translations for the familiar Russian terms *tolkach* and *blat* that epitomize the importance of informal rather than formal mechanisms in enabling Soviet planning to function (Ledeneva, 1998). This may, as implied by Ledeneva, reflect very deeply-rooted cultural phenomena. The implication is that there was no need to reinvent regulation by formal rules in Czechoslovakia after 1989. It had survived through the four preceding decades.

Acceptance of formal rules, particularly in conditions of relative price stability, meant that banks could play a role within central planning. The state bank had the status of a major organ of economic policy, as clarified in laws in 1965 and 1970. Its job was to check that enterprises kept to spending limits and used resources in line with central decisions. The more an enterprise was dependent on credit rather than its own sources of finance, so the greater the bank's ability to exercise control. It had powers to impose financial penalties by withholding credits and these could quickly impinge on an enterprise's wage bill.

This was by no means a perfect basis for the subsequent development of a market system: enforcement was inevitably weak when no enterprise could face bankruptcy. Its significance was put to the test in the 1980s when economic difficulties were met by tighter financial discipline. The bank was thereby taking on a more active role in deciding which projects should be financed. Later in the decade it was frequently exercising its power to refuse further credits when old debts were not repaid (Revenda, 1991, pp. 90–91). Some enterprises were able to ignore this, running up unpaid bills leading to a growing chain of bad debt. The originators, however, were the most powerful and prestigious enterprises. Across much of the economy cuts were made to comply with central bank rules. It could even be argued that at least 'a part of the economy' in pre-1989 Czechoslovakia was coordinated through the market (Klaus and Tříska, 1988, p. 825).

Even if this is an exaggeration, the role of banking under central planning did have important implications. It had prestige and a solid position that was carried forward into a strong voice after 1989. Its activities had something in common with those of both commercial and central banks in market economies, including the fastidious checking of company accounts and the focus on caution and macroeconomic balance. Many of its leading officials felt a loyalty to the pre-war tradition and to pre-war economists who had written on the monetary system. This was not a bad framework for the emergence of an orthodox central bank.

The importance of finance in Czechoslovak central planning can be illustrated by figures on the volumes of credit relative to NMP (Net Material Product), the available indicator of national income under central planning. These show an increase from 32 per cent in 1960 to 69 per cent in 1969 and 87 per cent in 1983 (FSÚ, 1985, p. 142). This had fallen slightly to 83 per cent in 1989 (FSÚ, 1990, p. 182), following the efforts to impose austerity. Table 7.1 provides a comparison with other transition economies using available figures from the IMF. These differ slightly from domestic statistical sources, but the general picture remains the same. Thus in Poland credits to the socialist sector of the economy reached 111.8 per cent of

NMP in 1975. By 1988, after the inflationary chaos throughout much of that decade, the figure had fallen to 37.3 per cent (GUS, 1990, p. 119, 148).

There was also particularly strong continuity from the former Czechoslovakia in that credits continued to go to the enterprise sector. They did not, either before or after 1989, and in contrast to Russia and also Hungary, go on a significant scale to the government. Continuity into the 1990s, when market conditions gave credits a rather different significance, was almost inevitable. Enterprises were bound to the banking system by their debts from the past.

Personal savings were also more important in Czechoslovakia, presumably reflecting higher living standards and greater macroeconomic stability. The consumer price index in 1989 was officially recorded at only 20 per cent above the 1953 level. Total savings deposits increased steadily from 3.3 per cent of NMP in 1954 to 44.8 per cent in 1989. A relatively small proportion of this was matched by personal loans so that, in macroeconomic terms, these savings were balanced by investment from the enterprise sector. In Poland savings deposits relative to NMP grew more slowly, reaching 24.7 per cent in 1980 and then peaking at 30.8 per cent in 1981, the year when NMP fell by 12.0 per cent. The following years of inflation saw savings relative to NMP falling to 14.8 per cent in 1988. The habit of putting deposits in a trusted domestic bank was clearly better established in Czechoslovakia.

BANKS IN THE CZECH TRANSFORMATION

As in Russia, a prominent theme in economic transformation was the liberalization of relations and elimination of central controls. The government's initial conception of economic reform lacked any coherent policy towards the banking sector as such. The main policy documents on economic reform did not even mention banking and nor was the point taken up by its many critics (Myant, 1993, pp. 174–83). No alternative was developed to a conception, occasionally made explicit, that liberalization, privatization and competition would solve the problems for this sector, as for others.

However, the two key centres of power tempered this with more coherent conceptions. The government may not have had a clear view on how banking should be transformed but, as is indicated below, it soon developed a clear vision of the role banking would play in the transformation of the economy as a whole. This led it to favour considerable organizational continuity, with a few large banks under partial state control.

The central bank concentrated on maintaining stability, an objective which also pointed towards organizational continuity. The legal framework, as amended in 1989 in preparation for a reform of central planning,

Table 7.1 Deposits and credits as a percentage of GDP

		Deposits	Credits	
			total	to private sector
Russia	1993	17.3	25.9	11.8
	1997	13.0	26.6	9.6
	2000	15.9	24.0	12.2
Poland	1987	34.4	48.1	4.4
	1993	29.5	40.7	12.2
	1997	30.8	34.8	17.0
	2000	38.0	37.8	26.0
Hungary	1987	35.2	102.1	—
	1993	38.5	97.0	28.2
	1997	34.6	65.2	23.9
	1999	39.0	52.5	23.0
Czechoslovakia	1987	—	68.8	5.8
Czech Republic	1993	62.0	72.0	50.1
	1997	62.7	73.0	67.6
	2000	64.9	57.3	49.7
Slovakia	1993	58.4	75.3	72.4
	1997	57.8	68.4	42.1
	2000	60.2	60.2	30.7

Source: Calculated from *IMF International Financial Statistics, Yearbook*, 1994 and 2001.

gave it the power to oversee newly emerging banks and took away its former powers to take deposits and grant credits. It retained the same management structure as in former years, with a nominally independent board and a head appointed by the President, following a recommendation from the government. Only in 1993, following a law passed in December 1992, was the bank given full formal independence from the government when the law gave the power of appointment to the President alone. It was a change of little immediate practical significance, but there was a gradual divergence in conceptions between the government and central bank which was to contribute to open conflicts later in the decade. The latter became more concerned at problems in the banking sector and saw a greater need for regulation, the importance of which had been underestimated on all sides when the main emphasis was being put on liberalization.

The initial weakness of the regulatory framework opened the way for some rapid changes in the banking sector, but some of the basic statistics point also to important elements of continuity from the past. Thus credits remained stable and high, as indicated in Table 7.1, with a strong bias towards businesses. These accounted for almost 93 per cent of the total in 1991 and still for 90 per cent in 1999: an approximate 50:50 split between businesses and households is usual in the UK and other mature market economies. Deposits were predominantly from households, 60 per cent in 1991 and 67 per cent in 1999, implying that their savings were financing the needs of the business sector. Comparisons with Hungary and Poland also show the great importance of bank credits in Czech enterprise finance, partly reflecting a burden from the past and partly the slow development of other forms of finance (Chvojka, 1999).

The total number of banks peaked at 55 in 1994. Four 'big' banks, with 86 per cent of deposits and 64 per cent of credits in 1995, were created by the transformation of institutions that existed under central planning. There was some discussion of whether to pursue a model of universal or specialized banking. A combination of wanting to build on past history, an atmosphere favouring liberalization and practical difficulties that would be imposed on any bank restricted to certain parts of the economy, all led to an acceptance that the four state-owned banks should become universal, commercial banks (Revenda, 1991, pp. 104–12).

The 'small' bank sector, peaking at 22 banks in 1993, was made up of new banks, created from scratch. This process was referred to as an 'explosion'. In fact, the number of banks created is small by international standards and minimal when compared with the 2500 at one time in Russia, but in line with experience elsewhere in east-central Europe (cf. Helmenstein, 1999). The larger Polish economy saw private bank numbers peak at 77 in 1993, with the total number of banks at 104. In Slovakia the total number peaked at 33 in 1996.

Czechoslovak rules for new bank formation were extremely lax. At first the only requirement was the equivalent of a manual worker's annual pay plus the names of board members. At least these rules do appear to have been enforced: only one application in ten was accepted (Matoušek, 1998, p. 25). New banks never held a major share of bank assets, with a peak of 8.8 per cent in 1994. Moreover, rules were tightened and no new licences were granted from 1993. The central bank intervened to eliminate small banks, reducing the number operating to two by 1999, as their financial difficulties grew following incompetence, naivety and very often corruption. The same trends can be observed across east-central Europe, albeit with a less dramatic rise and fall.

These small banks are the closest to the 'parasitic' model that was so important in Russia. Their relatively small representation reflects three key differences from conditions in that country. The first is that there was no incentive for large established enterprises to set up their own banks: they were tied in to the existing big banks by past credits, by the need for more credits and by the need for security for their own deposits. In short, the established banks offered a functioning system that alone served their needs.

The second difference is that, unlike a certain period in Russia, there was no disintegration of the established big banks with local branches setting up on their own. This too would have made little sense when customers were attracted to the large and established banks.

The third difference was the behaviour of the central bank. By mid decade more small businesses had been formed and voucher privatization had created scope for enrichment from share dealing and speculation. A base might then have existed for a genuine explosion in bank numbers, but the central bank had become aware of the dangers and was beginning to assert itself.

It even sought to encourage foreign banks to enter the market by buying existing Czech small banks, a solution that was actively blocked in Russia from 1992 onwards by the then powerful banking lobby (Johnson, 2000, pp. 119–21). Progress was at first slow, but foreign banks' share in total bank assets grew to 11.3 per cent in 1994 and 27.2 per cent in 1999. They were very cautious and initially worked almost exclusively with branches of multinational companies involved in inward direct investment.

In mid decade, then, the 'big' banks were left to dominate the sector. Three were partly privatized in the first voucher wave in 1992–93, leaving the state with a dominant share. The government's representatives hardly ever intervened openly, but managements were aware that they had been put in place by the government with the expectation that they would develop as modern, universal banks.

Voucher privatization in turn opened up new possibilities and banks established the investment funds that dominated the two voucher waves. They may have played an active role in some cases (Schütte, 2000), but generally allowed free rein to existing managements, at least until serious problems became apparent after 1997 (Myant, 2001). Shares were also a relatively small part of their assets, although their principal link to enterprises was through credits.

Some wanted to encourage banks to become the key force in directing and controlling enterprises, among them the country's IMF delegate (Jonáš, 1997). The idea that banks could fill a gap in corporate governance made sense within the framework of neo-classical economic theory in which the key problem is to control managers by imposing the right incentive structure. A disciplining force would ensure that managements 'look to the benefits of enhanced economic efficiency' (Frydman, Gray and Rapaczynski, 1996, Vol. 1, p. 2) after which the system should function satisfactorily. This, however, underestimates the complexity of management's tasks, the range of choices available that do not reflect incentives alone and the need for expertise in both performing and monitoring management's role (Myant, 1999).

An active role for banks in enterprise management was therefore not a realistic possibility. A bank pursuing a rational and self-interested business strategy would probably have trusted very few enterprises. It would have lent very little when there was no means of judging the reliability of clients and would have avoided the long-term commitment implied by share ownership. Becoming a substitute for entrepreneurship would have implied more knowledge and expertise than enterprise managements. Bankers' past experience probably left them with less. The result was a paradox of an apparently very substantial position in the economy alongside a lack of the expertise required to use it effectively.

Initially, to some extent aware of their own shortcomings (cf. Salzmann, 1990), Czech banks behaved cautiously. Soon, however, banks came under strong pressure from the government to be generous in granting credits to new small businesses, to large firms in financial difficulty and to individuals seeking credits to finance privatization. They were accused of 'putting their own interests before the interests . . . [of] the state budget or other entrepreneurs' (L. Válek, *Hospodářské noviny*, 22 June 1993) and chastized by Minister of Finance Ivan Kočárník for choosing 'the route of excessive security of credits with property and the like' (*Hospodářské noviny*, 31 March 1993). He blamed this on their 'inexperience with assessing business risk', with the questionable implication that they should cope with their low level of expertise by being more, rather than less, generous.

The banking system thus became central to the whole strategy of rapid transformation to a market system. In the words of one leading banker, the assumption was that 'in our thoroughly under-capitalized land everything was to be replaced by credit'. Banks thereby became the 'buffer, which absorbed the majority of the shocks from liberalization of prices, from privatization and from the mass emergence of the entrepreneurial sector' (Kunert, 1999, pp. 307–8).

Banks were for a time willing accomplices, buoyed up by the widespread optimism that the transition to a market economy would lead to rapid growth and increased prosperity. They had the resources to lend, thanks to a high and rising level of deposits, they knew no other form of profitable activity and they believed that good times in the future would lead to the repayment of most loans.

Needless to say, much of the credit granted by Czech banks was unsound. The proportion of 'classified' loans (including risky and loss-making loans) in the Czech Republic reached 37 per cent of the total in 1994 (Matoušek, 1998, p. 23). A figure around 2 per cent is normal in advanced market economies, with figures around 10 per cent often associated with a banking crisis. The figures in Hungary and Poland reached this range early in the decade – with, of course, a lower level of importance for credit in financing enterprises anyway – but the subsequent tendency was for decline. Privatization in Poland was a slower process and in Hungary there was a greater emphasis on selling to foreign companies. Banks were therefore less involved. They were able, and expected, to develop more as orthodox banks, with a primary responsibility to clients and shareholders.

The difference was confirmed by privatization strategies that included, in the Polish case, an aim to 'twin' with an established western bank. Sale of minority, and eventually more substantial, stakes to foreign banks developed as the aim from 1992 in Hungary and from 1993 in Poland. There was always some political opposition to this and policy in both countries evolved with some twists and turns (Bonin et al., and Górski, 2001). In the Czech Republic foreign participation in major banks was resisted until 1998.

There was, however, a catch in the Czech banks' generosity. They had to comply with central bank rules, derived from western European practice. Thus they had to comply with international accounting standards and to raise capital to 8 per cent of risk-weighted assets by the end of 1996. Reserves had never been a requirement under the risk-free conditions of central planning.

The conflict between these two pressures was resolved for a time by a generous approach to granting credits alongside a wide margin on interest rates between deposits and credits. That, however, was ultimately no substitute for checking creditworthiness. Moreover, it made it harder for businesses – especially the new, small ones – to keep up repayments.

DIVERSITY AMONG THE BIG BANKS

Just as there is no universal model of bank behaviour in transition economies, so too each of the Czech big banks had its own individual characteristics. These reflected their different pasts, hints from the government on how they should behave and choices made by their managements.

ČS (Česká spořitelna), the Czech Savings Bank, emerged from voucher privatization with the state holding 53 per cent of the voting shares and no other owner able to wield significant influence. It inherited a network of branches and a substantial body of personal savings. In December 1995 it still had 35 per cent of total deposits. The rate of personal savings increased after 1989, giving ČS a surplus of resources for investment with credits less than half the level of deposits in 1995. However, it had no background in contacts with enterprises. Before 1989 it had lent to households, but that was considered too complex. Government pressure too pointed it in a different direction. It started lending to some big and small enterprises and, above all, it funded the rapid expansion of the small banks that lacked the public trust required to build a deposit base of their own. This was presented as a positive step towards helping the development of a diversified banking sector.

When set in a historical context this behaviour is truly remarkable. In the inter-war period there had been 7000 cooperative and small savings banks in Czechoslovakia with deposits five times the level of the 23 joint-stock banks. These, however, were largely involved only in taking in deposits. Their funds were then used for credits by the few large banks that developed long-term relationships with business and that had the expertise to take the major decisions on credit (Mervart, 1996, p. 29, and Lacina, 1994, p. 36). The behaviour of the ČS in the early 1990s appeared as a reversal of this and rather implied that decisions on credit were being taken by those with the least chance of acquiring adequate expertise.

KB (Komerční banka), the Commercial Bank, emerged with 52 per cent of shares in state hands. The remainder were scattered over 103000 individuals with some concentration into 10 investment funds with 35 per cent of the shares between them. The bank's own funds controlled 3.4 per cent of the shares, which was insufficient to wield any serious power. The KB inherited close links with established enterprises. At the end of 1995 it still accounted for 26 per cent of total credits, but had also reached the same share in deposits. Its status meant that it came under the strongest pressure to accept its 'responsibility' to the economy as a whole. It lent to new small businesses and to established enterprises, both of which activities pleased the government. It subsequently became clear that no serious efforts had been made to control credit decisions. Many were unsound and investigations suggest that bribes to branch managers may have been routine (D. Šístková, *Právo*, 9 August 2000).

ČSOB (Československá obchodní banka), the Czechoslovak Foreign-Trade Bank, remained under a form of full state ownership until 1999. It was the most cautious, with a management experienced in international banking practice, and accounted for less than 10 per cent of both credits and deposits in December 1995. It avoided identification with politicians and proved capable of resisting pressures from government. It may have been helped by an ownership structure that gave 50 per cent of the shares to the Czech and Slovak central banks rather than to the Czech government. It was the most successful at raising loans from foreign banks and stands as the example for what could have been had all banks followed rules from international practice.

IPB (Investiční a poštovní banka), the Investment and Postal Bank, developed out of the Investment Bank set up under the reform proposals of 1989. Privatization initially left the state with a 48 per cent share. It had to fight from a position of initial weakness and proved itself innovative, aggressive and unorthodox. It established a deposit base partly by merging at the start of 1994 with the newly-established Postal Bank which took in deposits at post offices. This gave it 16 per cent of total bank deposits in December 1995 against 15 per cent of credits.

It aimed for a bias towards investment banking and used investment funds to acquire shares in a wide range of companies. The management's great innovation was then to mastermind its own 'privatization by stealth', using control over investment funds to acquire shares in the bank itself. The state, for reasons that remain unclear, failed to take part in new share issues, reducing its total share to 36 per cent in 1994. These additional shares found their way to owners allied to the management. It was for a time unclear what was happening, as the IPB management was keen to protect the privacy of these owners, individuals who were allegedly shy of publicity. This was a consideration that rarely troubled owners of other banks (Mervart, 1998, p. 131). Behind this was a symbiotic relationship. A number of emerging businesses benefited from IPB help with generous credits and purchases of new share issues. In return, they took shares in the IPB and supported the bank's management.

There were close links between the bank's management and Václav Klaus, Czech Prime Minister from 1992 to 1997, and evidence that the bank supported enterprises that in turn funded his party (P. Kohout, *Hospodářské noviny*, 26 June 2000). However, a clear distinction can be made from banking in Russia. The IPB was not controlled by enterprises – its management used their support to cement its own position – and nor did it control politicians. Its core activities were the normal banking practices of taking in deposits and granting credits, supplemented by share ownership as a further method intended to yield a future profit. As would be expected in view of its inevitable lack of experience, it did not perform these roles very well. Hints from politicians may have encouraged lending to some ultimately unsuccessful businesses, but the IPB was capable of ignoring such advice and also of making its own mistakes. The central bank began expressing concern from early 1994 that it was pursuing a dangerous strategy of widespread, and apparently random, share acquisitions at prices that appeared excessively generous.

The management was able to find a means to survive growing external pressure, especially from the central bank. It persuaded both the government and the central bank to accept a form of full privatization in March 1998 that gave a controlling minority share to the Japanese investment bank Nomura. This, however, was never to be a strategic investor and was always intending to sell the IPB within a few more years.

BANKS AND ECONOMIC CRISIS

In mid decade the government felt able to boast that the Czech transformation had been a great success. The economy had recovered from the 'transformation depression' of 1991–92 and GDP growth reached 5.9 per cent in 1995 and 4.8 per cent in 1996. Banking seemed to be at the centre of the 'Czech road' in which the bulk of the economy was privatized into domestic ownership. Problems in small banks were dismissed for as long as possible as a few isolated incidents within a generally healthy sector. Big banks were said to be covered against possible losses with adequate reserves.

The only unfinished business was full privatization of the banks and there appeared to be no need to rush. If anything state ownership was seen as an advantage. Big banks' managements were complacently satisfied that they had done an excellent job and saw no need for new owners. International agencies gave high ratings to Czech banks, partly because state ownership carried an implicit guarantee of help should things go wrong. Klaus was also reassured that partial state ownership ensured a clear link to the interests of the domestic economy. In other words, it meant that they could grant credits that a private, and certainly a foreign, bank would have considered too risky. Although eventually persuaded to act over the IPB, he was generally happy to procrastinate in the hope that powerful Czech business groups would in time emerge to take over the remaining banks. Privatization would then mean a further strengthening of a specifically Czech capitalism rather than sale to foreigners.

That 'golden age' ended very abruptly before the end of the decade. Growth had not been based on improved industrial competitiveness and had brought with it rapidly rising imports, especially of sophisticated consumer goods. The current account deficit rose towards the dangerous level of 10 per cent of GDP in early 1997. Criticisms from the IMF and a loss of international confidence in the Czech currency forced the government to accept currency devaluation and to adopt two austerity packages in mid 1997. These were followed by a fall in GDP of 3.4 per cent over the 1997 to 1999 period.

This, then, was very different from Russia's problems in 1998. It was not primarily the result of financial problems or of banks' behaviour. They were, however, an important part of the process. Already before 1997 they had become more cautious and this contributed to the slight fall in growth after 1995. They gradually stopped lending to small banks, to much of the new small business sector and to a number of established enterprises (Buchtíková, 1999). Thus although they had at first been amenable to government pressure, they were not prepared to continue lending to firms that clearly could not repay loans from the past.

The big Czech banks, and particularly the IPB, faced additional difficulties as the prices of some of the shares they owned began to drop. These had been held up by substantial trading in the aftermath of voucher privatization but particularly those in engineering were falling by late 1996. There was also a squeeze on credit opportunities as foreign banks became more willing to lend to the safest Czech companies, such as utilities, on terms that the Czech banks could not match.

The austerity packages of 1997 were also accompanied by a tougher approach from the central bank which forced banks to increase their reserves to cover against possible losses. With this, lending to much of the Czech economy effectively ended. A 'credit crunch' hit very hard those enterprises, largely in engineering, chemicals and metallurgy, which were the most dependent on the kind of risky credits offered by Czech banks.

Still buoyed up with a healthy domestic deposit base, ČS and KB sought new opportunities abroad, with the former choosing to speculate on the Russian capital market. The resulting losses were catastrophic. By the end of 1998 the ČS faced a situation so serious that it was threatened with the withdrawal of its licence. KB was in a similar situation a year later.

This suddenly gave a new impetus to ideas of bank privatization. From late 1998 the government, by then a minority Social Democrat administration, saw no alternative to reestablishing majority state control followed by speedy sales to established foreign banks. The majority of ČSOB shares were sold to the Belgian bank KBC. ČS required a rescue package to cover for past losses that were greater than the price ultimately received for a majority share from the Austrian Erste Bank Sparkassen. The state's shares in KB, by then 60 per cent of the total, were set for sale to the French bank Société Générale in late 2001. The IPB suffered a remarkable fate. Mounting losses, primarily the fruits of past irresponsibility but also exacerbated by the sale of some valuable assets to the benefit of Nomura, ended in the central bank imposing direct control in June 2000. It then handed the bank over to the ČSOB under conditions that would oblige the state to cover for losses. This, it was argued, was the only means of preventing disruption to the payments system.

Thus, a completely new banking structure is being created, based on foreign ownership. The same end result is emerging across east-central Europe, albeit by different routes. There will be no return in the Czech Republic to the easy lending practices of the early 1990s, but the state budget will have to foot the bill for covering the banking sector's losses. The scale of this remains unclear, but the highest estimates suggest that it could be around one-quarter of GDP, or one-half of state spending in a single year.

CONCLUSIONS

The experience of banking in Russia and east-central Europe confirms some of the most general lessons of economic history. It confirms that there is no universal model of the activities undertaken by institutions called banks. Their role and nature is heavily dependent on the wider environment and, under the conditions following the end of central planning, there is no reason to suppose that they will play a positive role in terms of the development of the economy as a whole.

Three broad models can be identified. The first is the cautious orthodoxy displayed largely by foreign banks. The ČSOB was close to this model, suggesting that this kind of behaviour was possible from state-owned banks. However, it would have been politically extremely difficult to restrict all Czech banks to such caution when they demonstrably were awash with deposits and when new and established businesses alike were crying out for credits.

If all Czech banks had behaved like the ČSOB, there would have been less rapid growth in new activities and the difficulties that were to engulf much of the enterprise sector towards the end of the decade would have been apparent much sooner. It would probably have involved state aid to enterprises in preparation for sale to foreign firms. Costs of covering for past losses, and of covering enterprises' past debts could have led to substantial budget deficits, covered in part by borrowing from banks.

There were advocates of a privatization strategy based much more on sale to foreign companies (Myant, 2001). It was a theoretical possibility, albeit a politically unacceptable one in the early 1990s. It would have had much in common with the solution chosen in Hungary. The difficulties of advocating such a course in Russia would have been, and still are, much greater in view both of the attitudes towards foreign companies and of the low level of attractiveness to multinational companies of much of Russian industry. If an approach of cautious orthodoxy were to be successfully imposed by a central bank on the Russian banking sector it would therefore leave great uncertainties over the transformation of much of the rest of the economy.

The second possible model of banking, based on liberalization and *laisser faire*, has led into an emphasis on the parasitic role. Despite the undeniable benefits of a market system in general, the fact remains that banking is very heavily regulated throughout the world. It is too important to the economy, the beneficial functions that it can perform are too difficult and the temptation to move to play a negative role too great for the sector to be left to uncontrolled free enterprise. Experience across all transition economies seems to point unequivocally to the benefits of firm central constraints on how banks can behave. That is clearly made much more difficult where the number of banks escalates and where organizational continuity from the past is broken.

The third model of banking sees it used as part of wider economic policies. Inspiration for this can be derived from the history of banks playing a crucial role in economic development. There are, however, two important reservations. The first is that banks in the past played substantial roles as part of their profit-seeking strategies. They did not substitute for this different aims, such as economic growth or the development of new businesses, or at least when they were persuaded to do so the outcome was often serious difficulties for the banks themselves. The second reservation is that banks played a substantial role in the development of some European countries because they alone had the knowledge and experience to assess business risk. There is no analogy here to the conditions in a transition economy where banks, perhaps more than any other enterprises inherited from the past, have to learn completely new activities and completely new ways of working.

It is difficult to translate this into recommendations for other transition economies. The conclusion seems to be that banks should be seen as a 'dependent' as much as an 'independent' variable. Rather than expecting them to play a leading role in transforming a planned economy, the best may be to ensure, by the adoption of orthodox practice from elsewhere, that a stable payments system is created and maintained and that their activities do not take a form that is positively harmful to the economy as a whole.

NOTE

1. I would like to acknowledge support for this research from the British Academy in arranging an exchange visit to the Economic Institute of the Academy of Sciences of the Czech Republic in August and September 2000.

REFERENCES

Aoki, M. (1994), 'Towards an economic model of the Japanese firm', in K. Imai and R. Komiya (eds), *Business Enterprise in Japan: Views of Leading Japanese Economists*, Cambridge, MA: The MIT Press.

Batyrev, V. M. and V. K. Sitnin (1947), *Finanční a úvěrová soustava SSSR*, Prague: Orbis.

Bonin, J., K. Mizsei, I. Székely and P. Wachtel (1998), *Banking in Transition Economies: Developing Market Oriented Banking Sectors in Eastern Europe*, Cheltenham, UK and Northampton, USA: Edward Elgar.

Buchtíková, A. (1999), 'Empirická analýza financování podniků a úvěrových aktivit bank v ČR v letech 1995–1997', Prague, ČNB sekce měnová, VPč.14.

Chvojka, P. (1999), 'Financing enterprise restructuring', in M. Myant (ed.), *Industrial Competitiveness in East-Central Europe,* Edward Elgar: Cheltenham, UK and Northampton, MA, USA.

Collins, M. (1998), 'English bank development within a European context, 1870–1939', *Economic History Review*, 51, pp. 1–24.

Edwards, J. and K. Fischer (1994), *Banks, Finance and Investment in West Germany since 1970*, Cambridge: Cambridge University Press.

Feldman, G. (1991), 'Banks and the problem of capital shortage in Germany, 1918–1923', in James, Lindgren and Teichova.

Frydman, R., C. Gray and A. Rapaczynski (eds) (1996), *Corporate Governance in Central Europe and Russia* (2 vols), Budapest: Central European University Press.

FSÚ (Federální statistický úřad) (1985), *Historická statistická ročenka ČSSR*, Prague: SNTL.

FSÚ (Federální statistický úřad) (1990), *Statistická ročenka České a Slovenské federativní republiky 1990*, Prague: SNTL.

Górski, M. (2001), 'The new banking and financial sector: its role, potential and weaknesses', in G. Blazyca and R. Rapacki (eds), *Poland in the New Millenium*, Cheltenham, UK and Northampton, USA: Edward Elgar.

Gerschenkron, A. (1962), *Economic Backwardness in Historical Perspective*, New York: Praeger.

GUS (Główny urząd statystyczny) (1990), *Rocznik Statystyczny, 1990*, Warsaw.

Helmenstein, C. (ed.) (1999), *Capital Markets in Central and Eastern Europe*, Cheltenham, UK and Northampton, USA: Edward Elgar.

James, H., H. Lindgren and A. Teichova (eds) (1991), *The Role of Banks in the Interwar Economy*, Cambridge: Cambridge University Press.

Johnson, J. (2000), *A Fistful of Rubles*, Ithaca: Cornell University Press.

Jonáš, J. (1997), *Bankovní krize: zkušenosti a příčiny*, Prague: ČNB Institut ekonomie, VP č.78.

Klaus V. and D. Tříska (1988), 'Ekonomické centrum, přestavba a rovnováha', *Politická ekonomie*, 36.

Kunert, J. (1999), 'České bankovnictví – určitě ne v roce nula', *Finance a úvěr*, 49, pp. 307–14.

Lacina, V. (1994), 'Banking system changes after the establishment of the independent Czechoslovak Republic', in A. Teichova, T. Gourvish and A. Pogány (eds), *Universal Banking in the Twentieth Century*, Aldershot, UK and Brookfield, USA: Edward Elgar.

Ledeneva, A. (1998), *Russia's Economy of Favours, Blat, Networking and Informal Exchange*, Cambridge: CUP.

Matoušek, R. (1998), *The Czech Banking System in the Light of Regulation and Supervision: Selected Issues*, Prague, ČNB sekce měnová, WP No. 5.

Mervart, J. (1996), *České bankovnictví do roku 1936: charakteristika, inspirace*, Prague: ČNB Institut ekonomie, VP č.52.

Mervart, J. (1998), *České banky v kontextu světového vývoje*, Prague: Nakladelství Lidové noviny.

Mosser, A. and A. Teichova (1991), 'Investment behaviour of industrial joint-stock companies and industrial shareholding in Österreichische Credit-Anstalt: inducement or obstacle to renewal and change in industry in interwar Austria', in James, Lindgren and Teichova.

Myant, M. (1989), T*he Czechoslovak Economy 1948–1988: The Battle for Economic Reform*, Cambridge: CUP.

Myant, M. (1993), *Transforming Socialist Economies: The Case of Poland and Czechoslovakia*, Aldershot, UK and Brookfield, USA: Edward Elgar.

Myant, M. (1999), 'The barriers to restructuring of Czech enterprises', *Prague Economic Papers*, 8, No. 2, pp. 163–77.

Myant, M. (2001), 'Whatever Happened to Voucher Privatisation?', Managing Economic Transition Working Paper, Manchester Metropolitan University.

Preiss, J. (1912), *Průmysl a banky*, Prague: Nákladem ústavu ku podpoře průmyslu.

Revenda, Z. (1991), *Banky a měnová politika*, Prague: Nad Zlato.

Řezníček, J. et al. (1978), *Základy vědeckého řízení ekonomiky*, Prague: Práce.

Ross, D. (1996), 'Commercial banking in a market-oriented financial system: Britain between the wars', *Economic History Review*, 49.

Salzmann, R. (1990), 'Nová role obchodních bank', in *Banka a podnik v roce 1990*, Prague: Komerční banka.

Schütte, C. (2000), Privatization and Corporate Control in the Czech Republic, Cheltenham, UK and Northampton, USA: Edward Elgar.

PART III

Economic and Global Aspects

8. Predicting Russia's currency and financial crises

Sheila A. Chapman and Marcella Mulino

1. INTRODUCTION

According to one traditional approach currency crises can be explained by either 'first'- or 'second-generation' models. In canonical 'first-generation' models (Krugman, 1979; Flood and Garber, 1984; Agénor et al., 1992; Flood and Marion, 2000; Dooley, 2000) crises are explained as the result of a fundamental inconsistency between domestic policies and the attempt to maintain a fixed exchange rate. The original source of problems is a persistent money-financed budget deficit, with the central bank trying to peg the exchange rate using a (limited) stock of foreign exchange reserves. This policy being ultimately unsustainable, foresighted speculators anticipating the inevitable collapse generate a speculative attack on the currency well before reserves are exhausted: when reserves fall to some critical level the central bank is forced to abandon the fixed exchange rate.

'Second-generation' models differ from one another in a number of crucial aspects. In general they model situations in which crises do not follow policy inconsistencies but may be explained as self-fulfilling bad outcomes (Obstfeld, 1994; Cole and Kehoe, 1996; Bensaid and Olivier, 1997). Accordingly, governments face a trade-off between policy objectives and choose to abandon a pegged exchange rate once the benefits of maintaining the exchange regime are outweighed by the costs of higher debt or lower output. As the cost of defending a fixed exchange rate grows when expectations that it might be abandoned spread, these models envisage the possibility of self-fulfilling crises and of multiple equilibria.[1] Some second-generation models suggest that crises may occur as a consequence of pure speculation against the currency, as agents follow a herding behaviour and/or foreign exchange markets are subject to contagion effects.

More recently yet another framework has been put forward. It stresses the fact that currency crises are often part of broader financial crises. The two elements interact with one another, giving life to what have been dubbed the 'twin crises' (Chang and Velasco, 1998b; Kaminsky and

Reinhart, 1999). In this approach financial intermediaries play an active role in generating large capital inflows, but in doing so they raise the risks of a sudden reversal of capital flows and of a bank run.[2] In 'twin crises' these two elements are intertwined: if agents expect a devaluation, early withdrawals will be beneficial. This generates financial panic and raises the risk of a bank run. On the other hand, a run against the intermediaries generates a sudden demand for foreign exchange reserves that may force currency devaluation.

This paper attempts to sketch a framework for understanding the Russian crisis. While not fitting entirely into any pre-existing model, it shares many elements of the schemes outlined above. On the other hand, it shows distinctive features that are linked to the country's situation as an economy in transition. Our thesis is that what occurred in Russia in the summer of 1998 was largely due to inconsistent policies (which recalls 'first-generation' models) that exacerbated systemic weakness and made the crisis spread from the currency sphere to the banking sector (as in the 'twin crises' framework). Less importantly, there were also herding and contagion effects which determined economic losses that were possibly larger than were warranted by underlying fundamentals.

Following standard IMF stabilization policies, monetary policy in Russia was strictly devoted to fighting inflation. From mid-1995 on the authorities adopted a moving nominal anchor consisting of a pre-announced exchange rate devaluation schedule. This policy was directed towards stabilizing inflation and, indeed, in this respect it proved to be successful. However, a strong ruble made the current account worsen; a stable ruble contributed to raise capital inflows. The role played by exchange rate movements and capital flows is examined in Section 2. Over time the government's inability to raise fiscal revenues determined growing debt accumulation and prevented interest rates from falling as intended (see Section 3). In addition, the banking system was heavily indebted *vis-à-vis* foreign creditors and recorded dangerously low levels of actual liquidity, as discussed in Section 4. In late 1997 international market turmoil leading to confidence loss made foreign capital flee the country. As interest rates rose in an effort to resist speculation, public finances were caught in a trap of the 'unpleasant monetarist arithmetics' type. Russian authorities, possibly believing that the confidence loss was short-lived and that nominal interest rates would soon fall, stuck to the nominal anchor keeping money supply tight. Eventually, inconsistency among a growing fiscal debt, tight monetary policy and a pegged exchange rate made devaluation inevitable (see Section 5). In Section 6 we use the insights of our analysis to link the Russian episode to existing theoretical frameworks and we draw some conclusions on the effectiveness of the stabilization policy.

2. REAL EXCHANGE RATE APPRECIATION AND CAPITAL FLOWS

Many models (Kaminsky and Reinhart, 1999) stress that currency and banking crises have common causes, underlining that usually in exchange rate-based stabilization programmes there is a cumulative real exchange rate appreciation, as inflation converges to international levels only gradually. If the increase in imports is financed by borrowing abroad, the current account deficit continues to widen, raising the issue of its sustainability and fuelling an attack against the domestic currency. As stabilization is often coupled with financial liberalization which raises access to international capital markets, banks are usually able to borrow abroad to finance imports and economic activity, notwithstanding the domestic tight monetary stance. Therefore when capital inflows become outflows and asset markets crash the banking system caves in.

Russia shares only part of this story. In 1995 Russian monetary authorities pegged the exchange rate as a nominal anchor to reduce domestic inflation.[3] In doing so they pushed up the real exchange rate. After the sharp real appreciation against the dollar of 1995 (60 per cent in the period May–December 1995, based on CPI), in the following years there was a creeping appreciation (5 per cent in 1996 and 4 per cent in 1997). The loss of competitiveness, however, was much wider, as the ruble continued to appreciate against most European currencies (40 per cent in 1996 and 15 per cent in 1997 against the Deutschmark) and unit labour costs rose more rapidly than the CPI-based measure. Largely due to the sharp fall in international prices of the country's major exports, the terms of trade worsened by more than 25 per cent from early 1997 through July 1998. The loss of competitiveness made imports rise continuously despite a cumulative fall in real incomes; however, it did not lead to trade or to current account deficits, but rather to a tendency of the surplus to deteriorate. This was due to the low level of economic activity and domestic absorption and to the composition of Russian exports, made up more than 80 per cent by energy and other natural resources.

Trade surpluses recorded in the face of an overpriced exchange rate point to a sort of 'Dutch disease', linked to the switch to non-CIS markets and to world prices for natural resource exports. In effect, while total export growth rates halved in 1996 with respect to 1995 and turned negative (−2.3 per cent) in 1997, the dynamics of different commodity groups diverged significantly: oil and gas exports to non-CIS countries rose by more than 38 per cent in 1996 and fell by 1.5 per cent in 1997 (due to falling world prices), while non-energy export growth rates kept falling. Export dynamics, coupled with a low but rising domestic absorption,[4] and with an increasing

Table 8.1 Current account of the Russian Federation (US$ billion)

	1997			1998		
	Jan.–June	July–Dec.	Total	Jan.–June	July–Dec.	Total
Current account	3.7	−0.8	2.9	−5.0	7.4	2.4
of which:						
Trade balance	9.6	7.7	17.3	2.5	14.8	17.3
Services balance	−2.2	−3.0	−5.2	−2.4	−0.8	−3.2
Net income	−3.4	−5.1	−8.5	−4.9	−6.5	−11.4
of which:						
Investment income	−3.3	−4.9	−8.2	−4.8	−6.4	−11.2
Net current transfers	−0.3	−0.3	−0.6	−0.2	−0.1	−0.3

Net capital flows into the Russian Federation (US$ billion)

	1997			1998		
	Jan.–June	July–Dec.	Total	Jan.–June	July–Dec.	Total
Capital account	−0.3	4.6	4.3	9.5	−4.0	5.5
of which:						
FDI	−0.9	2.8	3.7	0.5	0.7	1.2
Portfolio investment	14.1	3.1	17.2	7.3	0.5	7.8
Other investments[a]	−5.6	−8.3	−13.9	0.3	−8.6	−8.3
Changes in reserves[b]	−9.4	7.5	−1.9	1.7	3.6	5.3

Notes:
[a] Include largely official and bank loans, trade credits, foreign exchange current accounts and cash.
[b] The sign (−) indicates an increase in reserves.
* Net of the restructuring of the public debt to the London Club worth $28.2 billion.

Source: CBR, *Balance of Payments of the Russian Federation*, 1997 and 1998.

negative balance on investment income, led in 1997 to a sharp erosion in the current account surplus, which eventually turned into a deficit in the second and third quarter of the year. This trend continued in the first half of 1998 when the current account showed a remarkable deficit (see Table 8.1).

Although by the end of 1997 the Russian currency appeared to a growing extent overvalued, it is nevertheless difficult to argue that these features alone might have led agents to believe that the stabilization programme was no longer sustainable. As far as capital inflows are concerned, Russia attracted significant capitals starting from the last quarter of 1996; in 1997 the capital account showed a surplus, after several years of deficits mainly due to capital flight.[5] Successful rescheduling agreements with Paris and London Club creditors in 1996 and 1997 respectively improved Russia's access to international markets sharply. Although FDI increased in 1997 as well, a large part of the surge in capital inflows – in particular in the first half of 1997 – was due to short-term portfolio private inflows. Unlike standard models, Russian external borrowing cannot be explained by the financing of imports and of economic activity, given trade balance surpluses, dwindling economic recovery and no lending boom (see section 4.2). In fact, short-term foreign capitals went especially to the Russian government securities market, attracted by consistent interest rate differentials and a perceived low exchange rate risk. In addition, commercial banks were actively tapping international credit markets as a source of liquidity.

The purchase of government securities by non-residents was officially allowed at the beginning of 1996. Thereafter temporary restrictions limiting repatriation of ruble proceeds from the GKO–OFZ market were gradually lifted and fully relieved at the end of 1997.[6] As the inflation rate declined nominal yields of ruble denominated Treasury bills fell steadily until August 1997; however, interest rates remained high with respect to international ones. Significant interest differentials emerged as the combined result of a tight monetary policy and a loose fiscal stance. Therefore foreign investments in the Russian government debt market quickly increased: in the first six months of 1997 net foreign investments amounted to $8.8 billion; in September 1997 they represented nearly one-third of the $60 billion outstanding GKOs and OFZs. Moreover, the state sector raised foreign capitals through loans and the placement of Eurobonds. For the first time in 1997 also regional governments placed their securities in the international capital market. Altogether in 1997 nearly 30 per cent of the federal budget deficit was financed from foreign sources (IMF, 1999).

Starting in 1997 foreign investors became more active in the corporate securities market; in the third quarter of 1997 they were estimated to control no less than 10 per cent of the shares in the Russian stock market,[7] whose capitalization was above $100 billion. Following the privatization process Moscow's equity market steadily increased from the second half of 1996, when its index rose by 132 per cent, and recorded a spectacular boom in the first seven months of 1997, as the index rose by a further 184 per cent also thanks to the growth in foreign investments.

It is unlikely that foreign investors would have assumed the same level of exposure to Russia if derivative instruments had not been available. Some foreign banks accepted GKOs as collateral supporting total-return swaps; similarly, foreign investors were willing to invest in GKOs in part because they were able to use forward contracts with large Russian commercial banks to hedge their ruble exposure. On the other hand, Russian banks used repurchase agreements with foreign financial institutions as a means of leveraging their GKO holdings, seizing the interest rate differential but assuming the exchange rate risk. However, the availability of derivative instruments also raises opportunities for speculation, allowing transactions to be funded by a limited margin and making adequate scrutiny more difficult. Short-term speculative finance exposes recipient countries and their currencies to sudden changes in investors' confidence; vulnerability to capital reversals also arises from a mismatch of the term-structure of foreign liabilities and assets. These risks are higher in countries like Russia, that have widely liberalized capital account movements for residents and non-residents,[8] but whose financial systems are weak and poorly supervised. As speculative activities picked up, Russia lacked both a legal framework regulating the activities of credit institutions in the forward market and an efficient system for monitoring commercial banks' operations with financial derivatives.

3. FISCAL PROBLEMS AND PUBLIC DEBT DYNAMICS

While large capital flows from abroad represent a common feature of most crisis countries, as far as the public deficit is concerned records differ widely. While East Asian countries presented almost good fiscal records, Mexico and Russia had persistently high budget deficits.

High fiscal deficits have been a common problem for transition economies but in the case of Russia their reduction proved particularly difficult to achieve, owing to institutional weakness in tax collection capacity, lack of tax discipline among politically influential firms and perverse incentives in tax administration arising from the sharing of tax bases between different levels of government. The erosion of revenue forced massive expenditure compression, which reached a level that could not be further reduced in the short run; it led to extreme measures such as the sequestration of budget spending, delays in paying wages and pensions, growing arrears for goods received and underinvestment in infrastructure and public services.

Over the period under examination Russia's enlarged government collected over 30 per cent of GDP in revenues.[9] The figure is low compared to other European countries, but similar to that of the United States and Japan and considerably above the average for other countries with Russia's income level. Moreover, taking into account that at least 25 per cent of Russia's reported GDP was estimated by Goskomstat to represent the untaxed unofficial economy, enlarged government revenues were a burden of over 40 per cent for the registered economy, meaning that the tax burden on registered activity was actually high by world standards.

From 1992 to 1997 tax revenues to the consolidated budget fell by nearly 4 percentage points with respect to GDP.[10] This was largely due to a huge drop in federal tax revenues which fell from 16.6 per cent to 12 per cent. The two main sources of revenue in the consolidated budget are VAT and the profit tax; both fell as a share in total revenue since 1994. The fall in profit tax revenues was strong (from 23 to 11 per cent) as profits reported by enterprises fell substantially more than Goskomstat's estimate (Treisman, 1999), indicating that profits were increasingly sinking underground.[11] Personal income taxes represent a minor source of total revenues (about 8 per cent in 1997),[12] due to the low level of administrative competence and lack of more-or-less voluntary compliance by the majority of taxpayers. In conclusion, Russia collected a high proportion of taxes from a few sectors where the government was able to keep a close eye on levels of production, such as oil and gas extraction and pipeline transportation. The fuel and pipeline sectors, which together contributed 12 per cent of GDP, paid one-quarter of all taxes in 1997 (RECEP, 1997a).

The quantitative decline of tax revenues went hand in hand with a qualitative deterioration, as non-cash tax receipts (in the form of promissory notes – *vekselya*[13] – or other non-monetary payments) reached 26 per cent of taxes in 1996 and 20 per cent in 1997. Difficulties in tax administration are witnessed also by tax arrears, which grew dramatically over time. Total arrears as a proportion of collected taxes accumulated faster in the federal than in the regional budgets, probably as it was less costly for regional governments than for the federal government to accept payment in forms other than money. The government was itself a guilty party in the arrears problem, as it has been estimated that 'federal government debts to the economy may be almost as high as the stock of tax debts to the federal budget' (RECEP, 1997b). Tax 'offsets' – that is, the mutual settlement of budgetary and tax arrears, often on a multilateral basis – were widely used between enterprises and all levels of government. In general, they envisaged discounts that actually operated as a rolling partial tax amnesty. On one side this seriously affected taxpayer discipline; on the other it exacerbated the government's problems in meeting cash obligations on time, distorting expenditure patterns and leading to overpricing of goods and services delivered to the government.

Perverse incentives in the tax system follow from the fact that the main taxes are shared at relatively even rates between the federal budget and regional ones. Recent economic literature (Keen, 1997; Boadway et al., 1998) stresses that, to the extent that cooperation between levels of government is necessary to collect taxes effectively, each level has an incentive to shirk and free ride on the others' efforts. In the case of Russia it was argued (Treisman, 1999) that obligation to share official tax revenues with the federal government prompted regional governments to seek covert deals with local enterprises in order to conceal part of the tax base in return for under-the-table contributions. Moreover, regional governments used their growing leverage over regional collection agencies both to prioritize regional revenues and to protect regional enterprises from federal extraction.

On the other hand, the non-interest expenditure of the enlarged government declined from 57 per cent of GDP in 1992 to 39 per cent in 1997. However, less progress was made in actually reducing government absorption than is suggested by cash spending estimates. In fact the Ministry of Finance had no effective mechanism for controlling (let alone measuring) expenditure commitments, while suppliers, particularly in the energy sector, continued to supply goods to non-paying spending units, increasingly resorting to non-transparent off-budget practices.

Altogether the enlarged government fiscal balance showed a tendency to swing: the deficit/GDP ratio fell in 1995, in the wake of stabilization policies, but rose again in 1996 and fell to a smaller extent in 1997. The bulk of the deficit came from the federal government balance, as local government and extra-budgetary funds were in surplus until 1996, showing afterwards small and slowly deteriorating deficits. The latter were financed largely by issuing *vekselya.*[14] Federal deficit financing underwent dramatic changes in 1995–96, when the newly independent central bank, strictly devoted to fighting inflation, ruled out monetary financing of the deficit and the Russian government was compelled to resort to massive issues of high yield, short-term government securities. Domestic financing came mostly from credits from the commercial banking system in 1996 and from securities held both by non-bank and bank sectors in 1997. Starting from 1996 the share of foreign financing of the enlarged government deficit kept growing, reaching about one-third of outstanding public debt in 1997.

Debt financing succeeded in curbing inflation but introduced new weakness in the Russian economy: on the one hand it made it vulnerable to the withdrawal of market funding. The latter was particularly likely given the difficulties in the process of fiscal consolidation. On the other hand, as nominal interest rates were extremely high during most of the period under consideration, debt financing contributed to a very rapid build-up of costly debt. By mid-1997 the stock of GKOs and OFZs reached 12.5 per cent of GDP – a seemingly tolerable level – but, more worryingly, it was about as large as total federal budget receipts over the same period. In 1997 debt servicing absorbed nearly 85 per cent of new emissions. Interest payments rose rapidly from 2 per cent of GDP in 1994 to 6 per cent in 1996 (that is, respectively, from 17 to 47 per cent of fiscal revenues). In the first nine months of 1997 efforts to raise revenues and to cut expenditures,[15] coupled with the fall in nominal GKO yields, thanks to declining inflation, improved the ratios both of the federal deficit and of debt servicing to GDP (see Table 8.2). However, the sizeable increase in GKO yields at the end of the year – linked to the CBR's efforts to defend the exchange rate – raised the cost of servicing domestic debt. In its 1997 *Annual Report* the CBR admits that such a cost exceeded the gross returns from the sale of government securities for the first time in December 1997.

4. THE RUSSIAN BANKING SYSTEM

In 'twin crises' models the fragility of the banking system adds up to the system's overall weakness. A bank run can generate a sudden demand for foreign reserves that may force the exchange rate collapse. On the other hand, an expected devaluation makes early withdrawals potentially beneficial for those who withdraw deposits, adding pressure on the banking system.

In theory bank runs may occur as self-generating events, irrespective of the bank's actual health (Diamond and Dybvig, 1983). Experience, however, shows that runs generally occur in the presence of some form of mismanagement (excessive exposure, insufficient capitalization or the like). The key to banks' self-protection is, naturally, liquidity. A bank with substantial liquidity – large liquid reserves and/or ready access to liquidity – is not likely to be subject to a run (Feldstein, 1999). However, a bank could be temporarily illiquid but still remain solvent in the longer run – that is, assets in value are higher than liabilities. If a temporary assets–liabilities mismatch points to illiquidity, that is generally faced by central bank intervention. If carried on over time illiquidity may be perceived as insolvency, leading to confidence loss and, eventually, to a run. A banking system as a whole is said to be insolvent when 'bank debt holders at all, or many, banks . . . suddenly demand that banks convert their debt claims into cash (at par) to such an extent that the banks suspend convertibility of their debt into cash' (Calomiris and Gorton, 1991, p. 112).

Although often representing the crucial factor for a run, illiquidity and/or insolvency are not easily assessed. Depending on a number of qualitative features, they may not show from banks' balance sheets; sometimes healthy-looking balances conceal rather poorly shaped banks. Apart from false reporting, this may occur whenever the market value of banks' assets and/or liabilities departs markedly from the face value, for instance because bad loans and investments curtail the true value of assets.

Table 8.2 Federal government budget (%)

	1995	1996	1997	1998	1997		1998	
					Jan.–June	July–Dec.	Jan.–June	July–Dec.
Revenues/GDP	12.7	11.5	12.0	10.2	10.3	13.4	10.7	9.6
Expenditures/GDP	18.1	19.4	19.1	15.2	18.7	19.4	16.0	14.3
Debt Service/GDP	3.4	5.6	4.6	4.0	5.6	3.8	5.2	2.9
Deficit/GDP	5.4	7.9	7.1	5.0	8.4	6.1	5.2	4.7
Debt Service/Exp.	19.1	29.2	23.8	26.2	29.8	20.0	32.8	21.3

Source: RECEP, 1999a.

Table 8.3 Selected indicators of the Russian banking system (%)

Ratios	31 Dec. 1995	31 Dec. 1996	31 Dec. 1997	1 June 1998
Capital/loans	25.7	32.8	31.3	29.7
Leverage ratio*	5.0	4.0	4.0	4.2
Capital adequacy**	20.0	25.0	25.0	23.8

Notes:
* Assets to capital.
** Capital to assets.

Source: CBR, *Analytical Accounts of Credit Institutions*, 1995, 1996, 1997, 1998.

In some sense this appears to have occurred in the Russian banking system in 1995–97. While press reports point to impending disaster well before July 1998 (see *The Economist*, 1997–98), CBR data indicate an underdeveloped and uncompetitive system, but a very cautious one as well. The indicators that generally assess the health of a banking system point to a relatively high capital base, expanding healthily in 1996–97 and falling only slightly in early 1998, and in any case remaining remarkably high by Western standards well into June 1998, at the very eve of the crisis (see Table 8.3).[16] So-called leverage ratios (the ratio between overall assets and banks' capital) were low and stable, implying low average returns on capital but also smaller fluctuations in banks' returns, and hence lower illiquidity risks. The inverse of the leverage ratio, the capital adequacy ratio, for which the minimum standard BIS requirement is 8 per cent, was three times this figure – twice if one considers that higher-risk countries are sometimes advised to bring the minimum ratio to 12 per cent. True, from July 1997 on the nominal value of Russian banks' assets fell below that of liabilities. In aggregate, however, banks' capital managed to cover the gap and still allow a positive net worth, meaning that the system as a whole remained solvent even in the summer of 1998.[17]

However, a closer look at the system's official consolidated balance sheet makes it possible to trace evidence of systemic fragility building up already in 1997, before and independently of the East-Asian crisis.

4.1 Banks' Liabilities

The weakness of the Russian banking system is often seen as stemming from the liability side. It comes first of all from the lack of comprehensive deposit insurance, then from the fall in domestic sources of funds and their rising costs. Thirdly, it stems from the growing volatility of funds.

Table 8.4 Foreign assets and liabilities of commercial banks (US$ million)

	1995	1996	1997	mid-1998
Foreign liabilities	5125	9204	19236	20481
Foreign assets	8818	10155	12078	12426
Liabilities/assets (%)	0.58	0.91	1.59	1.65
Short-term liabilities	4310	8047	15574	15906
Short-term liabilities/total liabilities (%)	84.10	87.43	80.97	77.66

Source: CBR, *Consolidated Dynamics of Foreign Assets and Liabilities of the Banking System of the Russian Federation*, various years.

The most striking feature of Russian banks' liabilities is the low and falling share of deposits. From 1995 to 1997 deposits fell by some 11 per cent, reaching 49 per cent of overall liabilities. Without household deposits going to Sberbank – the large state savings bank absorbing some 75 per cent of household deposits – the ratio of deposits to liabilities was much lower, well below 30 per cent. Also, the composition of deposits changed, the contraction concerning mainly long-term ones (time and savings deposits, including currency ones). The overall fall in deposits harmed Russian banks inasmuch as it reduced access to a cheap source of liquidity; moreover, as the public turned to more volatile forms of deposit, banks became more exposed to sudden liquidity shortfalls due to confidence loss.

Another feature of Russian banks' liabilities is the modest share of other domestic items. In 1997 money market instruments were at the same level in percentage terms as mid-1995; government deposits were lower.[18] The share of credits by the central bank fell by over one-half from mid-1995 to 1997; in the first seven months in 1997 it contracted in nominal terms by 7 per cent as the CBR tightly geared monetary policies to contain inflation, following IMF-agreed programmes.

In this context Russian banks consistently resorted to the only source of funds that was actually expanding, international markets. Foreign liabilities started being important for Russian banks in 1997. Before then flows from abroad had been rather stable, averaging some 10 per cent of overall liabilities. In 1997 they reached 17 per cent, growing strongly especially towards the end of the year. The flow of funds from abroad was encouraged by the low interest rates prevailing in industrial countries, by capital account liberalization and financial deregulation and by a stable exchange rate which lowered the risk premium on dollar-denominated debts.

In absolute terms, however, the level of Russian banks' foreign liabilities was never very high, although it was with respect to banks' foreign assets.

The ratio between liabilities and assets was high – 0.9 in 1996, 1.6 in 1997 and 1.7 in June 1998 – and growing fast.[19] This means that from early 1997 Russian banks were borrowing from foreign credit institutions but lending to domestic agents. The currency mismatch between liabilities and assets implies a potential risk in case of exchange rate pressure. If markets anticipate the higher value of liabilities in foreign currency terms, creditors could refuse to roll-over existing lines of credit, precipitating a banking crisis. The exposure to markets' confidence is even deeper when the maturity structure of foreign flows is considered. Russian banks had access essentially to short-term sources of funding; in 1995–97 these reached over 80 per cent of total foreign liabilities, approaching 90 per cent in 1996.[20]

4.2 Banks' Assets

Russian banks' assets presented various peculiarities with respect to their Western counterparts as regards structure and dynamics. Reserves were relatively high (10–11 per cent of overall assets); due to the lack of comprehensive deposit insurance, they were high also compared to deposits. The ratio between total reserves and demand deposits (the most volatile component in deposits) was over 50 per cent in 1996–97 but fell by over 10 per cent in the first half of 1998.

Another peculiarity was the big share (over one-third) of claims on the general government, the overwhelming component of which – 86 per cent in 1996, 80 per cent in 1997 – was investments in state securities.[21] Purchases were especially large in 1996 when yields skyrocketed; they crowded out loans to enterprises but allowed banks to reap big interest rate differentials on low-yield deposits from enterprises and government agencies. This originated the year's exceptionally high level of banks' profitability – 5.1 per cent as of 1 January 1997, equal to 32.9 trillion rubles.[22] Investments in state securities continued to expand in the first half of 1997, notwithstanding the decline in yields. Strong investment in state securities runs counter to the standard behaviour of Western banks but can hardly be viewed as risky.

By far the most peculiar indicator of Russian banks' activity was their lending record. Lending to the private sector as a percentage of GDP was low (on average some 8.4 per cent) even with respect to other transition or emerging economies, and showed only minor signs of expanding. Lending to production (that is, to private and to state enterprises) was low too (on average 11 per cent). This may reflect a number of causes: first, the shrinking role of state enterprises; secondly, a newly-born private sector smaller in size than in other comparable countries. Apart from special cases firms generally had limited ability and/or experience in resorting to banks for credit. Possibly credit was not so important for firms that operated in an economy largely dominated by barter and by monetary surrogates. On the other hand, an important part of Russia's banking system (almost all the large Moscow-based banks) was affiliated to financial–industrial groups which involved shareholdings in many enterprises and often also in other financial institutions and companies. Some credits granted to loss-making enterprises within the group (especially longer-term ones) could not be registered in banks' balance sheets.

Even taking these elements into account, Russian banks' loans to production were low by any standards This may not be good for growth in general, but appears prudent. Without adequate regulation, strong lending on behalf of commercial banks is considered as one of the main factors determining bank fragility and hence lying behind a run (Sachs et al., 1996; Goldfajn and Valdés, 1997; Corsetti et al., 1998a). The argument goes as follows: a bout of financial liberalization generally makes lending expand sharply. This reduces banks' ability to screen marginal projects and amounts to a greater proportion of non-performing loans in banks' portfolios. In Russia evidence of a lending boom is scant, especially if compared to data relative to emerging markets. A lending boom is commonly measured by the growth rate of the ratio between bank lending to the private sector and GDP (for example Sachs et al., 1996). During 1995–97 in Russia the lending boom indicator equalled 1.5 per cent, far too low to indicate growth of any relevance. The hypothesis of a lending boom must again be ruled out even if banks' claims on state enterprises are included.

4.3 Liquidity, Nominal and 'True'

Measuring bank liquidity is no easy task. First, the very notion of bank liquidity is more complex than it appears at first sight. Apart from a day-to-day dimension, it reflects also funding requirements under various scenarios and with respect to each individual currency in which a bank is active (BIS, 2000). Accurate evaluation of bank liquidity accounting for these aspects requires an amount of detailed information which is extremely difficult to obtain – in the case of Russian banks almost impossible. In the second place, bank liquidity in a strict sense should be calculated only in relation to an individual bank, the general picture on systemic fragility resulting from the number of illiquid banks and their relative importance in the economy. Aggregate data may at best provide an indicative picture of overall liquidity.

With these caveats in mind, a very tentative assessment of Russian banks' liquidity is shown in Table 8.5. Estimates are based on aggregate data; no account is taken for the time or currency structure of banks' activities.

Table 8.5 *Nominal and 'true' liquidity of the Russian banking system (billion rubles)*

	31 Dec. 1995	Dec. 1996	Dec. 1997	1 July 1998
A) Nominal liquidity;				
Assets	342 272.4	500 460.5	622 834.3	623 875.5
Liabilities – Capital	253 408.0	359 823.0	490 479.3	499 393.7
Difference	88 864.4	140 637.5	132 355.0	124 481.8
B) 'True' liquidity (net of the 'bad loans effect')				
'True' assets	283 399.2	429 657.6	535 774.9	539 900.4
Liabilities – Capital	253 408.0	359 823.0	490 479.3	499 393.7
Difference	29 991.2	69 834.6	45 295.6	40 506.7
C) 'True' liquidity (net of the 'Treasury bills effect')				
'True' assets	—	420 584.2	518 120.6	504 695.6*
Liabilities – Capital	253 408.0	359 823.0	490 479.3	499 393.7
Difference	—	60 761.2	27 641.3	5 301.9
D) 'True' liquidity (net of the 'exchange rate effect')				
'True' assets	—	—	519 459.6′	506 289.9+
'True' liabilities – Capital	—	—	493 535.3″	505 184.3^
Difference	—	—	25 924.3	1 105.6

Notes:
* Partly estimated.
′ Reflecting a 2 per cent rise in the face value of foreign assets.
″ Reflecting a 2.2 per cent rise in the face value of foreign liabilities.
\+ Reflecting a 2.2 per cent rise in the face value of foreign assets.
^ Reflecting a 5.5 per cent rise in the face value of foreign liabilities.
(These percentage increases are calculated from CBR information and reflect the different maturity structures of assets and liabilities).

Source: Based on CBR, *Analytical Accounts of Credit Institutions*, 1996, 1997, 1998.

Throughout the period under consideration the Russian banking system as a whole kept a positive (even if falling) net worth, pointing to apparent liquidity. This reflects only the book values of balance sheets and says nothing about market (or 'true') values. For instance, as far as banks' claims on enterprises are concerned, it is important to account for the quality of the loans involved. As banks channel funds to enterprises a share could go to finance unprofitable projects, making future repayment difficult or impossible and curtailing the 'true' value of assets.

In the case of Russia information concerning the amount of bad loans is either lacking or inaccurate; estimates are purely tentative and vary wildly. Official data put non-performing loans of Russian banks respectively at 9 per cent and 8 per cent of total loans in 1996 and in 1997. In July 1998 the CBR calculated that overdue loans totalled 6 per cent of banks' total loans (climbing to 11 per cent by the end of the year) (CBR, 1998). By general consent these figures blatantly underestimate actual arrears. Underestimation occurs because banks roll-over or renegotiate bad debts in order to avoid write-offs; or else they convert existing credits by creating new loans and so on. Alternative estimates (OECD, 1997) accounting for these practices put the proportion of bad loans in bank credit around 30 per cent in 1996–97, the share growing over time. 'True' liquidity allowing for one-third of loans to be written off continued to be positive: it was at its lowest in 1995 (when the banking system underwent a crisis) but recovered later and fell somewhat in 1997, hitting some 45 000 billion rubles.

Further evaluation of the 'true' value of assets must also account for large state security holdings. While investing in state securities is generally considered safe, nominal yield fluctuations expose banks to potential losses in capital accounts and/or to liquidity problems if securities are used as collateral. 'True' liquidity reflecting both the market value of banks' holdings in state securities as reported by the CBR plus the 'bad loan' effect mentioned above falls further and reaches 28 000 billion rubles in 1997.

Also, exchange rate fluctuations are important for evaluating 'true' liquidity, as the market values of foreign assets and liabilities change with exchange rate fluctuations. Accurate calculations of the exchange rate effect would require detailed information on the maturity structure of different assets and liabilities, which is practically impossible to obtain for Russian banks. Rough calculations accounting for nominal exchange rate fluctuations, however, change the overall picture only marginally. While in 1995 and in 1996 'true' liquidity could have been slightly enhanced by the exchange rate effect, in 1997 on the contrary it was reduced and banks' 'true' liquidity fell to some 26 000 billion rubles. 'True' liquidity, however, had been even lower in the previous months, falling as low as 22 000 billion rubles in November 1997 and calling for CBR intervention.[23]

5. ASIAN CRISIS CONTAGION AND POLICY RESPONSES

Like most emerging markets Russia was affected by the turmoil on international financial markets stemming from the Asian crisis. The latter spread to Russia both through financial links (portfolio reshuffling) and also because investors began to reassess risk across all emerging markets. Russia suffered from a sharp loss of confidence; foreign capital started to flee the country and the ruble came under pressure. National authorities combatted the crisis with some success, considering it a temporary shock that would not affect economic fundamentals. By January–February 1998 the crisis was seemingly over and contagion appeared to be fading.[24] Its most immediate effect was that of having deepened structural weaknesses and imbalances of the economy.

As soon as the effects of the East-Asian crisis spread to Russian financial markets, the flow of foreign investment turned around. The stock market was hardest hit: in October 1997 the Moscow stock exchange index dropped by 34 per cent and by another 11 per cent by the end of December; the fall carried on in January 1998. Foreign capitals fled the Treasury bill market as well: foreign investors' share of GKO–OFZ fell to 27.5 per cent at the end of December 1997. By adding downward pressure on the currency, already suffering from households' shift to foreign currency as a precaution against the issue of redenominated rubles, the exodus of investors became self-reinforcing.

Russian authorities were extremely reluctant to give up the pegged exchange rate in which so much domestic and international credibility had been invested and which was strongly sustained by the IMF.[25] The CBR promptly supported the exchange rate first by buying rubles and later on by substantially raising the refinancing rate. In November 1997 alone international reserves fell by $6.3 billion (see Table 8.6), while the refinancing rate was raised from 21 per cent to 28 per cent and then to 39 per cent in early February 1998.

In the meantime a target value for the exchange rate over the period 1998–2000 was announced with the hope that, by reducing the expected exchange rate risk, it would help restore the confidence of both external and domestic investors. Downward pressure on the ruble continued instead to build up as an increasing part of financial markets considered the Russian exchange rate as unsustainable. The peg appeared unjustified also with regard to the poor performance of Russia's foreign trade,[26] which turned the current account balance into a growing deficit.

However, by the end of February 1998 the situation seemed to have somewhat stabilized: monetary authorities confirmed their willingness to

Table 8.6 Foreign exchange reserves (US$ billion – end of period values)*

	March	June	Sept.	Dec.
1995	4.1	10.1	10.9	14.3
1996	16.1	12.8	11.4	11.3
1997	12.4	20.4	18.7	12.9
1998	11.9	11.1	8.8	7.8

Notes: * Excluding gold.

Source: CBR, *Foreign exchange reserves*, 1995, 1996, 1997, 1998.

defend the ruble even at the expense of exceptionally high interest rates (and the linked debt service costs) and depletion of foreign reserves. From October 1997 to February 1998 the CBR lost nearly 45 per cent of its foreign reserves. In the same period the refinancing rate doubled, reaching 42 per cent in early February, even if it fell marginally later in the month. Average yields on GKOs followed a smoother, but continuously growing, pattern.

Albeit reflecting an expensive and purely myopic approach, these policies contributed in the short run to keeping foreign investors' exposure to Russia high. In early 1998 Russia continued to attract foreign banking funds: BIS-reporting banks raised their exposure by $3.3 billion in the first quarter of the year. One major factor behind the flow of banking funds to Russia was the granting of officially supported long-term credits by continental European banks. International investors' willingness to assume Russia's risk in the face of large budget deficits, increasing debt burden, falling international reserves and banks' fragility could follow from the belief that international institutions would not allow Russia to default on its government debt ('Many investors thought Russia was too big to fail'. Fischer, 1999) and that the central bank would act as lender of last resort for the banking system. The expectation that private creditors would be protected from adverse outcomes by the official sector, both domestic and international, was rooted in past experience of international financial crises, when private investors were bailed out in order to avoid contagion to lending countries' domestic financial systems.[27]

Improvements, however, were short lived as these policies ended up by deepening structural fragility. Support of the exchange rate weakened the banking system, reduced public debt sustainability and curtailed international liquidity. Possibly linked to divergences in the domain of economic policy was the March decision by President Yeltsin to sack Prime Minister Chernomyrdin and to name the virtually unknown Kirienko as acting

Prime Minister. It took exactly one month and three attempts for the Duma to approve the nomination, which opened a political void at a crucially difficult moment and substantially weakened the future credibility of the new government.

5.1 Effects on Banks' Financial Conditions

As far as banks are concerned, the Asian crisis worsened an already difficult situation. In its 1997 *Annual Report*, the CBR acknowledged that in November 1997 the share of 'problem banks' rose by 1.3 per cent following the Asian crisis. As of 1 January 1998 more than one-third (33 per cent) of credit institutions were not 'financially stable' and a further 41 per cent presented 'shortcomings in their operations'. Nevertheless, for the CBR the increase was only temporary and 'by the end of the year the share of financially stable banks had been restored' (CBR, 1997, p. 81).

This may be generally true for the immediate aftermath of the Asian crisis but does not consider the overall impact on bank liquidity. In its 1998 *Annual Report*, the CBR admitted that in the first half of the year the share of problem banks continued to grow: banks were increasingly affected by dwindling deposits, growing shares of bad loans (even by official reports), falling profits and high external borrowing. Past huge purchases of Treasury bills made Russian banks extremely dependent on the evolution of the government debt market, both because securities were used as collateral against foreign loans and because interest rate increases curtailed the market value of bonds. Banks suffered also because they were generally 'unable (or late) to rearrange active and passive operations mainly because they were unwilling to sell government securities at market prices, which they considered too low' (CBR, 1998, p. 87). In July 1998 estimates of the 'true' level of bank liquidity accounting for the fall in Treasury bills value were as low as 5000 billion rubles.[28]

The two standard indicators that signal pre-panic periods – the percentage growth of deposit withdrawals and the ratio of reserves to deposits (Calomiris and Gorton, 1991) – show that deposits started falling in May 1998; from May to July demand deposits fell cumulatively by almost 10 percentage points. The dynamics of the reserve ratio were somewhat less straightforward, as one would generally expect illiquid banks to draw upon their reserves to meet panic-driven withdrawals. Yet throughout 1998 the Russian banking system recorded a ratio of reserves to deposits that was high and stable; it fell to some extent only in August, at the very outset of the run, when it collapsed from 20 per cent to 15 per cent.

Also, capital adequacy and related indicators remained remarkably stable well into crisis-ridden July 1998. However, in many ways aggregate banking capital was low with respect to the system's needs. In July 1998 bank obligations under currency forward contracts hedging foreign investors' currency risks reached almost $23 billion (excluding Sberbank), which exceeded aggregate capital by some 1.2 times.[29] Before the crisis, Russia's aggregate banking capital (119.2 billion rubles in July 1998, without Sberbank) was smaller than that of any of the top 20 Western banks. On the other hand, Russian banks actively invested abroad. Foreign assets, which had grown already in late 1997, picked up from April on and were especially high in June–August, reaching cumulatively 21 billion rubles. This raised demand for foreign exchange and added pressure on CBR reserves.

As banks' liquidity (both nominal and 'true') reached record-low levels in the beginning of summer, in August the situation became unsustainable following the joint CBR–Russian Government decision to reschedule short-term government debt maturing before the end of 1998 in the amount of some $40 billion. This resulted in a virtual freeze of over 30 per cent of total banking assets and brought many Russian banks to the verge of illiquidity, affecting also large Moscow banks including Sberbank, which holds some 80 per cent of household savings and invests heavily in government debt. Operations in the interbank market came virtually to a halt. Exchange rate depreciation raised banks' burden in meeting foreign obligations, especially under forward contracts, notwithstanding the 90-day moratorium on repayment of private financial institutions' debt to non-residents. In July and August alone withdrawals from commercial banks (excluding Sberbank) reached some 10 per cent of their value; total bank reserves fell by 25 per cent (over 12 billion rubles) as banks tried to combat the mounting run.

5.2 Effects on Public Deficit and Debt

Given the large stock of outstanding GKOs and OFZs, the sizeable increase in GKO yields at the end of 1997 made the budget costs of servicing domestic debt soar. In the first quarter of 1998 interest payments on public debt rose to more than 46 per cent of federal budget revenues and to 5.1 per cent of GDP. In the second quarter, the ratios reached respectively 53 per cent and 5.7 per cent. Owing to the massive use of GKO financing the maturity structure of the debt became highly unbalanced: almost 75 per cent of the debt had to be repaid within one year and 45 per cent within five months (Komulainen, 1999). This obliged the government to raise an estimated average of 8 billion rubles a week (that is $1.3 million) to roll-over maturing public debt. The additional expenditure for every percentage point increase in GKO yields was estimated to be around 1 billion rubles (EIU, *Country*

Report, second quarter 1998). While in the first quarter of the year domestic financing of the deficit was achieved by placing securities with the bank and non-bank sectors, in the second quarter banking sector financing turned negative, as banks increasingly faced difficulties in meeting foreign liabilities falling due and sold part of their GKOs even at huge losses (IMF, 1999).

The growing interest burden nullified the efforts to cut the federal budget deficit: in the second quarter of 1998 the deficit picked up again mainly due to interest payments. From February to May the budget recorded – nearly for the first time – a primary surplus. This followed Parliament's decision to give the government the facility to cut expenditures in line with the dynamics of revenues in order to stop borrowing activity. However, the gaps between revenues and expenditures carried on together with declining revenues: federal tax revenues in the first six months of the year fell to 8.9 per cent of GDP, compared with 9.3 per cent in the first six months of 1997.

The federal debt/GDP ratio climbed to more than 50 per cent in the first months of 1998. Although this may not be considered high by international standards,[30] it allows the possibility of a debt trap. The latter could derive from the steep increase in the debt due to the need to keep real interest rates on growing issues of GKOs at an exorbitant level coupled with a fiscal deficit that was only artificially restrained by temporarily freezing expenditures to counterbalance declining revenues. Russian authorities were therefore obliged to offer higher and higher yields on Treasury bills, in a self-reinforcing spiral.[31] While new emissions had the sole purpose of servicing the old ones, private agents' expectations of debt unsustainability were growing.

5.3 Effects on Foreign Debt and International Illiquidity

The choice to support the peg forced the CBR to run out of its foreign reserves and added strength to pre-existing financial imbalances, particularly with respect to the foreign currency situation.

International illiquidity is defined as a maturity mismatch between international assets and liabilities of domestic banks, financial institutions and the central bank.[32] According to this definition liquid international assets include also foreign reserves. As far as short-term international liabilities are concerned, it has been argued that in a fixed exchange rate regime demand deposits in domestic currency are effectively obligations in foreign currency and should be included in the stock of short-term international liabilities (Chang and Velasco 1998b). International illiquidity in Russia, both with and without demand deposits in domestic currency, fell sharply from the second half of 1997 and reached dangerously low values in mid-1998 as liabilities grew faster than assets (see Table 8.7).

Table 8.7 Financial fragility indicators

	M2/FR	Short-term loans[a] (% of FR)	Assets/liabilities[b]	Assets/liabilities[c]
End-1996	4.57	234		
Mid-1997	3.95	187	0.60	0.41
End-1997	5.28	251	0.45	0.31
Mid-1998	6.22	312	0.38	0.27

Notes:
[a] Short-term loans from international banks.
[b] Short-term foreign assets and liabilities (short-term foreign debt, demand deposit in foreign currency).
[c] Short-term foreign assets and liabilities as above, including demand deposit in domestic currency.

Sources: BIS, 1998; CBR, 1998, 1999.

International liquidity appears important inasmuch as, according to more traditional evaluations, Russian foreign debt showed no serious problems in terms of sustainability.[33] BIS–IMF–OECD–World Bank joint statistics on external debt, giving details on maturity, creditors and type of funds, point to a situation that was far from dangerous. The share of Russian short-term external debt (due within a year) was not overwhelming: at the end of June 1998 it was lower than a year earlier: 36 per cent against 47 per cent (see Table 8.8).

However, the picture changes when short-term external debt is related to foreign reserves. In the case of Russia this ratio was very high and rose steeply from the second half of 1997, going from 191 per cent in June 1997 to 315 per cent in June 1998.[34] Also, the ratio between short-term loans from international banks and foreign reserves suggests a financially fragile situation: throughout the period considered this ratio was substantially above 180,[35] reaching 312 in mid-1998 (see Table 8.7). It is worth noting that the deterioration of these ratios stems mostly from the fall in foreign reserves linked to the commitment to support the exchange rate.

In a context of liberalized capital flows a useful indicator of the adequacy of a country's international reserves is the ratio of broad money to foreign reserves, since in the event of an exchange rate crisis or panic potentially all the money in circulation may have to be converted into foreign exchange (Calvo, 1996; Sachs et al., 1996). Thus the ratio of M2 to foreign reserves measures the ability of the central bank to cover its liquid

Table 8.8 Russian foreign debt (US$ million)

	Dec. 1995	June 1996	Dec. 1996	June 1997	Dec. 1997	June 1998
External debt – all maturities:	78466	—	87327	81274	99810	96574
Debt due within a year:	22001	24396	27101	38977	32907	35214
Ratios:						
Short-term debt/total debt (%)	28.04	—	31.03	47.11	32.97	36.46
Short-term debt/foreign reserves (%)	152.90	—	240.30	191.10	252.80	315.60
Debt-service/foreign reserves (%)	—	—	—	—	52.10	—

Sources: *Joint BIS-IMF-OECD-World Bank statistics on external debt*, http://www.oecd.org/dac/htm/debtstat.htm, World Bank, 1998. *Joint BIS-IMF-OECD-World Bank statistics on external debt*. World Bank, *Global Development Finance*, 1998.

liabilities, both direct ones – the monetary base – and commercial banks' liquid liabilities, demand deposits. In Russia the M2/foreign reserves ratio was high by international standards (on average above 4 in 1996–97)[36] and rising sharply from mid-1997 on, recording a value above 6 in mid-1998.

However, if the central bank is called upon to serve as lender of last resort, its available resources are international reserves net of short-term government liabilities which may be called in at a time of trouble. So the ability of monetary authorities to combat a sudden decline in the demand for domestic assets is best measured by the ratio between M2 plus outstanding short-term Treasury bills and international reserves. The EBRD estimated this ratio for Russia to have a value near 10 in March 1998. It confirms that the huge stock of short-term public debt, coupled with peg support efforts depleting international reserves made the Russian economy particularly fragile.[37] According to EBRD calculations even after the conversion of $6.5 billion worth of GKOs into eurobonds at the end of July 1998 domestic government debt maturing at the end of the year was around $16.5 billion, still well in excess of the central bank's foreign exchange reserves at the time ($13.8 billion).

5.4 Russian Policy Response

In the aftermath of the East-Asian crisis Russia's economic policy failed to address the country's deepening fragility; rather it carried on along traditional IMF lines, centred on a fixed exchange rate acting as a nominal anchor, to be pursued through high interest rates and intervention on foreign currency markets. In defending the exchange rate the CBR chose not to fully sterilize the fall in foreign reserves. The monetary base started to fall from the end of October.

The political world on its part showed no sign of being able – or wanting – to face the country's immense fiscal problems. In spring, Parliament repeatedly failed to enact a reformed Tax Code that was meant to raise revenues, despite urgent recommendations to do so by the IMF and major international organizations. Skyrocketing interest rates gave a further blow to the already shaky budget balance. Apart from debt consolidation, either voluntary or compulsory, two possibilities were then open. One was forced monetization of the public deficit, which was incompatible in the medium run with a fixed peg. The other was immediate devaluation. Spreading expectations of impending devaluation made the ruble/dollar exchange rate in six-months forward contracts rise with respect to the nominal rate by as much as 24 per cent in June; from the end of May the interest rate differentials between outstanding GKOs and currency-denominated bonds widened sharply and reached some 85 percentage points in late June.

Domestic agents consistently shifted to the good that traditionally represented a shelter in times of trouble – foreign currency. From mid-May on, money flows from the 'government securities markets to the foreign exchange market intensified' (CBR, 1998, p. 61) and brought the ruble under attack. Even the July attempt to restore international credibility was unable to contrast the crisis. The IMF-agreed package converting some 30 billion rubles worth of Treasury bills into eurobonds and ensuring a package of higher-than-expected additional assistance (some $22.6 billion, including contributions from the World Bank and Japan) ironically seemed to push the confidence crisis to its highest limit. The crisis reached its peak a few weeks later: the peg was abandoned and the exchange rate regime shifted to a dirty float.

6. CONCLUSIONS

The analysis outlined above shows that the Russian episode does not fit entirely into any pre-existing framework. Rather it lies between 'first-generation' and 'twin crises' models. It shares important features of 'first-generation' models inasmuch as it was largely due to policy inconsistencies. However, unlike canonical models, in the case of Russia the inconsistencies did not stem from a fixed peg and monetization of the public deficit, but rather from a fixed exchange rate and a debt-financed fiscal deficit that was getting out of control in a context of liberalized capital flows. This means that standard IMF stabilization and liberalization policies were probably incompatible with the structural weaknesses that Russia was facing in its difficult transition process.[38] Therefore, the attack on the ruble that eventually led to the peg being abandoned was essentially determined by economic policies conflicting in the longer term with the fixed exchange rate. Rational foreign and domestic agents simply anticipated an unavoidable devaluation and had every incentive to pull out of the country.

On the other hand, by touching both currency markets and the banking sector, the Russian episode falls within the 'twin crises' framework. In this respect Russia followed a pattern common to many currency and banking episodes, in a self-reinforcing spiral going from the currency sphere to banks. This suggests 'that existing banking problems were aggravated or new ones created by the high interest rates required to defend the exchange-rate peg or the foreign exchange exposure of banks' (Reinhart and Kaminsky, 1999, p. 472).

In substance the core of the Russian crises appears to lie in the strenuous defence of the ruble, which was backed by IMF guidance but was becoming increasingly unsustainable. Keeping the (overvalued) exchange rate fixed was justified on the grounds that a devaluation would have had a number of negative effects outweighing the positive ones: in the first place it would have strongly destabilized Russian banks, worsening their foreign position; it would have created a confidence crisis among foreign investors that were important for debt financing of the budget; it would have made inflation pick up again; last but not least, it would have raised the country's foreign debt burden. However, given the conflict among a pegged rate, a debt-financed fiscal deficit and liberalized capital flows and given that markets increasingly anticipated a devaluation, possibly a controlled devaluation at the beginning of spring – when the turmoil following the East-Asian crisis was over – would have been a better policy option. To begin with it would have allowed the Russian authorities to signal to markets that someone indeed was in charge of the economy; it would have reduced foreign reserves losses enabling Russia to meet payments on at least part of its foreign debt. Possibly a devaluation carried out in spring would have been smaller than the one markets imposed in August–September. Some of the most disruptive effects of the August crisis could have then been averted or at least limited. For instance, interest rates could have been lower, bringing benefits to the Treasury bill market; eventually even the August *de facto* moratorium on GKOs could have been avoided, easing banks' immediate liquidity problems[39] and limiting investors' losses. Moreover, in the short and medium run the devaluation could have brought traditional textbook benefits to the real economy, from improving the price competitiveness of exports, discouraging imports and promoting domestic production through import substitution. Revenues from taxes on exports and on profits could have grown and this would have somewhat improved the fiscal balance. By and large all these events occurred in 1999, by far Russia's most successful year since the beginning of transition. A few months after the crisis the Russian economy started witnessing impressive growth rates in industrial production, especially in exporting and in import-competing sectors (over 20 per cent per annum); overall, GDP grew by 3.2 per cent. Inflation fell while fiscal revenues rose, leading to a growing primary surplus. Eventually the deficit/GDP ratio was cut by one-half in comparison with the pre-crisis level.

NOTES

1. It has been stressed, however, that 'this possibility holds true only for certain ranges of the fundamentals' (Aziz et al., 2000) so that even in 'second-generation' models some fundamentals play a critical role in generating crises.
2. There may also be a moral hazard problem associated with financial intermediaries when the latter are poorly supervised and monetary authorities act as lenders of last resort. See Krugman (1998); Corsetti et al. (1998b).

3. In mid-1996 the fixed exchange rate corridor was replaced by a 'crawling-band mechanism', that is a sloping exchange rate corridor, with the 'slope' reflecting the expectations of the domestic inflation rate. The limits of the corridor were fixed in advance for six months and later on for a whole year. In November 1997 monetary authorities 'announced the transition from setting short-term (up to one year) limits on ruble exchange rate variations to establishing medium-term targets for ruble exchange rate dynamics' (CBR, 1997, p. 68). As a guide for the period 1998–2000 the CBR set a central target rate of 6.2 redenominated rubles to the dollar, allowing the exchange rate to fluctuate up to 15 per cent around it.
4. 'Currently, 48 per cent of retail sales consist of imports, an extraordinarily high share for a country as large as Russia' (RECEP, 1998).
5. Capital flight from Russia has been an ongoing process since the move to a market-oriented economy. The main channels of capital flight have been the non-repatriation of export proceeds, uncovered import advances and currency purchases by the population. Estimates of the phenomenon vary significantly: recent estimates put capital flight from Russia at $17 billion annually since 1994 and evaluate that Russian residents accumulated about $68 billion abroad between January 1994 and September 1997. See Abalkin et al. (1999); Mulino (2000). The CBR's highly tentative estimates of capital flight indicate $14.1bn per annum during 1994–98.
6. GKOs are short-maturity (less than one year) ruble-denominated Treasury bills, while OFZs are longer maturity bonds.
7. According to the CBR in 1997 the Russian corporate securities market was heavily dependent on non-resident investors, in particular Western investment funds (CBR, 1997, p. 30).
8. Russia accepted the obligations of the IMF's Article VIII in June 1996 and until the August 1998 crisis its exchange system was largely free of restrictions on both current and capital transactions.
9. The 'enlarged government' includes the federal government as well as the regional and local ones.
10. The consolidated budget refers to the 'enlarged government' budget plus a number of extra-budgetary funds: the Pension Fund, the Social Insurance Fund, the Employment Fund and the Medical Insurance Fund.
11. One way in which reported profits were reduced in Russian industry was barter. The latter has reportedly spread widely in recent years: OECD (1997) underlines a steady increase in the share of barter in industrial sales, close to 40 per cent by the end of 1996 and over 45 per cent in April 1997; more recent estimates put it over 50 per cent in 1998, peaking at 54 per cent in August (RECEP 1999b). The hypothesis that a large share of profits were unreported was also proved by the fact that sectors where the unofficial economy is relevant and measurement problems are more daunting, such as retail trade and agriculture, paid far less taxes than would be expected on the basis of their contribution to GDP.
12. In other transition economies personal incomes are widely taxed and the average ratio of the income tax revenue to GDP is about 8 per cent, while in Russia it does not reach 3 per cent of GDP.
13. Money surrogates ('*vekselya*') are issued by banks and other financial institutions, enterprises, local and federal authorities. They started growing rapidly around 1993 in the context of a general payment crisis. OECD (1997) reports that some estimates of the total amount of outstanding '*vekselya*' put it at about two-thirds of ruble M2 in the spring of 1997.
14. In 1997 for the first time some more fiscally sound regions began to gain access to foreign capital markets and proceeded to issue eurobonds to finance their budget expenditures.
15. In 1996–97 an especially created 'Emergency Committee' under Deputy Premier Chubais managed to extract payments from some major tax debtors, but not enough to reverse the revenue decline for more than a few months.
16. The relatively high levels of capital of Russian banks are strictly not comparable with Western banks' records, given that apart from Sberbank, the big state savings bank, Russian deposits are not insured.

17. This reflects information of the CBR concerning the consolidated banking sector. It says nothing about the state of individual banks, some of which were on the verge of disaster. According to the CBR 'a number' of credit institutions recorded negative capital in 1997; in 1996, 46 per cent of credit institutions were not 'financially stable' and 23 per cent presented 'shortcomings in their operations' (CBR, 1997, p. 78 and p. 81).
18. Government accounts at commercial banks recovered slightly towards the end of 1997 when high securities sales raised the liquidity in the hands of the government. Accounts were distributed very unevenly among banks, as the government had privileged relationships with a few large Moscow banks. The spring 1997 suggestion to shift most government accounts into branches of the National Treasury stirred up discontent among several banks and its application was delayed.
19. The figures recorded by Russia were in line with those of some East-Asian countries hard-hit by the crisis: during 1993–97 the ratio ranged from 1.14 to 1.71 in the Philippines, from 1.51 to 1.61 in Singapore, from 0.83 to 2.23 in Malaysia. See Corsetti et al. (1998a), p. 34.
20. In East Asia the shares went from 67 per cent in Korea to 65 per cent in Thailand, 61 per cent in Indonesia and 58 per cent in the Philippines. These figures are defined as 'particularly problematic' by Corsetti et al. (1998a), p. 34.
21. Including Sberbank, a strong investor in state securities. Calculated from CBR data.
22. See CBR (1997), p. 82. Profitability is defined as the ratio of profits to assets. By comparison, average profitability in 1990–94 was 1.7 in Hong Kong, 0.6 in Korea, 0.7 in Indonesia, 1.3 in Malaysia, 1.3 in Thailand, 1.4 in Argentina, 0.1 in Brazil, 1.3 in Mexico, 0.8 in the United States, 0.1 in Japan and 0.2 in Germany (see Goldstein and Turner 1996, Table 5, p. 29).
23. In November–December 1997 the CBR raised credit to the banking system, a measure that is typically employed to fight illiquidity, by over 8 000 billion rubles. CBR intervention ceased in early 1998, when liquidity had somewhat recovered.
24. 'The crucial period in assessing the impact of East-Asian contagion on the transition economies of CEE and the CIS is thus the period from 20 October 1997 (collapse of the Hong Kong stock exchange) to the end of January 1998' (Fries et al., 1999, p. 540).
25. However, a 1999 report of the Council on Foreign Relations suggests among other things that 'the IMF and the G-7 should advise emerging economies against adopting pegged exchange rates and should not provide funds to support unsustainable pegs' (De Cecco, 1999, p. 235).
26. A growing part of the industrial oligarchy was in favour of a devaluation to boost competitiveness and to reduce its domestic debt (see Buchs 1999). In addition the adverse effect of low prices on Russian exports was worsened by the overvalued ruble, and the leading Russian export sectors would have greatly benefited from a devaluation.
27. Only recently both G-7 countries and the IMF changed this approach. During the G-7 Cologne Summit in June 1999 it was stated that 'Market discipline will work only if creditors bear the consequences of the risks that they take' (De Cecco, 1999). This new attitude was stated by S. Fischer while addressing the question of moral hazard: 'officially financed bail-outs can encourage imprudent lending in the future. This makes financial crises more likely to happen and more severe when they do. So we should not offer any promise that countries will always be able to service all their external debts' (Fischer, 1999).
28. 1 100 billion rubles if the effects of the exchange rate depreciation are included (see Table 8.5, line D).
29. The first case of a Russian bank failing to fulfil its foreign obligations was that of Tokobank, in May; its licence was revoked, together with that of Bank Imperial, before August. In July Inkombank and in early August SBS-Agro became effectively insolvent and appealed to the Bank of Russia for help.
30. In 1997 Poland, Hungary and Bulgaria recorded a debt/GDP ratio over 50 per cent (see Fries et al., 1999).
31. At the beginning of August, five-month GKO yields skyrocketed to 135 per cent. Russian federal deficit was financed 'by an unsustainable high-yielding pyramid-type treasury bills market' (Westin, 1999).

32. 'A country's financial system is internationally illiquid if its potential short-term obligations in foreign currency exceed the amount of foreign currency it can have access to on short notice' (Chang and Velasco, 1998b, p. 18).
33. For instance, according to World Bank data, in 1997 the ratio between external debt and GDP was low by international standards (30 per cent) albeit slightly higher than in 1996. The debt-service ratio was low as well, falling to 7 per cent in 1997. The World Bank considers a country with an external debt/GDP ratio of more than 60 per cent as being heavily indebted. In June 1997 the Russian ratio was lower than those of many other transition countries (see Fries et al., 1999). The corresponding percentage values for East-Asian countries in 1996 were: Korea: 28.4; Indonesia: 56.7; Malaysia: 40; Philippines: 49.7; Singapore: 10.7; Thailand: 50; Hong Kong: 15.4; China: 15.4; Taiwan: 10.1 (see Corsetti et al., 1998a).
34. In mid-1997 the same ratio was 206 for Korea, 170 for Indonesia and 145 for Thailand, while it was below 100 for the other East-Asian countries (see Chang and Velasco, 1998a).
35. Even at the end of 1997 – not to mention in mid-1998 – this ratio was higher in Russia than in Korea, Indonesia, and Thailand at the end of 1996 (EBRD, 1998).
36. The corresponding values for the East-Asian countries in 1996 are: Korea: 6.51; Indonesia: 6.50; Malaysia: 3.66; Philippines: 4.50; Singapore: 1.03; Thailand: 3.90; Hong Kong: 4.25; China: 8.55; Taiwan: 5.78. According to Corsetti et al. (1998a), these values were 'dangerously high'.
37. Pre-crisis Asian countries showed far lower levels, ranging from around 6 for Indonesia and Korea to 5 for Malaysia, Philippines and Thailand in June 1997 (EBRD, 1998).
38. Among others, we may mention permanent budget difficulties, inadequate regulation of financial markets, a scarcely monetized economy, weak corporate governance, poorly defined property rights, inadequate restructuring of production and so on.
39. At the end of 1998 the CBR estimated that 720 banks – around half of those operating – were insolvent, some 18 large banks were in serious difficulties, while five of the country's ten largest banks were believed to be insolvent (EIU, *Country Report*, first quarter 1999).

REFERENCES

Abalkin, A. and J. Whalley (1999), 'The Problem of Capital Flight from Russia', *The World Economy*, 22.

Agenor, P. R., J. S. Bhandari and R. P. Flood (1992), 'Speculative Attacks and Models of Balance of Payments Crises', *IMF Staff Papers*, 39/2.

Aziz, J., F. Caramazza and R. Salgado (2000), 'Currency Crises: In Search of Common Elements', *IMF Working Paper*, 00/67.

Bank for International Settlements (BIS) (1998), *Quarterly Review*, International Banking and Financial Market Development, November.

Bank for International Settlements (2000), *Sound Practices for Managing Liquidity in Banking Organisations*, February.

Bensaid, B. and J. Olivier (1997), 'The Instability of Fixed Exchange Rate when Raising the Nominal Interest Rate is Costly', *European Economic Review*, 41(8).

Boadway, R., M. Marchand and M. Vigneault (1998), 'The Consequences of Overlapping Tax Bases for Redistribution and Public Spending in a Federation', *Journal of Public Economics*, 68.

Buchs, T. D. (1999), 'Financial Crisis in the Russian Federation. Are the Russians Learning to Tango?', *Economics of Transition*, 7(3).

Calomiris, Charles W. and Gary Gorton (1991), 'The Origin of Banking Panics: Models, Facts and Bank Regulation', in Glenn Hubbard (ed.), *Financial Markets and Financial Crises*, Chicago: University of Chicago Press, pp. 110–57.

Calvo, Guillermo A. (1996), 'Varieties of Capital Market Crises', mimeo, University of Maryland.

Central Bank of the Russian Federation (CBR) (1998), *Annual Report, 1997*, http://www.cbr.ru/eng/.

Central Bank of the Russian Federation (1999), *Annual Report, 1998* http://www.cbr.ru/eng/.

Central Bank of the Russian Federation, *Analytical Accounts of Credit Institutions*, http://www.cbr.ru/eng/dp/komb_98_engl.htm.

Central Bank of the Russian Federation, *Balance of Payments of the Russian Federation*, http://www.cbr.ru/eng/statistics/credit_statistics/htm.

Central Bank of the Russian Federation, *Foreign exchange reserves*, http://www.cbr.ru/eng/statistics/credit_statistics/htm.

Central Bank of the Russian Federation, *Interest Rates*, http://www.cbr.ru/eng/statistics/credit_statistics/htm.

Chang, R. and A. Velasco (1998a), 'Financial Fragility and the Exchange Rate Regime', *NBER Working Paper* , Cambridge, MA, 6469, March.

Chang, R. and A. Velasco (1998b), 'The Asian Liquidity Crisis', *NBER Working Paper*, Cambridge, MA, 6796, November.

Cole, H. and T. Kehoe (1996), 'A Self-fulfilling Model of Mexico's 1994–1995 Debt Crisis', *Journal of International Economics*, 41.

Corsetti, G., P. Pesenti and N. Roubini (1998a), 'What Caused the Asian Currency and Financial Crises?', mimeo, September.

Corsetti, G., P. Pesenti and N. Roubini (1998b), 'Paper Tigers? A Model of the Asian Crisis', mimeo, September.

De Cecco, M. (1999), 'The Role of the Private Sector in the New Financial Architecture', *Economies et Sociétés*, 9–10, pp. 229–44.

Diamond, D. W. and P. Dybvig (1983), 'Bank Runs, Deposit Insurance, and Liquidity', *Journal of Political Economy*, 91.

Dooley, M. P. (2000), 'A Model of Crises in Emerging Markets', *The Economic Journal*, 110.

European Bank for Reconstruction and Development (EBRD) (1998), *Transition Report,* London.

European Commission (1998), *Economic Reform Monitor*, DGII, No. 5, March.

Economist Intelligence Unit (EIU), *Russia. Country Report*, various issues.

Feldstein, M. (1999), 'Self-Protection for Emerging Market Economies', *NBER Working Paper*, Cambridge, MA, 6907, January.

Fischer, Stanley (1999), 'Learning the Lessons of Financial Crises: The Roles of the Public and Private Sectors', *Speech at the 'Emerging Market Traders' Association' Annual Meeting*, New York, 9 December.

Flood, R. P. and P. M. Garber (1984), 'Collapsing Exchange-rate Regimes: Some Linear Examples', *Journal of International Economics*, 17, pp. 1–13.

Flood, R. P. and N. P. Marion (2000), 'Self-fulfilling Risk Predictions: An Application to Speculative Attacks', *Journal of International Economics*, 50.

Fries, S., M. Raiser and N. Stern (1999), 'Stress Test for Reforms. Transition and East Asian "Contagion"', *Economics of Transition*, 7(2).

Goldfajn, I. and R. O. Valdés (1997), 'Capital Flows and the Twin Crises: the Role of Liquidity', *IMF Working Paper*, 97/87, July.

Goldstein, M. and Ph. Turner (1996), 'Banking Crises in Emerging Economies: Origins and Policy Options', *BIS Economic Papers*, Basle, 46, October.
IMF (1998), 'Memorandum of the Government of the Russian Federation and the Central Bank of the Russian Federation on Economic and Financial Stabilization Policies', 16 July.
IMF (1999), 'Russian Federation: Recent Economic Developments', *IMF Staff Country Report*, 99/100.
Kaminsky, G. L. and C. M. Reinhart (1999), 'The Twin Crises: The Causes of Banking and Balance-of-Payments Problems', *The American Economic Review*, 89(3).
Keen, M. (1997), 'Vertical Tax Externalities in the Theory of Fiscal Federalism', *IMF Working Paper*, WP/97/173.
Komulainen, T. (1999), 'Currency Crisis Theories: Some Explanations for the Russian Case', *BOFIT Discussion Paper*, 1.
Krugman, P. (1979), 'A Model of Balance of Payments Crises', *Journal of Money, Credit, and Banking*, 11(3), pp. 311–25.
Krugman, P. (1998), 'What Happened to Asia?', MIT, mimeo, January.
Joint BIS–IMF–OECD–World Bank statistics on external debt, http://www.-oecd.org/dac/htm/debtstat.htm.
Mulino, M. (2000), 'Determinants of Capital Flight from Russia', UIC, mimeo.
Obstfeld, M. (1994), 'The Logic of Currency Crises', *NBER Working Paper*, Cambridge, MA, 4640, February.
OECD (1997), *Russian Federation*, OECD Economic Surveys, Paris.
OECD (2000), *Russian Federation*, OECD Economic Surveys, Paris.
PLANECON REPORT (1998), *Russian Economic Monitor*, XIV, 9–10, April.
RECEP (1997a), *Russian Economic Trends*, October.
RECEP (1997b), *Russian Economic Trends*, December.
RECEP (1998), *Russian Economic Trends*, April.
RECEP (1999a), *Russian Economic Trends*, April.
RECEP (1999b), *Russian Economic Trends*, November.
Sachs, J., A. Tornell and A. Velasco (1996), 'Financial Crises in Emerging Markets: the Lessons of 1995', *Brookings Papers on Economic Activity*, 1.
Treisman, D. (1999), 'Russia's Tax Crisis: Explaining Falling Revenues in a Transitional Economy', *Economics and Politics*, 11(2).
Westin, P. (1999), 'One Year after the Crisis: What Went Right?', *RECEP, Russian Economic Trends*, September.
World Bank (1998), *Global Development Finance.*

9. The political economy of banking reform and foreign debt

Claudia M. Buch, Ralph P. Heinrich, Lusine Lusinyan and Mechthild Schrooten

MOTIVATION*

A sustained recovery from the 1998 crisis will depend critically on restoring confidence in the banking system for two reasons. First, the financial sector has so far barely contributed to the growth of the economy. In 1999, credit to the private sector stood at less than 12 per cent of GDP, one of the lowest values observed in transition economies and certainly well below the levels of developed countries (IMF, 2000b, Table 35).[1] In the first half of 2000 alone, real domestic credit contracted by an additional 12 per cent (DIW and IfW, 2000b). After the crisis, the economy recovered, largely on the basis of investment financed from retained earnings. However, the limits of this approach began to show in early 2001, when rising real wages started to squeeze profits, and current and future profit opportunities started to diverge. As a result, it will be key to create a system of financial intermediation which is capable of providing attractive savings incentives for households and of efficiently channelling those savings into productive new investments in the private sector.

Secondly, Russia will need to restore access to international financial markets in order to be able to sustain its economic recovery. Typically, the domestic banking system is a major channel through which emerging market economies integrate into international capital markets. Without thorough reform, the inefficiency and lack of development of its banking sector will be an obstacle to Russia's integration into the global economy. Worse, the inefficiency of the domestic financial system is one reason why capital flight remains prevalent.

Yet, progress on reforming the banking sector has been disappointing so far (IMF, 2000a). The present chapter discusses the political economy of the problem. In finding a solution to the banking crisis, it is important to take into account the fact that the failure of the government to service its – domestic and foreign – liabilities was one trigger of the crisis. The debates about foreign debt rescheduling and banking reform are therefore closely linked.

Part two gives a brief overview of the twin crisis in the balance of payments and in the banking system, its origins, and solutions currently being discussed. The third part discusses the political economy of banking reform in the context of ongoing negotiations on foreign debt rescheduling. It argues that excessive foreign debt may prevent efficient banking reform because of a positive externality which banking reform generates for foreign creditors. Hence under certain conditions, foreign debt rescheduling can benefit both sides by improving the incentives of the government to engage in banking reform. In particular, tax reform can complement banking reform. The fourth part concludes.

TWIN CRISIS RUSSIAN STYLE

The Banking Sector

The banking sector was hit particularly hard by the crisis of 1998 because of its heavy exposure both to government debt and to foreign currency debt. Prior to the crisis, about one-third of the assets of the banking system had been invested in government bonds (Table 9.1). Even after taking account of the fact that a substantial number of GKOs are held by the state-owned savings bank, Sberbank, GKO investment by the rest of the banking system still amounts to 15–20 per cent of total assets. Thus when the government responded to the crisis by essentially defaulting on its domestic debt, a significant portion of the banks' assets and income were wiped out.

In addition, large banks had borrowed quite extensively on international capital markets, particularly in 1996 and 1997. In mid-1998, net foreign assets amounted to a negative 5 per cent of banks' balance sheet totals. At the same time, domestic liabilities accounting for about 12 per cent of the balance sheet were denominated in foreign currency. As a result, the drastic devaluation of the ruble during the crisis dramatically increased the ruble value of banks' liabilities. The banks had tried to hedge against the resulting exchange rate risk by denominating about 45 per cent of their domestic loans in foreign currency. This explains why, measured in ruble terms, domestic credits increased quite substantially after the financial crisis of August. Yet, to the extent that the recipients of these loans had revenues in rubles, these loans were only a very imperfect hedge against foreign exchange risks.

In addition to exchange rate risk resulting from on-balance-sheet activities, there were also off-balance sheet liabilities. To a substantial degree,

Table 9.1 Balance sheet indicators of banks, 1994–2000

	1994	1995	1996	1997	1998 (June)	1998	1999	2000 (proj.)
	(as % of balance sheet total)							
Foreign assets	23.9	13.5	14.6	11.8	11.6	23.5	23.9	21.1
Claims on the government	5.2	18.3	30.3	31.5	33.0	27.8	28.2	23.3
Claims on the priv. sector	35.9	39.1	31.6	38.2	40.0	37.1	33.7	38.4
Other assets	35.1	29.1	23.5	18.5	15.4	11.6	14.2	17.2
Demand deposits	15.8	20.3	17.5	26.3	21.8	16.0	16.1	19.6
Foreign currency deposits	18.1	16.1	13.9	13.0	12.4	20.5	18.7	18.6
Foreign liabilities	7.0	8.8	11.8	16.9	16.9	21.8	14.4	11.0
Capital accounts	12.7	19.5	24.9	23.3	25.1	16.9	18.9	19.3
Other liabilities	46.4	35.4	31.8	20.5	23.8	24.9	31.9	31.4
Memorandum:								
Net foreign assets	16.9	4.8	2.8	−5.1	−5.3	1.8	9.5	10.1
Nonperforming loans[a]	—	15.6	17.9	18.5	16.4	—	13.4	6.8[b]

Notes:
End of period. Data include Sberbank and those activities of Vneshekonombank which are not performed in its function as a foreign debt manager of the government.
[a] Share in total loans in per cent.
[b] October 1.

Sources: IMF (2001), CBR (1998a, 2001a).

foreigners had hedged foreign exchange risks from GKO investments through forward contracts with Russian banks as counterparts. According to data provided by the CBR (1998), liabilities resulting from forward contracts in foreign currency alone exceeded on-balance-sheet activities of Russian banks by a substantial margin at the beginning of 1998. By the middle of the year, on- and off-balance-sheet activities were roughly of equal volume. At least according to the official data, off-balance-sheet liabilities were hedged by and large through off-balance-sheet assets. Yet, the reliability and usefulness of these data are likely to be poor because many of these hedges involve a substantial counter party risk. Moreover, capital adequacy regulations restrict the foreign exchange exposure of commercial banks, which provides incentives for fictitious transactions.

Overall, foreign bank loans to Russia had increased until mid-1998 (Table 9.2). Although the share of loans raised by commercial banks had come down considerably as compared to the early 1990s, it still accounted for more than 50 per cent of the total, according to data of the Bank for International Settlements (BIS). This is roughly in line with values

Table 9.2 Structure of foreign bank loans, 1992–2000

	1992	1993	1994	1995	1996	1997	1998 (June)	1998	1999	2000 (Sep.)
					(billion US-dollars)[a]					
Total loans to Russia	56.8	51.4	48.0	51.5	57.3	72.2	75.6	60.3	48.1	39.7
Loans to Russian banks	43.3	40.2	41.5	43.8	43.0	40.3	39.0	38.1	29.7	19.6
					Share of loans granted to commercial banks (%)[a]					
Asia	39.0	40.4	41.4	42.6	43.3	40.4	37.0	34.7	30.3	36.6
Latin America	25.2	26.9	24.7	24.5	24.2	26.1	23.7	20.9	18.4	18.0
Eastern Europe	71.1	72.4	70.6	70.3	64.2	52.6	49.2	56.1	50.5	41.2
Russia	76.2	78.3	86.5	85.0	75.2	55.8	50.9	63.2	61.7	49.5
					Share of short-term loans (%)[a]					
Asia	62.3	62.8	62.9	63.5	61.5	60.3	53.0	52.5	51.0	46.7
Latin America	45.5	50.0	51.3	52.4	53.7	55.0	55.2	50.8	48.7	49.2
Eastern Europe	32.2	37.2	35.2	39.2	44.2	43.4	44.1	35.7	32.0	33.4
Russia	29.2	35.6	35.8	39.7	46.3	44.9	45.0	29.3	22.7	26.0
					(billion US-dollars)[b]					
Foreign liabilities of Russian banks (total)	—	3.0	3.2	5.9	9.6	19.6	20.5	14.6	11.8	12.1
Other investments	—	2.5	2.5	5.1	8.7	17.6	18.5	13.7	10.7	10.7

Notes:
End of period.
[a] Consolidated cross-border claims in all currencies and local claims in non-local currencies of banks in the BIS reporting area. 1992 and 1993 = Former Soviet Union.
[b] CBR data not including Vneshekonombank transactions in its capacity as manager of the federal government's foreign debt and assets.

Source: BIS (2001), CBR (1998b, 2001a); authors' own calculations.

observed in the rest of Eastern Europe but clearly exceeds corresponding shares for Asian or Latin American countries. Presumably, however, the BIS data include debt of the former Soviet Union such as loans raised by the state-owned Vneshekonombank. Using data provided by the CBR, which exclude these loans, gives a share of liabilities of Russian commercial banks *vis-à-vis* foreign banks of about one-fourth of the total.

After the onset of the crisis, foreign lending to Russian banks collapsed both in dollar terms and as a share of total foreign lending to Russia, reflecting the loss of international creditworthiness of the banking system. Thus the banking crisis fed back into the capital account and further aggravated the balance of payments crisis. At the same time, depositors lost a substantial part of their pre-crisis deposits in real terms due to the fact that their ruble accounts had been temporarily frozen in the state savings bank while the ruble was losing a large part of its value. Similarly, foreign creditors of the Russian banks lost their claims almost entirely.[2]

Meanwhile banks did benefit from the economic upswing following the crisis by expanding their deposit and lending businesses and charging high spreads of lending over deposit interest rates. This allowed the banking industry to be marginally profitable on current operations in the first three quarters of 2000. However, the industry still incurred aggregate losses when taking liabilities from previous years into account (CBR 2001a), and its capital base remained weak (RECEP 2001). High spreads may eventually allow banks to regain their solvency.[3] But they are an inefficient way of achieving this, as they amount to cross-subsidization of past losses from current operations, and as such distort current deposit and lending decisions.

Policy Responses

After a series of emergency measures including ad hoc injections of liquidity and the transfer of deposits from a number of private banks to the state savings bank Sberbank, progress on a systematic and lasting clean-up of the banking industry remained disappointing.

A bank insolvency law came into effect in March 1999, but enforcement remained uneven at best. Also in early 1999, the Agency for Restructuring of Credit Organizations (ARCO) was set up. However, its contribution to efficient bank restructuring remained limited. Through mid-2000 it had been accorded only 4 billion rubles for its voluntary restructuring programme, half of which had been disbursed. This amounts to a mere 0.2 and 0.1 per cent of total banking assets, respectively. It took until 2001 to pass a series of bills to expand the supervisory powers of the Central Bank, to streamline the bankruptcy procedures for credit organizations and to revise the legal responsibilities of bank shareholders and managers (RECEP 2001).

As we argue in the remainder of this chapter, the foreign debt burden has been a major reason for the sluggishness of banking reform and for the lack of fiscal resources committed to it.

The Foreign Debt Burden

Following the substantial devaluation of the ruble in the wake of the currency crisis of 1998, most foreign debt indicators worsened significantly. Measured in relation to GDP, Russia's debt burden had been below the average of developing countries (33–35 per cent) prior to the crisis but considerably exceeded the average afterwards.[4] In early 1999, foreign debt stood at more than 100 per cent of GDP. Other debt indicators worsened as well. Foreign currency reserves, for example, were extremely low: the ratio of currency reserves to debt fell from 14 to 6.6 per cent as compared to an average value of over 28 per cent for developing countries.

Almost half of the external debt originates from Soviet times (IMF 1999). After the collapse of the Soviet Union in 1991, Russia, as the biggest successor country, assumed foreign liabilities and a substantial share of foreign assets of the former USSR. After several restructuring arrangements and repayments, the face value of these obligations as of the end of 1998 totalled around $100 billion, or 55 per cent of total foreign currency debt. New credits raised by the Russian government and non-sovereign borrowers amounted to 30 per cent and 17 per cent of total debt, respectively.[5]

Debt obligations against multilateral creditors (47 per cent) and eurobonds (29 per cent) constituted the largest shares in the post-Soviet debt, while debts against the Paris Club official lenders (40 per cent) and against the London Club of private lenders were the major components of the Soviet-era debt. Credits of the Paris Club have not been securitized, while London Club claims have been restructured into tradable securities that correspond to the nominal value of the credits (PRINs – principal notes) and to the capitalized interest payments (IANs – interest arrears notes).

Overall, the Russian Federal Government is the main debtor to foreigners. In the group of non-sovereign debtors, Russian banks have had the largest share, with almost two-thirds of total foreign debt. They also experienced serious problems in their foreign debt servicing. As a response to the August 1998 financial crisis, temporary restrictions on capital account foreign exchange operations by residents were imposed. This, first of all,

Table 9.3 Foreign currency debt burden of the federal government, 1994–99

	1994	1995	1996	1997	1998	1999
			(% of cash revenues)			
Total foreign currency debt service due	59.2	51.9	46.9	27.1	53.3	69.9
Total (external and domestic) debt service paid	17.2	32.4	64.8	46.8	50.4	47.3

Source: IMF (1999), BEA (1999), IMF (2000b) p. 80; authors' calculations.

included bank and corporate debt to foreign creditors estimated at $40 billion at that time, and forward contracts of about $10 billion.

The crisis of August 1998 was triggered by a default of the federal government on its domestic and part of its foreign debt. And indeed the main debt problem was not so much the size of the overall debt, but the size of the federal debt, relative to federal cash revenues. Foreign currency debt service commitments of the federal government were close to or even exceeded half of cash revenues in three out of four years before the crisis (Table 9.3). The low value for 1997 reflects partly a temporary decline in the dollar value of payments due in that year. However, it also reflects the overvaluation of the ruble. After the forced devaluation, the debt burden reached nearly 70 per cent of cash revenues in 1999. The problem was exacerbated by the high levels of domestic debt. Even though the foreign debt had not been serviced in full even before the crisis, actual payments made on external and domestic debt together consumed almost two-thirds of cash revenues in 1996, and around half of cash revenues in 1997 and 1998.

Debt Repayment Schedule and Renegotiations

In the years 1994–98, Russia paid $30 billion in foreign debt service or 10 per cent of debt service due (Buch et al., 2000). Principal repayments tended to decrease, whereas interest payments increased. Post-Soviet debt was serviced on time, but Soviet-era debt was partly repudiated. As of the end 1998, arrears totalled 11 per cent of the Soviet-era obligations. In 1999, total debt service due amounted to $17.5 billion (DIW et al., 1998).

In the years 2001–2010, projected debt-service of the government amounts to around $11 billion annually.[6] A sharp increase in payments to $16 billion is expected in the year 2003 due to a redemption of eurobonds.

Debt service will be distributed relatively equally between principal repayments and interest service, while the latter will exceed the former until 2002, and will fall short of principal repayments after 2003. A decrease in debt service is expected only after 2009. To this, foreign debt service to the tune of $5–6 billion annually by the private sector must be added. However, since these credits are mostly short term, their amount will decline relatively quickly.

Since the break-up of the former Soviet Union and Russia's acceptance of the Soviet Union's external liabilities, both the Paris and London Club debts have been subject to a number of rescheduling arrangements.[7] However, those arrangements did not prove to be a sustainable and sound solution to the external debt problem. In addition, the financial crisis in mid-1998 showed the extreme vulnerability of Russia's external debt position and necessitated urgent resumption of debt restructuring negotiations with all its creditors.

A temporary agreement with the Paris Club was reached in August 1999. According to the agreement, about $8 billion of payments due between 1999 and 2000 will be repaid over 15–20 years. In 1999–2000, Russia had to pay only some $600 million. At the time of writing, no agreement had been reached with the Paris Club about debts falling due in subsequent years.

By contrast, an agreement was reached with the London Club in February 2000. It entails a write-off of 37.5 per cent of the face value of PRINs and of 33 per cent of those of IANs. The remainder will be restructured into a 30-year-maturity eurobond with a seven-year grace period. The following section discusses the impact which debt rescheduling may have on the restructuring process of the banking sector from a political economy point of view.

BANKING REFORM AND FOREIGN DEBT

In its most recent Staff Report, the International Monetary Fund (IMF) identifies banking reform as a key area where progress has been disappointing. At the same time, the IMF notes of the discussions between the Russian government and its sovereign creditors that

> [The authorities] emphasized the fiscal dimension of the problem, expressing concern that the heavy debt burden from Soviet-era obligations on the federal budget could severely circumscribe policy options in the future, especially in light of the fact that key expenditure categories like health, education, and social transfers were already very compressed and that the budget would have to mobilize additional resources for reform-related expenditures in the future. They felt that an easing of the debt burden would significantly enhance the prospect for

> reform, not only by easing fiscal constraints, but also by signalling strong support by the international community of the government's reform plans.[8]

Similarly, the finance minister issued a press release in January 2001 to the effect that Russia needed to postpone debt service to the Paris Club in order to finance necessary structural reforms and to improve its ability to handle foreign debt payments in the future (BOFIT, 2001).

These statements suggest that Russian-style banking reform has a substantial political-economy component, and that negotiations about foreign debt service play a significant part in this. In what follows we therefore analyse the impact which the debt negotiations have on the incentives of the government to press ahead with banking reform.

As regards the sustainability of the foreign debt situation, it might be argued that the dependence of export revenues on the oil and gas sector and thus on the development of world market prices for these commodities leaves relatively little room to manoeuvre for domestic policy. At the same time, sustained economic growth, and thus debt service capacity in the medium to long term, will depend on progress made with banking reform.[9]

However, in order to reap the benefits of banking reform tomorrow, resources must be committed to it today. Moreover, since successful banking reform will enhance debt service capacity, its eventual benefits will have to be shared with foreign creditors. This creates a positive externality and thus provides scope for negotiations between foreign creditors and the government about the distribution of the costs and the benefits of the reform.

The Impact of the Post-Crisis Economic Upswing

After the crisis of 1998, GDP rebounded strongly, investment picked up and the balance of payments strengthened (Table 9.4). The recovery has been traced not so much to successful structural reforms, but to improvements in the external economic environment. Most notably, the ruble was devalued drastically and the terms of trade improved dramatically as world energy prices rose.[10] This was underpinned by a 33 per cent decline in real wages in the period 1998–99 (DIW and IfW, 2000a). As a result, the real effective exchange rate based on unit labour costs declined by roughly 70 per cent after the crisis (IMF, 2000b). While real wages had almost recovered to their pre-crisis levels by the end of 2000 (DIW and IfW, 2000b), the nominal exchange rate held fairly steady so that the real effective exchange rate remained significantly below its pre-crisis level even in mid-2001 (RECEP, 2001). The decline in real unit labour costs made enterprises vastly more profitable and provided them with a ready source of funds to finance new investments.

Table 9.4 The post-crisis recovery

	1999	2000	2001[a]	2002[a]
GDP growth (% yoy)	5.4	8.3	5.0	3.5
Investment growth (% yoy)	5.3	17.4	8.0	9.0
Current account balance (% GDP)	13.0	18.4	11.2	6.6
Foreign reserves and gold (USD bn)	12.5	28.0	38.0	45.0
Federal budget deficit, total (% GDP)	−1.4	2.3	1.4	1.3
Federal budget deficit, primary (% GDP)	2.0	4.7	4.6	3.9

Note: [a] Forecasts.

Sources: CBR (2001b, 2001c), Goskomstat (2001), Ministry of Finance (2001), Goldman Sachs (2001).

At the same time, the fiscal situation of the federal government improved dramatically as well (Table 9.4). This was due primarily to an increase in the tax rate on exports, to shifts of VAT revenues from the local to the federal budget and to improved tax compliance (IMF 2000b). By contrast, the improvement in the external environment turned out to be approximately neutral in terms of federal budget revenues because of the adverse effect of the real devaluation on the non-tradables sector. However, the combination of stronger federal budget revenues and a stronger balance of payments significantly improved the government's ability to service its foreign debt while at the same time expanding its domestic expenditures.

The consequences of these developments for banking reform are ambiguous. To be sure, the economic recovery of 1999–2001 does not obviate the need for reforming the banking system. Indeed, due to the fact that real wages rebounded strongly in 2000 and 2001, enterprise profits began to decline in early 2001. In step, the first quarter of 2001 saw the first prolonged decline in investment since the recovery started in mid-1999. This suggests that it will be critical for the sustainability of the economic recovery that workers be encouraged to save, and that these savings be made available to enterprises through efficient financial intermediaries.

At the same time, the improvement in the fiscal position should make financing banking reform easier. However, the economic recovery may also lessen the pain of (temporarily) living with an inefficient banking system, thereby reducing the incentives for reform. In particular, positive externalities conveyed to foreign creditors are not the only obstacles to banking reform from a political economy point of view. The costs and benefits of the reform are also likely to be unevenly distributed within Russia. For instance, creating an efficient banking system will reduce the dominant role currently played by the state savings bank Sberbank. Inter alia, this will reduce the government's ability to channel financial funds to preferred uses and will thus diminish rent-seeking opportunities.[11] Whether and when a political consensus on reform is achieved within Russia will depend on the relative opportunity costs of the status quo which different interest groups face, as well as on the distribution of reform benefits between them.

Formally, the political economy of the problem could be thought of as a war of attrition as in Alesina and Drazen (1991). In their model, the party which concedes first obtains a smaller share of the net benefits of the reform than the party which holds out longer. Uncertainty about the opponent's opportunity cost leads to uncertainty about when the opponent might give in. This creates a trade-off between conceding early, thereby bringing forward the benefits of reform, but receiving a smaller share of them, and holding out longer, thereby delaying reform, but (possibly) receiving a larger share of its benefits once it is finally implemented. Each period which ends in disagreement conveys new information about the true opportunity costs of the parties.

Casella and Eichengreen (1996) have shown how an anticipated *permanent* increase in the net benefits of the reform can result in either an acceleration or a delay of the reform depending on whether the anticipated increase materializes in the near future or is a longer way off. A *temporary* increase in the utility the parties derive from the status quo, by contrast – such as a temporary economic recovery – would unambiguously delay the reform by reducing the opportunity cost of holding out.

OUTLOOK

The severe real and financial crisis of 1998 has left Russia with an aggravated foreign debt problem. Traditional debt indicators have worsened, the country lacks access to international capital markets, negotiations with foreign creditors are protracted, the fiscal situation of the government remains precarious and capital flight continues. At the same time, the banking system is only beginning to recover from the collapse of 1998. Finding a way out of this deadlock has been difficult: foreign creditors are unwilling to lend new funds unless the government has proven its ability to reform, and the government procrastinates reforms as it fears their short-term costs.

As regards the sustainability of the foreign debt situation, this chapter has focused on the fact that the bulk of the foreign debt is owed by the government. At the same time, fiscal revenues are still relatively low, and the recent recovery rests precariously on the real devaluation, the effects of which are already beginning to be eroded by wage growth and inflation, and on high world energy prices, which are likely to come down as the world economy slows down. Institutional reforms, and among them banking reform, are crucially important in order to put the economy in general, and government finances in particular, on a sustainable path.

This chapter has focused in particular on the decision of the government to invest or not to invest in banking reform. For the government, the basic trade-off is between the efficiency losses due to an unreformed banking system and the fact that any efficiency gains will have to be shared with foreign creditors. Foreign creditors may be able to encourage reforms by rescheduling debt or even by granting debt relief.

Foreign creditors, in turn, face the trade-off that debt restructuring affords the government additional resources that can be spent on economic reform while, at the same time, current claims are forgone. The decision of the London Club to write off and restructure Russia's inherited debt will benefit the creditors only if banking restructuring and other institutional reforms are thereby encouraged and prove to be sufficiently effective. Technical assistance might be used to achieve this goal. Additionally, foreign creditors can influence the decision of the government by making default more costly through, for instance, cross-default clauses on the renegotiated debt.

In the meantime, empirical estimates of the trade balance have shown the importance of oil price and real exchange rate developments for Russia's net exports and thus its debt servicing potential (Buch et al., 2000). Since the development of oil prices must be taken as exogenous by policymakers, ensuring the (price) competitiveness of domestic producers by an appropriate exchange rate policy thus enhances Russia's ability to service its foreign debt. This requires, most importantly, a coordination of monetary, fiscal and institutional reforms with exchange rate policies. If such coordination is not achieved, competitiveness erodes, and a new crisis becomes all the more likely. In addition to institution building, sound and consistent macroeconomic policies are thus the key to successful debt restructuring.

NOTES

* The authors thank Paul Gregory as well as the participants of the conference 'The Russian Banking Sector: Evolution, Problems and Prospects' for helpful comments on an earlier draft. All remaining errors are our own.

1. Calculations by Jaffee and Levonian (2000) give an impression of the degree of underdevelopment of the Russian banking system. Compared to a benchmark banking system structure, the Russian banking system has only 11 per cent of the assets of comparable

countries. According to these figures, Russia would be highly overbanked at the same time, the number of banks being five times as high as would be expected for a country of its structure and size. See also Table A9.1 in the Appendix.

2. For instance, the foreign creditors of Inkombank have sold their claims to Rosbank of Russia for less than 10 per cent of their face value.
3. Indeed, by October 2000, those banks which did have positive equity averaged a capital adequacy ratio of 22.6 per cent, clearly above the minimum standards set by the BIS accords (CBR, 2001).
4. For these and the following comparisons see Buch et al. (2000).
5. The total does not sum up to 100 per cent because resident eurobonds and Minfins holdings are also included in the total debt, whereas non-resident holdings of GKOs/OFZs are excluded.
6. This figure assumes that no new borrowing takes place but takes the debt rescheduling agreements reached with the London Club in February 2000 into account.
7. See Buch et al. (2000) for details.
8. IMF (2000a), p. 26.
9. Other structural reforms, like tax reform and fighting corruption and the unofficial economy, are of course also important. See Buch et al. (2000).
10. From their trough at the beginning of 1999, the terms of trade improved by more than 50 per cent until early 2000 (IMF, 2000).
11. There is evidence that even during the immediate post-crisis recovery, a disproportionate share of investible funds was channelled to loss-making sectors of the economy (DIW and IfW, 2000a).

REFERENCES

Aleksina, A. and A. Drazen (1991), 'Why are Stabilizations Delayed?', *American Economic Review*, **81** (5), 1170–88.

Bank for International Settlements (BIS) (2001), *The Maturity, Sectoral and Nationality Distribution of International Bank Lending*, http://www.bis.org/publ/, Basle.

Bank of Finland (BOFIT) (2000), *Russian & Baltic Economies – The Week in Review*, various issues, http://www.bof.fi/env/eng/it/iten.stm, Helsinki.

— (2001), *Russian & Baltic Economies – The Week in Review*, 3, Helsinki.

Buch, C. M., R. P. Heinrich, L. Lusinyan and M. Schrooten (2000), 'Russia's Debt Crisis and the Unofficial Economy', Kiel Institute of World Economics, *Kiel Working Paper*, 978.

Bureau of Economic Analysis Foundation (BEA) (1999), 'The Russian Economy at the Turn of the Millenium: Current Issues and Prospects of Development', *Information Bulletin*, 15, June, Moscow.

Casella, A. and B. Eichengreen (1996), 'Can Foreign Aid Accelerate Stabilisation', *Economic Journal* **106** (436), 605–19.

Central Bank of Russia (CBR) (1998), *Bulletin of Banking Statistics*, various issues, Moscow.

— (2001a), *Trends in the Development of the Russian Banking System in January–September 2000*, http://www.cbr.ru/eng/analytics/bank_sys_e.htm.

— (2001b), Main Economic Indicators, http://www.cbr.ru/eng/statistics/credit_statistics/.

— (2001c), Gross International Reserves of the Russian Federation, http://www.cbr.ru/eng/statistics/credit_statistics/.

Deutsches Institut für Wirtschaftsforschung (DIW), Kiel Institute of World Economics and Institut für Wirtschaftsforschung (IWH) (DIW et al.) (1998), *Die wirtschaftliche Lage Rußlands – Krise offenbart Fehler der Wirtschaftspolitik*, Kiel Discussion Paper 330/331, Kiel Institute of World Economics, published also in *DIW Wochenbericht* 51 (1998) and in *IWH Forschungsreihe* 10/98.

Deutsches Institut für Wirtschaftsforschung (DIW), Kiel Institute of World Economics (IfW) (2000a), *Russische Wirtschaftspolitik setzt auf Investitionen*, Kiel Discussion Paper 360, Kiel Institute of World Economics, published also in *DIW Wochenbericht* 15 (2000).

Deutsches Institut für Wirtschaftsforschung (DIW), Kiel Institute of World Economics (IfW) (2000b), *Russlands Aufschwung in Gefahr*, Kiel Discussion Paper 372, Kiel Institute of World Economics, published also in *DIW Wochenbericht* 50 (2000).

European Bank for Reconstruction and Development (EBRD) (1998), *Transition Report*, London.

Finansovie Izvestija (1999), various issues, Moscow.

Goldman Sachs (2000), *Daily News and Views – New European Markets, Middle East and South Africa*, 14 February.

Goldman Sachs (2001), *EMEA Economics Analyst*, 01/13, 29 June.

Goskomstat (2001), National Accounts, http://www.gks.ru/scripts/free/1c.exe?XXXX25R.1.3.1.

International Monetary Fund (IMF) (1998), *Russian Federation – Staff Report*, Washington DC.

— (1999), *Russian Federation – Recent Economic Developments*, Washington DC.

— (2000a), *Russian Federation – Staff Report*, Washington DC.

— (2000b), *Russian Federation – Selected Issues*, Washington DC.

— (2001), *International Financial Statistics* on CD-Rom, Washington DC.

JP Morgan (1998), *Asian Financial Markets*, Second Quarter, Singapore.

Ministry of Finance (2001). Federal Budget Execution. http://www.eeg.ru/DOWNLOADS/tab01_e.pdf, http://www.eeg.ru/DOWNLOADS/tab00_e.pdf, http://www.eeg.ru/DOWNLOADS/tab99_e.pdf.

Russian European Centre for Economic Policy (RECEP) (2000), *Russian Economic Trends*, Monthly Update, December, Moscow.

— (2001), *Russian Economic Trends*, Monthly Update, June, Moscow.

10. Russian banks and foreign investments

Julia A. Solovieva*

INTRODUCTION

In all respects, 1998 marked a turning point in the cosy relationship between Western investors and Russia. The Russian Federation not only allowed the ruble to devalue, and defaulted on its domestic short-term obligations, but seriously damaged its relationship with foreign investors. Whereas prior to the crisis, every player in the financial markets had to do business in Russia, by the middle of 2000, there was a lot of scepticism and mistrust. Most Western banks had closed their offices in Russia, downsized them, or, at best, mothballed them. Credit lines for Russian counterparts were reduced and often cut completely. As a result, trades in Russian assets were possible only with Western counterparts, but not with Russian ones. Only in 2001, on the back of a recovery of the domestic economy and a remarkable upturn in the Russian eurobond market did Western investors begin to consider moving into Russia again, and applied for lines to be restored.

The aim of this paper is to establish where and why foreign investors[1] put their money into the Russian banking system, and how much they were able to take out after the crisis.

INVESTMENTS IN THE RUSSIAN BANKING SECTOR PRE-CRISIS

1. The Loan Market

Two types of foreign investor became involved with Russian banks. On the one hand, there were foreign banks that invested in equity and thus bought part of a Russian bank, while on the other hand there were Western banks that invested money in bonds issued by Russian banks or participated in loan syndications and thus became involved in the debt side of the business.

Table 10.1 Selected syndicated loans outstanding to Russian borrowers in August 1998

Borrower	Principal Outstanding (US$)	Signing Date	Maturity
Alfa-bank	77 million	31 October 1997	31 October 1998
Gazprombank	230 million	30 April 1998	30 April 1999
Inkombank	75 million	26 November 1997	26 November 1998
Inkombank	63.5 million	28 July 1998	28 July 1999
Bank Rossiiskii Kredit	125 million	28 August 1997	28 August 1998
Sberbank	225 million	2 December 1997	2 December 1998
SBS-Agro	113 million	20 November 1997	20 November 1998
Tokobank	60 million	29 August 1997	29 August 1998
Tokobank	65 million	28 November 1997	28 November 1998

Due to the different nature of these investments, the creditor normally has a much better chance of recovery than the shareholder, who at least in theory, is a partial owner of the company. This paper will first look at investments in securities such as bonds, loans, promissory notes, and so on, before investigating the level at which Western companies were involved on the equity side.

Around the time of the crisis, there were over $2 billion outstanding in syndicated loans to Russian banks.[2] Table 10.1 lists examples of deals and principal outstanding at the time crisis struck.[3] They illustrate the situation prevailing in 1997 and 1998. The above list illustrates a few interesting points: most of the banks that received loans from international banks were, of course, ranked among the top Russian banks. In retrospect, such rankings look very optimistic indeed, and most banks on the list (and this is true for most banks that were given loans in 1997 and 1998) are now in liquidation (Tokobank, SBS-Agro, Inkombank) or have restructured (Bank Rossiiski Kredit, Alfa-bank). Only the biggest and best supported banks have been able to repay their creditors in full and on time. It is surprising, however, to see how many Debt Origination desks and Research Departments were fooled into believing that investing in Russia was 'safe', given that the Russian crisis had been looming since at least the end of 1997. An indication that foreign currency reserves at the Central Bank of Russia were rapidly diminishing did not serve as a sufficient warning,[4] although the consequence of such an observation is often a run on and subsequent devaluation of a currency. This, in turn, negatively influences the ability of the state or the enterprise to repay hard currency loans as the cost of servicing the debt increases manyfold, unless the company is relying on hard currency income for servicing its debt (in the oil and gas industries, for example).

As illustrated in Table 10.1, it is clear that nothing could stop the euphoria of Western banks in lending money to their Russian counterparts. Tokobank did not have much difficulty attracting a second loan for a slightly higher amount just three months after it had received its first ever syndicated loan. Even more surprisingly, Inkombank creditors were happy to lend $63.5 million to the bank less than a month before the August crisis, although admittedly the proceeds of the loan were used to refinance a loan of $115 million that was maturing on 7 August 1998. Three weeks before the crisis, this loan was oversubscribed and increased from $50 million to $63.5 million. Maybe this is not surprising, given that the bank was classified as one of the largest private banks in Russia with a wide network of branches across the country. It is quite disturbing to find that the loan for $115 million was granted on an interest basis of Libor + 425 basis points, whereas the spread for the refinancing loan was just 50 basis points wider and stood at Libor + 475 basis points.

Who were the main participants in the loan sector? Table 10.2 shows the banks that were involved in loans to Russian banks around the time of the crisis of 1998.

Table 10.2 Banks active in the Russian loans market pre-crisis

Lender[5]	Participations[6]
Bayerische Landesbank	around 20
Bayerische Vereinsbank	around 18
Bank Austria	around 18
Moscow Narodny Bank	around 15
Bank of New York	around 12
London Forfaiting Company	around 11
Baden-Württembergische Bank	around 10
BCEN-Eurobank	around 10

It seems that Western banks, at least in the loan market, were more concerned with demonstrating that they were active in the Russian markets: unlike bonds, loans are relatively illiquid instruments, which means that a loan cannot easily be transferred from one owner to another. Sometimes, the loan agreement even specifies that the borrower's consent to a transferral is required. While this consent is not normally withheld (however, it needs time to contact the borrower and get a reply from him), loans are not traded frequently as there is no standard documentation and the purchaser of the loan has to invest considerable time and resources to check underlying loan documentation. Moreover, there are restrictions on trading loans imposed by regulatory financial authorities which means that a lot of due diligence needs to be done before buying a loan. Finally, most banks book loans at par value in their books and do not mark-to-market the value, which means that once the value of the loan drops, the bank will want to hold the loan to maturity as otherwise it would have to take a loss on the position. As a result of all this, one can say that a great number of banks that originally participated in the syndication of the loan will hold their share of the loan to maturity. The opposite is the case for bonds: often, their sale and purchase in the secondary market will settle via Euroclear or Cedel,[7] usually three days after the trade has been agreed. The issuer of the bond does not normally know who is holding the debt, whereas the borrower of a loan has more chance of finding out. The ease with which bonds are bought and sold has the further advantage that in a bearish market, banks will be keen to sell their bonds and cut their losses. This is almost impossible to do in the loan market for the reasons specified above. The risks of participating were thus relatively high, whereas opportunities were relatively limited, given that loans are not liquid instruments and the carry on them is mainly the interest rate they are paying.

2. Bonds

Bonds are much easier to trade than loans. They are usually marked-to-market, and the carry on them is thus not only the coupon they are paying but also the difference between the price at which the bond is bought and the price at which it is sold. This difference is not always positive. Despite this, the bond market did not develop at such a speed as the loan market, and by the time of the crisis, only a few banks had bonds outstanding: Alfa-bank, Uneximbank and SBS-Agro.[8] These deals were done generally in 1997, amounted to a total of $725 million and matured in 2000. Of these three, only Alfa-bank fully repaid its bonds. Uneximbank bondholders had their holdings restructured, and SBS-Agro bondholders did not see much light at the end of the tunnel until early 2001, as will be discussed in the second part of this paper. It is interesting that the bookrunners of the bonds were mostly American banks, whereas the loan market was very much dominated by European, and especially German, banks. The reason behind this might be the fact that the loan market is more attractive to commercial banks that then hold the asset, whereas bonds are mostly traded and thus are of more interest to investment banks. Geography certainly also plays a role: German banks keen to establish good relationships with their Eastern European neighbours would be more easily convinced to venture into these markets than commercial banks from countries geographically more remote. Also, a national (in this case Russian) bank would normally more easily turn to a commercial bank in a country that is trying to establish a good relationship with Russia.

Returning to the bonds themselves: the bonds issued pre-crisis were priced at between 385 and 425 basis points over comparable US treasuries (with one floating rate note issued by Uneximbank paying only 300 basis points over Libor). This attracted retail investors as well as financial institutions and the deals all went extraordinarily well. There was a huge appetite for Russia. However, what makes bondholders different from participants in loans is the ability to sell bonds relatively easily. Therefore it is impossible to judge which banks were left with their positions as the crisis struck. Moreover, the fact that no further bonds were issued in 1998 by Russian banks points to the fact that banks were starting to fear that due to the volatility of the bond markets, no new issues could be placed with investors. Thus, no one took any further mandates from Russian banks for fear of being left with huge, unwanted bond positions, and the Russian bond market that had only begun to emerge in 1997 came to a grinding halt at the end of the same year.

3. Equity Investments

Issuing bonds and borrowing through loans are means for a company to attract capital that will be used for different projects. This way of receiving cash is called debt financing, and holders of bonds and loans are creditors to the debtor, the Russian bank in this case. There exists a third means of attracting money, which is by issuing shares and selling them on to investors. Unless an investor sells his shares, he will never be returned his money, but he is usually paid a dividend. In order to make shares attractive and to support their price, the company will normally aim at paying dividends that offer a far greater return than yields on bonds and loans. By buying shares in a company, the shareholder automatically becomes one of the owners of the company, and this is not always in the (often populist) interests of the state, which might try to limit foreign ownership in domestic companies by law. In Russia, purchases of shares in domestic banks by non-residents must be approved by the Central Bank of Russia, which can take quite some time.[9] Moreover, existing shareholders – and this includes the state – are often reluctant to sell equity to foreigners as they fear interference in the way they manage the company. Also, many banks are owned by regions or commercial groups and serve a particular purpose (Gazprombank, for example). If they were to be sold to foreign companies, they would effectively lose their *raison d'être*.[10]

Foreign banks that are active in Russia would normally try to set up their own subsidiary or branch that would be incorporated in Russia and thus be considered a Russian bank. An example of this would be the above-mentioned Bank Austria (Moscow) or Dresdner Bank's Russian-incorporated OOO Dresdner Kleinwort Wasserstein. There are a few banks that belong to neither of these categories: Renaissance Capital, for instance, was set up in the mid-1990s by senior expatriates who had been working for Credit Suisse First Boston in Moscow. In 2001, around 80 per cent of shares belonged to the founders of the company, which is trying to re-establish itself as one of the top Russian banks. Another example is Moscow International Bank, which is owned 41 per cent by Bayerische HypoVereinsbank, 20.5 per cent by Merita Nordbanken and 10 per cent by the European Bank of Reconstruction and Development (EBRD).[11] Another bank that managed to attract the interest of foreign shareholders was Avtobank, which in 1997 was owned to 41.7 per cent by foreign companies (also, 8 per cent of Avtobank belonged to the EBRD).[12] As a result of the above-mentioned legal restrictions, however, the August crisis had only a limited effect on foreign equity investments.

ATTEMPTS AT RECOVERY POST-CRISIS

1. Equity

In part one of this paper, I considered the different ways in which a Western bank can invest money in a Russian bank. Investing money, however, is about getting a return on one's money, and this is precisely where things were starting to go wrong in post-crisis Russia. As mentioned above, the ruble devaluation increased considerably the cost of debt servicing of the Russian banks, and failure to pay the coupon or interest on their outstanding debt resulted in a number of defaults by Russian banks. In this part, we will analyse the returns that Western investors could expect after things had gone so wrong. For the sake of recovery, it does not make much difference whether one holds a loan or a bond. As it is simplest with equity investments, I will start off with these and will then analyse the fate of Russian banks and the ultimate recovery of creditors.

Loans and bonds can be secured by the assets of the company. They can have different rankings (seniority) which influence the amount the creditor would expect to be returned in the case of a bankruptcy. With equity, it is much easier. Equity holders are owners of the company and as such come last in the list of people who receive their money back. After the crisis, those who had invested in the equity of failing banks had very limited choices:

either they accepted that their investment had been lost or they tried to restructure the company. This often involves cash injections, and not every investor is willing to put even more money into a problem bank. In cases where the Russian Agency for Bank Restructuring (ARCO) came in, shareholdings were often diluted as ARCO took control over the bank and received the majority of shares. Other banks, such as Tokobank in which the EBRD had a stake, were bankrupted and ceased to exist, thus reducing the value of the equity investment to zero. Other banks, such as Renaissance Capital, had to downsize their operations and subsequently restructured their bank to make it viable once again. The same is true for banks owned by industrial groups but going into this in greater detail goes beyond the scope of this paper, as investments in these banks were made not by Western investors.

2. Bonds and Loan

a) The lucky ones

Far more interesting is to see what happened to creditors, as opposed to investors. As the first coupon payments post-crisis drew nearer, one could divide the banks into three groups. First, there were those that after initial difficulties were able to remain current on interest, and ultimately pay back their debt. A good example of this is Alfa-bank, whose eurobond matured in July 2000 and was fully redeemed. Other banks had to restructure their debt, and creditors were offered other bonds in return (Rossiiskii Kredit, Avtobank, Konversbank, Roseksimbank, Promstroybank St Petersburg, and so on). Finally, there were of course banks which, even by mid-2001 had not gone anywhere, and which were, if not already in liquidation, then at least on the way to bankruptcy. As at end-September 2001, banks that had not even reached a satisfactory deal with creditors included Bank Imperial and Inkombank. Others, such as Tokobank, had gone into liquidation and were in the process of being wound up. I will take one example from each category to illustrate the difficulties Western creditors faced after the August 1998 crisis.

It is easiest to begin with Alfa-bank. Debt prices for assets across all ranges, including Russian sovereign eurobonds, plunged from levels of around 100 per cent to as low as 0 per cent. To put this into perspective, one has to remember that even in autumn 1999, Russian sovereign eurobonds were trading in the teens, so there was certainly not much scope for higher prices for all other issuers or borrowers. Many banks used this opportunity to buy back their own debt in the secondary market from creditors who only wanted to get out of their holdings and close out their Russian positions. In order to achieve such a debt buyback without upsetting investors too much, an issuer or borrower can charge a player in the financial market with buying back the company's debt. Otherwise, it might choose to do so via a broker, or by directly addressing creditors. Alfa-bank openly admitted to having bought back chunks of their own debt. For the issuer/borrower, this is a very cheap way of reducing their debt, which at maturity they would have to redeem at par, whereas now they can buy it for, say, 20 per cent of the nominal. Creditors who want to exit at all costs, benefit from this in so far as they can get rid of their positions. However, they are unlikely to get more than current market value, which after a crisis such as the Russian crisis will be a bargain (for the issuer). Those creditors who had the nerve to hold their debt to maturity were compensated for the uncertainty by rising debt prices starting from autumn 1999 and, finally, in July 2000, full redemption in the case of Alfa-bank.

b) The cost of restructuring

Less fortunate were holders of Rossiiskii Kredit paper. ARCO took control of the troubled bank and acquired 25 per cent of its equity. The organization then provided loans to the bank to enhance liquidity, and took a further 50 per cent of equity as security for these loans.[13] In October 1999, a mandatory moratorium on claims was introduced, and ARCO determined that the balance sheet of Rossiiskii Kredit was negative, with assets being worth \$542 million and liabilities amounting to \$972 million.[14] A restructuring proposal was presented to creditors in April 2000, and the majority had accepted it by August 2000, as had the Moscow Arbitrage Court. The alternatives were liquidation and bankruptcy, with the prospect for foreign creditors, who rank last according to Russian bankruptcy law after domestic investors and government organizations, of receiving very little or even nothing at all.[15]

Most of the debt due to foreign creditors was in US dollars. However, the amount due was converted into Russian rubles on the day of the moratorium (19 October 1999) at an exchange rate of 25.8 rubles to one US dollar.[16] Creditors can think themselves lucky that by that time the exchange rate had already stabilized, otherwise they would have had to accept a huge exchange rate loss. The restructuring plan, or Amicable Settlement Agreement, provided for class three investors (which includes foreign investors) to receive 5 per cent of cash in US dollars seven days after the signing of the plan, plus a further 5 per cent of cash in US dollars three months later. Also, 20 per cent of the total claim was transformed into six-year, amortizing promissory notes denominated in US dollars, with a further 70 per cent being exchanged into 10-year non-amortizing ruble-denominated promissory notes.[17] The USD-denominated promissory notes are heavily back-loaded with 50 per cent of the principal repayments being made at maturity. Moreover, the first principal repayment is not due until the expiry of a three-year grace period, and amounts only to 5 per cent of the principal.[18]

What losses did foreign investors have to take? The eurobond issued by Rossiiskii Kredit would have matured in 2000, whereas the loan was due even earlier. From the date of the moratorium that came into being in October 1999, all liabilities of Rossiiskii Kredit stopped accruing interest. Thus, in effect, creditors lost a year of coupon payments,[19] plus they had to accept that their maturities would be extended significantly. The value of this extension is difficult to quantify, but in addition to this, creditors also lost out on the conversion of their holdings into rubles. The exchange rate at the date of the moratorium was used to convert all claims into rubles; however, when it came to paying out 10 per cent of these claims in US dollars, the exchange rate of the date of the approval of the restructuring plan by the Moscow Arbitrage Court (15 August 2000 at a rate of 27.69 rubles to one US dollar[20]) was used. On a total claim of $752 million, this meant a loss to creditors of about $50 million, or just over 6.6 per cent of their total claim. The USD note, issued by a special purpose vehicle called Snap Limited,[21] will pay a coupon of 1 per cent per annum in years one and two, and 2 per cent per annum subsequently. Since there is a grace period of three years, the coupons for years one and two are not going to be paid until the end of year three.[22] Given that the interest rate is so low anyway, it already does not make much difference that the coupon payments for the first two years are not even capitalized, that is, added to the principal and thus interest-bearing. The ruble notes start paying interest at 3.3 per cent annually in 2007 with the principal repayment not due until 2010.[23] This is not a great interest rate in comparison to the quality of the credit. It is difficult to quantify how much money an investor holding this note to maturity would lose, given that the interest rate is derisory for a ruble-denominated instrument, and that the value of the ruble in ten years' time is anyone's guess. A better indication of the value (as of autumn 2001) is the price at which these two assets are trading in the secondary market: the Snap ruble notes trade for around 4–6 per cent, whereas the dollar-denominated notes trade at 24–26 per cent.[24] That represents a loss of investment of 95 per cent for the ruble notes and some 75 per cent for the dollar-denominated notes, considering that the normal value for an investment should be around par.[25] Maybe investors take comfort in the knowledge that, should Rossiiskii Kredit do well, the value of the notes will be enhanced by additional payments.

c) The disaster scenario

When SBS-Agro launched its eurobond in 1997, the first ever by a Russian bank, the market appraised the launch with the following words:

'a complete and utter blow-out'.[26] Only a couple of years later, one could speak of a complete and utter blow-up. SBS-Agro defaulted on its obligations on the eurobond in July 1999 when the first 10.25 per cent coupon after the August 1998 crisis became due. The market had already been suspecting a default, and prices for the bond had fallen to about 10 per cent of nominal by early July 1999. A steering committee that had been working on a possible restructuring well before the actual default resigned in summer 1999 because they found it impossible to work with the chairman of the bank, Alexander Smolensky. According to him, SBS-Agro needed 46 billion rubles to restructure. At the same time, he said that the Soyuz group, which he was chairing[27] by then and that came into existence after the crash of SBS-Agro, was not in bad shape and that the entire banking group should be re-organized. SBS-Agro, as the name implies, was heavily involved in lending to the agricultural sector, and Smolensky suggested that all the risks of lending to agriculture should be handed over to the semi-state-owned Rosselkhozbank that the government was planning to set up.[28] What followed was a period of confusion. There were different options discussed, after the creditor banks refused to accept a restructuring plan put forward by Smolensky, under which he proposed that foreign creditors should get around 4–5 per cent of the nominal.

The main problem, apart from a chairman unwilling to cooperate with the steering committee of foreign creditors, was also that although ARCO had practically taken over the bank by acquiring 99.9 per cent of its shares in November 1999, the bank was too large for the organization to handle: ARCO had a capital of 10 billion rubles, of which they had spent 4 billion rubles by mid-summer 1999. SBS-Agro's losses, in comparison, were estimated to be around 46 billion rubles.[29] The Central Bank of Russia's stabilizing loans of several billion rubles were not much help either in reaching a satisfactory conclusion to restructuring. On top of this, there was a lot of political pressure, especially from the IMF which was unhappy about the way Russian banks were restructuring, and it was half expected that the restructuring of SBS-Agro would be the showpiece for reform in the banking sector.[30]

By the spring of 2000, creditors waited to hear of a new restructuring plan, which took considerable time to come forward. There were two creditor meetings in April 2000 and in November 2000, but it was not until January 2001 that a new settlement proposal was distributed to creditors,[31] who at the time were told that all they could expect was recovery of approximately 1 per cent of their investments, which is appalling by any standards. Private depositors, on the contrary, were always in another category and therefore slightly better off: under the current agreement, they are supposed to achieve a recovery of around 90 per cent with a maximum of 20 000 rubles being paid out, the rest being paid back with foreign currency loan bonds (for example, MinFin bonds).[32] SBS-Agro's assets have more or less all been transferred into OVK-Bank[33] which is controlled, unsurprisingly, by Smolensky.[34] That explains why the offer to foreign creditors could only be bettered to the extent that they will now receive promissory notes issued by SBS-Agro[35] with a maturity span of 25 years. Still, after all the time that had been spent negotiating a restructuring, this was enough for banks like Chase Manhattan, Société Générale and the EBRD to accept the proposals for a peaceful settlement.[36] The value of this is not much: in autumn 2001, SBS-Agro debt traded at 1–2 per cent.[37] Still, this was already remarkably 'high' in comparison to prices of 0.5–1.5 per cent in summer 2000.

CONCLUSION

By 1998, the loan market had developed quite satisfactorily in Russia. Banks were striving to establish a name in a potentially huge market, and 1997 had seen the beginning of a shift from loan financing to bond financing. However, this was cut short by troubles in South-East Asia that then began spreading to other emerging markets and culminated in the Russian government default in August 1998. Whereas prior to the crisis, many banks had tried to set up majority-owned subsidiaries in Moscow, not many banks had ventured into acquiring shares in Russian banks. This was partly due to political unwillingness on the Russian side to let foreigners acquire majority stakes in banks, but partly also due to the nature of the Russian banking sector where many banks were set up with the main purpose of servicing certain industrial branches. It was rather supranational banks such as the EBRD, dedicated and set up to do business in Eastern Europe, that seriously ventured into the world of equity investments,[38] which, however, often proved to be worthless after the crisis. This, and the turmoil in the share market in 2001, has certainly prevented Western banks and investors (up to the end of 2001) from expressing strong interest in Russian-domiciled bank shares. The risks associated with a banking sector that remains badly regulated and undercapitalized are simply too great.

Whereas equityholders can predict the outcome for their investments in the event of such a systemic crisis, it is more difficult for creditors to evaluate in advance what their chances of recovery are: incidentally, the bank that received the best press when it issued its eurobond in 1997 was SBS-Agro. We have seen that the rate of recovery for creditors of SBS-Agro was virtually nothing. In contrast, Alfa-bank that was appraised by the market as not carrying 'the same weight as SBS-Agro or Uneximbank' and thus being 'a harder deal to get sold'[39] managed to pay back its creditors on time and in full.

By summer 2001, however, foreign investors were seriously beginning to eye the Russian banking sector again. Very little had been done in the previous two years, but signs that Russian banks are beginning to come back to international markets are starting to show: a good example of this is Bank Zenit, which received a syndicated loan (the first after the Russian crisis) from foreign banks. The loan, signed on 15 May 2001,[40] had a tenure of 1 year with a put option after 180 days and paid a margin of 400 basis points.[41] The loan of $20 million was secured by Tatneft' eurobonds with the collateral representing 200 per cent of the principal, which indicates that, indeed, some lessons had been learnt from the crisis. This is especially important as emerging markets investors in 2001, in light of the unstable situation both in the Turkish and Argentine markets and the fear of a possible spillover to other emerging countries, sought refuge in Russian assets: high oil prices and soaring foreign currency reserves at the Central Bank of Russia have done much to put the country back in the minds of investors, but the unease still remains.

NOTES

* The opinions expressed in this paper are solely those of the author, and do not necessarily correspond with the opinion of Dresdner Kleinwort Wasserstein.

1. I will look in particular at Western banks as the most exposed group of investors because banks were the middle-man for many other investors, such as hedge funds and retail investors.
2. According to data available in Loanware (an electronic database that allows one to search for termsheets of syndicated loans). Due to the often bilateral nature of private placements, it is impossible to estimate how much more money might have flown into the Russian banking system as loans.
3. Again, these data are from Loanware and only serve to illustrate a few points. I have refrained from citing a full list of loans, since at the time of the crisis, there were just under 50 foreign currency loans outstanding to Russian banks.
4. There were, of course, several others, such as soaring interest rates, and so on.
5. No difference is made between different branches and subsidiaries. For example, in some loans, Bank Austria AG was involved, whereas in others, it was Bank Austria (Moscow). I have counted them as one, as they ultimately belong to the same banking group.
6. The numbers come from my analysis of the loan market as per data available in Loanware. There might have been private placements in addition to this.
7. Two clearing houses through which the greater part of bonds are settled. It has the advantage that it cuts down on risks for the transacting parties (such as counterparty risk where one party delivers the bonds but the other fails to pay the money), and it serves as a depository for bonds which avoids physical paper being passed around each time a bond is bought and sold.
8. Data as in Bondware (a similar system to Loanware but with data on bonds, notes and so on). There were other bonds and notes issued in 1997 but for short maturities which could be redeemed before the crisis.

9. *Russia/Central Europe Executive Guide*, 30 October 2000.
10. Ibid.
11. Ibid.
12. 'Rossiya: Balansovaya prybil' Avtobanka na 1 okt97g – 503.14mlrd r.', *Reuters Business Briefing, Reuters News Service* (29 October 1997).
13. This illustrates very well the point made above that shareholders often lost their investment when ARCO took control of the financial institution.
14. Stephen F. Evans, 'Rossiyskiy Kredit Bank Review of Restructuring Terms', *ING Barings High Yield Research* (15 September 2000), p. 2. Out of the $972 million in liabilities, $752 million were due to third group investors, that is, foreign investors. Ibid., p. 5.
15. Ibid., p. 2.
16. Ibid., p. 5.
17. Ibid.
18. A further 20 per cent and 25 per cent are due in October 2004 and October 2005 respectively. Ibid., p. 10.
19. For the sake of simplicity, I take an average interest rate of 10 per cent on the total class three claim to arrive at a figure of around $75 million in lost coupon payments.
20. Stephen F. Evans, 'Rossiyskiy Kredit Bank Review of Restructuring Terms', *ING Barings High Yield Research* (15 September 2000), p. 6.
21. In fact, the notes issued by Snap are credit-linked to the performance of promissory notes issued by Rossiiskii Kredit to Snap.
22. Stephen F. Evans, 'Rossiyskiy Kredit Bank Review of Restructuring Terms', *ING Barings High Yield Research* (15 September 2000), p. 6.
23. Ibid., p. 7.
24. See the Bloomberg page of 'Exotix Ltd.', Eastern Europe.
25. Of course, these are extreme figures and would only apply to those who bought the bonds well before the crisis and still hold them.
26. See Bondware, SBS-Agro USD 250 million eurobond.
27. 18 February 1999, 'Rossiya: Bankovskaya gruppa SBS-Agro menyaet nazvanie na Soyuz', *Reuters Business Briefing, Prime Tass*.
28. Igor' Moiseev, 'Novy stsenarii dlya SBS-Agro predusmatrivaet ego bankrotstvo, *Vedomosti* (12 October 1999).
29. Olga Zaslavskaya, 'Byt' ili ne byt', *Segodnya* (23 August 1999).
30. *Vedomosti*, ibid.
31. 'Russia: ARCO proposes new settlement offer for SBS-Agro', *Reuters Business Briefing* (15 January 2001).
32. 'Russia: ARCO likely to hand MinFin Bonds to SBS-Agro's Investors', *Reuters Business Briefing* (15 January 2001).
33. 'Rossiya: SBS-Agro vedet partiyu v bridzh', *Reuters Business Briefing – Vremya MN* (6 April 2000).
34. Very much the same happened with lots of other troubled Russian banks: Rossiiskii Kredit, for instance, transferred its assets into Impexbank. See *Renaissance Capital Weekly Monitor* (22 January 2001), p. 11.
35. Just compare the credit risk of MinFin bonds and SBS-Agro issued promissory notes.
36. 'Rossiya: Kreditory SBS-Agro soglasilis' na mirovuyu", *Reuters Business Briefing* (14 February 2001).
37. See the Bloomberg page of 'Exotix Ltd.', Eastern Europe.
38. Not surprisingly, the only bank currently listed on the Russian Trading System RTS is Sberbank, but its shares are not normally recommended as a 'buy'.
39. Bondware, Alfa-bank eurobond.
40. Loanware, Bank Zenit Term loan.
41. 'Bank Zenit tests appetite for Russian FI risk', *IFR*, 1371 (17 February 2001), p. 71.

11. Progress towards financial stability

Brigitte Granville[1]

INTRODUCTION

However unforeseen, the consequences of the Russian default on over $40 billion-worth of debt in August 1998 extended to a perceived threat to the stability of the global financial system. This perception was reflected in the actions of the US Federal Reserve in the autumn of 1998: rapid monetary easing, and the move to arrange a rescue for Long Term Capital Management (LTCM) from insolvency as a result of the Russian crisis. The experience of Russia and the other major emerging countries caught up in the financial market crises of 1997–98 has informed IMF-led attempts to develop Codes and Standards (C&S) and measures for financial crisis prevention and cure as part of a renewed 'International Financial Architecture' (IFA).[2] Standards of good practice have been codified in *Reports on the Observance of Standards and Codes* (ROSCs). The IMF's 'Article IV' report on Russia of July 2000 (made public by the Russian authorities in October 2000) referred to the fact that a ROSC had been completed.

This paper begins with an overview of the state of the Russian economy against the background of the 1998 crisis and hence the systemic risks contained in the problems of Russia's transition. This provides the necessary context for making sense both of detailed policy work related to the implementation of C&S and, in some areas, of the absence of any such work. In addition, the economic background is essential to distinguish the underlying factors driving (and hampering) Russia's economic performance from marginal improvements which might flow from more effective implementation of standards and codes.

ECONOMIC BACKGROUND

The external debt on the eve of the August debacle amounted to about $150 billion (about 35 per cent of annualized dollar GDP in January–August 1998). This was equivalent to one-third of the combined external debts at

Table 11.1 External government debt (US$ billion)

	1991	1992	1993	1994	1995	1996	1997	1998
Federal Government	96.8	107.7	112.7	119.9	120.4	125.0	123.5	147.1
Former USSR debt	96.8	104.9	103.7	108.6	103.0	100.8	91.4	95.2
To official creditors	62.2	69.2	68.1	69.9	62.6	61.9	56.9	59.5
To commercial creditors	32.9	34.0	34.0	37.0	39.3	38.8	33.9	35.2
Bonds	1.7	1.7	1.6	1.7	1.1	0.1	0.1	0.0
Debt accumulated:								
By the Russian Federation	0.0	2.8	9.0	11.3	17.4	24.2	32.1	51.9
To multilateral creditors	0.0	1.0	3.5	5.4	11.4	15.3	18.7	26.0
To official creditors	0.0	1.8	5.5	5.9	6.0	7.9	7.6	9.7
Bonds	0.0	0.0	0.0	0.0	0.0	1.0	4.5	16.0
Subnational governments	0.0	0.0	0.0	0.0	0.0	0.0	1.1	2.2
Total	96.8	107.7	112.7	119.9	120.4	125.0	124.6	149.3

Source: OECD, 2000, Table 6, p. 67.

the end of 1996 of the five Asian countries (Indonesia, Korea, Malaysia, Philippines, Thailand) and just 8 per cent of emerging markets' total external debts.[3] Russia defaulted on $44 billion of domestic debt of which one-third was owed to non-residents.

Russia's debt problem goes back much further than that default on part of the stock of short-term domestic T-bills that had been accumulated with ill-advised speed from virtually zero in 1995. A key part of the problem has always stemmed from the burden of inherited Soviet debt, the roots of which are to be found in the resource misallocation (fuelled by the demands of perceived Cold War threats, though in fact inherent in central planning) which took place in Soviet times. Therefore Russia launched its reform efforts with a large financing gap resulting from the Soviet debt it had inherited – loans, it should be recalled, that the West had extended to the system of central planning from which Russia was now trying to extricate itself. Refinancing was impossible, since access to international capital markets was blocked following the December 1991 default on foreign bank debt. With the capitalization of unpaid interest, Russia's external debt burden mounted rapidly (Ferguson and Granville, 2000).

The severity of the burden was acknowledged in long-term rescheduling agreements concluded with the Paris and London Clubs of official and commercial creditors, respectively. In April 1996 a comprehensive rescheduling agreement was reached with Paris Club creditors, covering about $38 billion of debt; and in December 1997 a 25-year rescheduling agreement covering approximately $24 billion was reached with the London Club.[4] However the collapse of Russian GDP in dollar terms (from about $430 billion to less than $190 billion) as a result of the 1998 ruble devaluation left Russia unable to make even these reduced payments. The ratio of foreign debt to $GDP increased from 26 to 113 per cent between December 1997 and December 1998.[5] If the full $17.5 billion due in 1999 had been paid, this would have cost Russia about 80 per cent of planned tax revenue. Russia therefore applied to both creditor clubs for further debt relief. The strategy to obtain debt relief was based on two principles: (i) to service post-Soviet Russian debt, amounting to $51.1 billion at the end of 1999, or one-third of the total; (ii) to secure a further comprehensive restructuring of all external obligations inherited from the Soviet era. These totaled $103.5 billion at the end of 1999 or two-thirds of total debt.

On 1 August 1999, an agreement was reached with official creditors covering arrears and maturities falling due on Soviet-era debt in the period July 1999 to December 2000 estimated at $8.1 billion. This flow rescheduling provided for a differential treatment between previously-rescheduled and non-previously-rescheduled debts as well as arrears. The new maturities were between 16 and 20 years with graduated grace periods and payments. On 11 February 2000 an agreement was reached with the London Club on a comprehensive debt and debt service reduction operation. The entire stock of $31.8 billion of Soviet-era debt owed to London Club creditors was agreed to be exchanged for $21.2 billion in new Russian eurobond issues, with concessional coupon payments in the early years. In total this operation will yield a 40 per cent reduction in Russia's private-sector debt.[6]

The Paris Club has proved much more reluctant to forgive debt, especially as the commodity price slump that had contributed to Russia's 1998 financial crash had been fully reversed by 2000, considerably boosting debt-service capacity.[7]

Russia therefore had little choice but to comply. After holding out for official debt relief, and even entertaining a tactical 'technical' default, the Russian authorities changed back in March 2001 by committing themselves to service Soviet-era Paris Club debt in full according to existing contracts based on the 1996 restructuring.

Indeed, as Table 11.2 shows, Russian macroeconomic indicators have improved dramatically since early 1999. Real GDP growth reached 7.7 per cent in 2000 and by mid-2001 was on course for a rate of 5–6 per cent for the year as a whole. This recovery was mainly due to the large ruble devaluation in 1998 (40 per cent) and the oil price increase. The devaluation and favourable global commodity price upswing were instrumental in transforming

Table 11.2 Key indicators of the Russian economy (%, 12-month growth unless otherwise stated)

	1996	1997	1998	1999	2000
GDP	−3.5	0.8	−4.9	3.5	7.7
Industrial production	−4.0	1.9	−5.2	8.1	9.0
Fixed investment	−18.0	−5.0	−6.7	1.0	17.7
Inflation	22.0	11.0	84.8	36.5	20.2
M2	30.0	29.5	36.3	57.2	62.4
Unemployment	9.3	9.0	11.8	11.7	10.2
Federal budget balance, % of GDP	−8.3	−7.0	−4.9	−1.2	2.5
Current account, % of GDP	3.0	0.5	0.3	13.5	20.0

Sources: Goskomstat, CBR, Ministry of Finance.

both the balance of payments and the fiscal position. The current account swung back into surplus in 1999 from near balance in 1998, and in 2000 the surplus surged to $46.5 billion (nearly 20 per cent of GDP), while the visible trade surplus of $60 billion was 25 per cent of GDP. International reserves reached $27.9 billion at the end of 2000, the equivalent of about six months of imports. State revenues have also benefited from buoyant commodity prices (captured in export tariffs in particular) and from the domestic output growth stemming from the effect of the devaluation in pricing out imports. Since the 1998 crisis, fiscal consolidation has been considered a priority for the Russian authorities, at first forced upon them by the disappearance of deficit financing sources, but since late 1999 positively adopted as a policy goal. Aggregate federal budget revenues rose to almost 16 per cent of GDP in 2000, from less than 11 per cent in 1999 and less than 9 per cent in 1998; and revenues are on target to exceed 16 per cent of GDP in 2001. The primary balance of the federal government went from being in deficit (−1 per cent of GDP) in 1998 to surpluses in 1999 and 2000 (+2 per cent and +5 per cent of GDP respectively), and this indicator is expected to stabilize at 4.4 per cent in 2001.

This turnaround in the public finances deserves pride of place in the improved macroeconomic picture since the 1998 crisis. Monetary policy has also been prudent, with twelve-month consumer inflation falling from 84.8 per cent in the crisis year of 1998 to 36.5 per cent in 1999 and 20.2 per cent in 2000 (set to be about 18 per cent in 2001). In short, devaluation and commodity price strength are not the whole story of the Russian economic recovery, which has also been underpinned by the strengthening of fiscal and monetary policies. This conclusion becomes inescapable on recalling how failure to rectify fiscal imbalances was the long-term source of the Russian crisis.

Table 11.3 Federal budget balance, inflation rate and T-bills financing

	Federal budget balance, (% of GDP)	12 months CPI (% change)	Debt service (T-bills financing)
1992	−44.6	2317.0	0
1993	−15.6	842.0	0
1994	−10.6	204.0	−0.2
1995	−5.6	132.0	−1.5
1996	−8.3	21.8	−4.0
1997	−7.0	10.9	−3.5
1998	−4.9	84.8	−2.2
1999	−1.2	36.5	—
2000	2.5	20.2	—

Note: The federal budget data for 1992 are very problematic, as the Russian Federation's nation budget system was taking shape in this year. Comparisons with 1991 are indicative and based on an assumed share of the RSFSR in the budget of the USSR.

Source: Goskomstat.

The figures in Table 11.3 may be summarized as follows. From 1992 to 1995, high inflation prevailed as large budget deficits were financed by monetary issue. The switch to an exchange rate stabilization programme accompanied by an IMF Stand By Arrangement (SBA) approved in March 1995 marked the beginning of relatively low inflation, which, however, was only achieved in practice by switching the financing of the budget deficit from central bank credits to treasury bills. August 1998 marked the failure of this policy and of the exchange rate-based stabilization programme. In the months leading up to August 1998, the authorities tried to stem the outflows of the foreign capital on which they depended for deficit finance given the inadequacy of available Russian domestic savings. But the putative lure of high interest rates combined with a pegged ruble ended up proving a repellent, as the high T-bill returns were vitiated by the increasingly unaffordable debt service, hence high default risk.

Against the background of this recent history, the present situation of a balanced budget, healthy balance of payments and managed floating exchange rate seems all the more remarkable. That said, there remains a vast unfinished agenda of structural reform. An important item on that agenda is reform of the banking sector.

Mention of the banking sector takes us back to the 1998 financial debacle. If the root cause of that collapse was the consistent failure to tighten fiscal policy sufficiently, the timing, on the other hand, was determined by the peculiarity of the flaws and distortions within the banking system and in banking supervision. At the IMF's behest, the CBR gradually withdrew from the system of fixed forward conversion rates from rubles back into USD for foreign investors in the domestic T-bill market. All restrictions on non-resident investors' access to that market had been lifted by January 1998. The banks, for their part, rushed into the currency forward business vacated by the Central Bank, apparently tempted by the easy gains in defiance of ordinary prudential principles of risk management. By mid-1998, leading Russian banks had sold billions of 'forward' dollars to foreign counter-parties hedging their GKO investments or other ruble exposures against a possible devaluation. The notional value of outstanding forward foreign exchange contracts was $365 billion (over 3000 per cent of the capital of the Russian banking system). The authorities were thus doubly hostage to the ruble peg – not only as the precondition for the required foreign refinancing of mushrooming short-term debt, but also because a devaluation would bankrupt almost all the major banks. This closed off the option of a controlled depreciation of the ruble and/or an orderly and voluntary debt restructuring process, and instead precipitated the collapse of August 1998, and general banking insolvency.

The urgency of banking sector and other structural reform is underscored by the recent slowing of Russia's economic recovery. Real GDP growth in 2001 looks set to be around 5 per cent.[8] The immediate cause of this slowdown is that the effect of the 1998 ruble devaluation has played itself out, with the currency appreciating 25 per cent in real terms since 1999. But the resulting uncompetitiveness and slackening of output in turn reflect slow progress in improving the investment climate and in microeconomic restructuring, especially at the enterprise level.

The challenge of laying the basis for sustainable growth is addressed in the present government's structural reform programme. This is a full agenda comprising *inter alia* tax reform, deregulation, land reform, judicial reform and natural monopoly restructuring. Banking and financial sector reform flow from underlying progress with the broader structural agenda.

If successful implementation of this structural reform agenda is essential for sustained economic growth, prolonging the existing recovery in the short to medium term will require continued improvements in macroeconomic management in the face of rising inflation and real exchange rate appreciation. Continued growth is all the more important in the run-up to the sharp spike in Russia's external debt service profile in 2003.

Debt repayments in 2003 will place considerable strain on federal finances. This increases the importance of continuing growth to reduce the effective fiscal burden of debt service. At the same time, sustained growth will fuel investor confidence, which in turn would reduce the cost for Russia of refinancing some of the debt maturing in 2003 in international capital markets in the event of any financing gap. But the chances of achieving

Table 11.4 Debt service due under existing contracts (US$ billion)

	2000	2001	2002	2003	2004
Total debt service	13.0	17.4	17.0	21.5	12.5
% of projected GDP	5.3	5.5	4.7	5.4	2.9
External debt service – total	9.6	13.2	13.5	18.2	11.8
Interest payments	4.2	6.9	6.8	6.4	5.8
Russian Federation debt	3.6	4.1	4.0	3.7	3.4
Eurobonds	—	2.7	2.8	2.8	2.7
IMF, WB, IFIs	—	1.0	0.8	0.7	0.5
Paris Club	—	0.4	0.3	0.2	0.1
Soviet debt	0.6	2.8	2.7	2.7	2.4
Paris Club	—	2.6	2.5	2.4	2.3
Amortization	5.4	6.2	6.8	11.8	6.0
Russian Federation debt	5.2	4.9	5.3	6.8	4.1
Eurobonds	—	1.0	0.0	1.6	1.0
IMF, WB, IFIs	—	2.0	3.5	3.7	2.2
Paris Club	—	2.0	1.8	1.4	0.9
Soviet debt	0.1	1.3	1.5	5.0	1.8
MinFins	—	0.0	0.0	3.5	0.0
Paris Club	—	1.3	1.5	1.6	1.8
Domestic debt service	3.4	4.3	3.5	3.3	0.7
Interest payments	2.1	1.5	0.8	0.3	0.0
Amortization	1.2	2.7	2.7	3.1	0.6
Nominal GDP, $billion	244.5	318.3	359.7	395.0	433.6
JP Morgan Assumptions:					
Real GDP growth	8.3	4.0	4.5	4.5	4.5
Ruble real appreciation, %	22.0	22.0	5.0	2.0	2.0
Ruble US$ rate	27.9	29.1	32.3	33.8	35.4

Source: Suppel and Ovanessian (May 2001), Global Data Watch, JP Morgan Research.

sustained growth will be weakened unless improvements are made in financial intermediation – primarily through a reform of the banking system.

TOWARDS GOOD CITIZENSHIP

Even without the publication of the IMF's first ROSC for Russia in 2000 due to some disagreements with the IMF, and despite the fact that the Russian authorities have not subscribed to the Special Data Dissemination Standard (SDDS),[9] considerable efforts have been made to improve conformity with the SDDS.

This is clear from the greater ease of access to data posted on the web sites of the CBR and government ministries. The CBR's time series of interest rates, base money and other macroeconomic data conform to international standards.[10] There are still a few exceptions, however. These include the CPI and PPI, quarterly volume measures of GDP and the production index, which are not disseminated in time series format that allows different periods to be compared. There is still a lack of coordination among statistics producing agencies – the State Committee on Statistics (Goskomstat), the Ministry of Finance and the CBR.

Monetary and budgetary policies are also more transparent. Still there is a need for more detailed disclosure on the CBR balance sheet as well as in the CBR's published data on the banking sector and the balance of payments. There is also a lack of consistency between CBR and Ministry of Finance data.

On the fiscal side, the execution of the budget is close to international standards. Examples of clear successes include the budgetary accounting of privatization proceeds and gold and other precious metal stockpiles

Table 11.5 Public sector finance (% of GDP)

	1995 actual	1996 actual	1997 actual	1998 actual	1999 actual	2000 estimate
Federal Budget						
Total revenues	12.8	13.8	12.5	10.7	13.2	16.2
Total expenditures:	18.4	22.1	19.5	15.5	14.4	13.7
interest spending	3.2	5.8	4.8	3.9	3.5	2.5
non-interest spending	15.2	16.3	14.8	11.6	10.8	11.3
Balance	−5.6	−8.3	−7.0	−4.9	−1.2	2.5
Primary balance	−2.4	−2.5	−2.2	−0.9	2.4	5.0
Regional and local budgets						
Total revenues	13.3	12.8	14.5	12.9	12.2	13.9
Total expenditures	13.8	13.8	16.0	13.2	12.2	13.4
Balance	−0.5	−1.0	−1.5	−0.3	−0.1	0.5
Off-budget funds						
Total revenues	9.4	9.9	11.9	9.6	9.8	10.1
Total expenditures	9.6	10.0	12.0	9.6	9.5	8.4
Balance	−0.2	−0.1	−0.1	0.0	0.3	1.7
Enlarged budget						
Total revenues	35.5	36.6	39.0	33.2	35.2	40.3
Total expenditures	41.8	46.0	47.6	38.3	36.1	35.6
Balance	−6.3	−9.4	−8.6	−5.1	−0.9	4.7

Source: Suppel and Ovanessian (May 2001), Global Data Watch, JP Morgan Research.

according to IMF standards. Considerably more work remains, however, to integrate these standards in the whole Russian budget system – which means extending them to the regional level. The main challenge here is to set regional and sub-regional budget accounting on a commitment (accrual) basis rather than the cash basis generally used at present because of the history of revenue and expenditure arrears. In addition, no data are available on the operations of regional and local government extra-budgetary funds. The main difficulty is still with local budgets and the issue of proper revenue assignment.

BANKING SECTOR

Progress has been achieved in banking supervision where major legislative amendments have been proposed by both the CBR and the Ministry of Finance to adapt the supervisory framework to international standards. But the framework still falls short of full conformity.

The Central Bank broadly observes recommended practices on promoting an open process for formulating and reporting financial policies. Some improvement would be welcome, however, such as developing formal arrangements for information sharing among domestic financial agencies.

The CBR's accounts are audited by one of the major international auditing firms (appointed annually by the State Duma), and in 2001 the CBR accounts will be drawn up according to International Accounting Standards (IAS) for the first time. But the financial statements of commercial banks are still compiled only in accordance with Russian Accounting Standards (RAS). The problem here is not that IAS (International Accounting Standards) are inherently more transparent than RAS (Russian Accounting Standards). But in certain key respects, such as loan provisioning rules, RAS does not permit a clear view of a bank's true net worth. The CBR is reluctant to force the transition, citing the difficulties of training banks' accountants in IAS. Other unstated reasons for this reluctance may be that the application of IAS provisioning norms would reveal many Russian banks to have negative capital, and that RAS involves the application of detailed rules and instructions rather than concepts as under IAS, facilitating bureaucratic control by CBR supervisors.

However, progress with bank restructuring has been disappointing and was clearly not a priority in 1999 and 2000.[11] In particular, a more determined response by the authorities might have prevented some of the asset stripping that occurred in major insolvent banks in the aftermath of the 1998 crisis. In addition, while licences of a large number of banks have been withdrawn, intervention in the situations with the large insolvent banks has been indecisive and ineffective, and the bankruptcy process seems to have been used to encourage restructuring rather than liquidation. The mobilization and efficient allocation of domestic savings is still a big issue – and will remain a problem as long as the taxation, banking, pension and insurance reforms are not completed. There is little trust from the public in existing financial institutions, and beyond them, in the state itself.

In light of these weaknesses, the IMF drew up a banking reform package aimed at tightening banking supervision, accounting standards and bankruptcy procedures. This package was approved in principle by both the government and the CBR in autumn 1999. But it took until June 2001 for the corresponding legislation to complete its passage through the federal parliament and be signed into law by the President. The package encompasses amendments to the Laws on the CBR, Banks and Banking Activity, and Bankruptcy of Credit Institutions. These changes aim to improve the transparency of the banking system and the CBR's control over the sector, increase the responsibility of banks' shareholders, and speed and tighten up bankruptcy procedures to protect the interests of depositors and creditors. The most significant change in practice may be that the CBR will now have the power to withdraw automatically a bank's licence as soon as its capital adequacy ratio falls below 2 per cent, triggering bankruptcy proceedings.

In addition, a Law on compulsory insurance of private household bank deposits is expected to be submitted to Parliament in 2002. At present there is an implicit guarantee of deposits in the CBR-owned Sberbank. This explains why about 75 per cent of household deposits are held in Sberbank. The proposed law 'on the system of bank deposits insurance' envisions establishment of a government agency through an initial 6.5-billion-ruble transfer from the government, with banks then being required to contribute 0.15 per cent of their deposits as reserves on a quarterly basis. This insurance, which would be mandatory for all banks other than Sberbank, would guarantee repayment of deposits in full up to 2000 rubles and to the extent of 90 per cent of deposits up to 10000 rubles.[12]

More drastic measures are needed to restructure the sector, rooting out the many insolvent banks and forcing transparency rules. At least some further opening of the banking sector to foreign institutions will be required for accession to the WTO – now an important stated objective of the Putin administration. Foreign institutions may inspire more confidence than Russian banks. The fact remains, however, that after the crisis year of 1998, Russia achieved three consecutive years of strong economic growth in the context of rudimentary financial intermediation from the banking system. Table 11.6 shows how small the banking sector is. Total bank lending in Russia is around 18 per cent of GDP compared to 38 per cent in Poland and 57 per cent in the Czech Republic. Household deposits total

Table 11.6 Comparative size of banking sectors (% of GDP, end 2000)

	Poland	Czech Republic	Germany	Russia
Bank lending:	38.5	57.4	107.9	17.9
to households	6.9	6.2	44.6	1.0
to corporates	21.0	46.5	40.0	13.9
in local currency	27.9	44.0	—	10.5
in foreign currency	6.7	8.7	—	7.4
Bank deposits:	40.7	66.6	109.8	13.5
of households	22.1	34.8	50.8	8.9
of corporates	7.9	30.8	31.0	4.0
in local currency	30.0	58.4	—	7.0
in foreign currency	3.9	8.2	—	6.5

Note: Czech Republic excludes insurance companies; Germany excludes savings deposits.

Source: Suppel and Ovanessian (February 2001), Global Data Watch, JP Morgan Research.

only 9 per cent of GDP compared to 22 per cent in Poland and 35 per cent in the Czech Republic. Bank lending finances only 3 per cent of fixed capital investment.[13]

CONCLUSION

The weakness of financial intermediation in Russia is an obvious obstacle to the achievement of sustained economic growth. Both household and corporate savings (especially the large cashflows of the natural resource industries) need to be mobilized and recycled for re-equipping the industrial base and for investment in new business, especially small and medium-size enterprises. Equally obviously, structural reform is the answer to this problem: but this reform needs to be defined broadly. The reform of the banking sector, whose existing flaws have been well detailed in the preceding papers in this volume, is clearly a necessary condition for ensuring effective financial intermediation – but not, in itself, a sufficient condition. The reason for this is that the absence of a deep, stable and long-term deposit base – and consequently, of long-term credit to the domestic real sector – is the result of perverse incentives and structural distortions which run much deeper than the inadequacies of the banking system itself.

On the liabilities side of the banking system's balance sheet, the fundamental deterrent to Russian citizens placing their savings in deposit accounts is a lack of trust. There is no mystery about popular distrust of private banks after the events of August 1998, and of Sberbank after the destruction of real savings balances in the inflation of 1990–92. But the problem would not be solved even if the full banking reform agenda were immediately implemented – that is, if the banks became properly capitalized, better regulated, more competitive and secure thanks to a credible deposit insurance scheme. The root of the problem lies in the citizen's distrust of the state. Part of this has to do with the state's dire and decades-long track record of monetary confiscation, supplemented in recent years by successive devaluations of the ruble.

This explains why Russian citizens prefer to save in foreign currency (in practice, US dollars) rather than rubles: but it does not fully explain the weak deposit base. After all, foreign currency deposit accounts have been legal since 1992; and Sberbank deposits carry an implicit state guarantee, which was honoured in practice after the financial crash of August 1998: so it should follow that a large volume of US dollar savings should be kept in Sberbank. Instead, such savings amount to only 5 per cent of GDP, with at least a further 15 per cent of GDP kept in the form of cash US dollar savings at home. The reason for this, and the deepest root cause of the entire problem, is that the distrust of the state extends to fear of state expropriation of wealth given that virtually all personal wealth has been accumulated without full payment of tax, and so is vulnerable. No wonder, then, that Russian households prefer to hide cash dollars under the mattress rather than place them in a bank deposit account where they might be discovered by law enforcement officials.

One solution to this problem would be a tax amnesty on household capital. But while there is a case to be made for such a move, the arguments are not absolutely clear cut, and it remains contentious. In any case, there are no indications (at the time of writing, at least) that the Putin administration seriously intends to go down this road. That leaves the solution of tax reform – and this is a road along which the Putin administration has made notable progress. By introducing a tax regime which is simple, fair and, above all, light, the state has incentivized households and businesses to abandon the grey economy. With time, therefore, people will obtain a track record of legality (the same effect which an amnesty could in principle achieve overnight), and gradually become inclined to place their savings in deposit accounts.

With the personal tax reform (including the celebrated 13 per cent flat rate of personal income tax) in force from January 2001, the deposit base grew notably in that year from 8.5 per cent to 10.5 per cent of GDP. But there is a long way to go, in keeping with the necessarily gradual impact of the tax reform on incentives and behaviour.

Turning to the assets side of the banking system's balance sheet, the lack of long-term lending to enterprises is largely the functional result of the weak deposit base. But there are other causes besides, which again stem from structural failings which extend far beyond those of the banking system itself. Chief among these is the lack of functioning commercial land and housing markets. As a result, firms and households have been deprived of the most obvious source of collateral for borrowing. Just as the tax reform is the key to restoring a normal deposit base, so another key structural reform of the first phase of the Putin administration can potentially solve this problem of collateral, namely land reform. A first key step was taken in 2001 with the adoption of the Land Code (signed into law by President Putin on 8 November). This Code gives enterprises the right to buy freehold title to the land on which they sit, and it defines a reasonable price scale to prevent the realization of this right falling victim to predatory local officialdom.

Against this background, there appears to be much sense in the way that the Putin administration has sequenced its structural reform efforts to start with the most fundamental items affecting financial intermediation, such as tax and land reform. For in the absence of these reforms, no amount of technocratic tinkering with the banking system would make much difference. To this extent, the frequent and typical reproach of Western commentators in recent years about the lack specifically of banking reform appears redundant. From now on, however, this reproach will become more relevant. The fundamental supply-side reforms now reaching the statute book have improved incentives for all economic agents in Russia. But if an improved investment climate is the *sine qua non* for restructuring and creating businesses, productivity gains and sustained growth, the potential ensured by that improved investment climate will be squandered without effective financial intermediation. In short, by the end of 2001, the time to begin reform of the banking system itself was most definitely ripe.

As if in acknowledgement of this, in September–December 2001, the Central Bank and the government worked up an agreed joint approach to banking system reform in a concept document. This document sets all the generally recognized objectives of reform, but envisages their implementation beginning in most areas only in 2003–04. This gradualist approach has disappointed many observers. However, a reasoned defence of the 'concept' was offered in a series of speeches and interviews in November–December 2001 by Tatyana Paramonova, First Deputy Chairman of the Central Bank of Russia.[14]

Mrs Paramonova presents the key to the whole reform as being the introduction of IAS from 1 January 2004. She argues that far from being gradualist, this is a tight timetable given the challenges posed by this change. These range from amending tax legislation (since the departing

RAS are geared to defining tax liabilities, to training not only bank accountants but also external auditors (all of whom the CBR will subject to an examination to verify their competence to sign off on IAS statements). Mrs Paramonova stresses that the key to this change is not the process but the result – which she predicted would be the disappearance of a 'very considerable number' of the 1 300 existing banks once IAS had revealed their true financial condition. (This will be due to IAS loan provisioning rules resulting in many banks' net worth turning negative.) Expanding on this theme, she said that to avoid having to close in 2004, many banks should act now either to recapitalize themselves, or merge with others, or attract foreign capital.

Greater openness to foreign participants is Mrs Paramonova's other main theme – tying in nicely with the inevitable requirement of any successful Russian negotiation on membership of the WTO. She says that the underlying reform in this respect would be first to align Russian banking supervision with international standards (and she specifically cited BIS prudential standards), and secondly to apply those standards equally to residents and foreigners. Key changes in this respect will be equalizing the minimum capital requirement of newly established banks (at five million euros), and equalizing the size of an acquisition of shares in a bank requiring CBR approval (at present foreigners need permission to buy any share whatsoever in a Russian bank). While stressing that all such existing restrictions are defined by law rather than CBR officials, Mrs Paramonova has not disclosed at what level the legislative amendments to be submitted to the Duma will seek to cap foreign participation in the banking system. She does say, however, that policy will be designed to prevent a single foreign 'mega-bank' coming into Russia and dominating the sector.

Senior officials of the Central Bank of Russia have also confirmed that legislation on a deposit insurance system will be staggered to allow Sberbank to join the scheme only after it is up and running for other banks selected for inclusion in it, and that thereafter the Central Bank would begin to divest its present controlling shareholding in Sberbank. This amounts to a reasonably coherent plan for ending the quasi-monopoly status of Sberbank, and introducing proper competition into the sector.

In most areas of practical implementation of IFA codes and standards, the picture is similar to that of broader structural reform: there is encouraging progress to report, along with much unfinished business. Examples of progress include data dissemination and capital market regulation, while notable blockages remain in accounting reform and financial sector supervision and restructuring. These efforts by the Russian authorities mean that data are more easily disseminated and more or less conform to international standards. Monetary and budgetary policies are more transparent and when weaknesses have been identified, they can be more easily rectified.

Of course, perfect conformity with the international codes and standards reviewed in this paper does not mean that financial crises will not recur and that Russia will never default again. No amount of transparency will suffice to service debt if budget revenues fall short. Repairing relations with creditors, as has been achieved both with the 2000 restructuring of Soviet-era commercial debt and the resumption of full service of Soviet-era official debt, is less decisive in ensuring solvency than the price of oil (and gas, which is linked to oil). The public finances depend heavily on the proceeds of taxes on oil extraction and export, and these revenues fluctuate in line with the oil price.

Still the authorities seem largely unperturbed and as of late 2001, this line was being backed by the IMF itself:

> Clearly, the macroeconomic performance has been very strong. The budget performance has been strong. People are looking out at the impact of lower oil prices on the fiscal situation, but it is our view and assessment at this point that it is not at a stage where it would cause us to change our view that the Russian fiscal and external situation over the next couple of years is sustainable, without need for recourse to the Fund or other forms of external support.[15]

This upbeat assessment clearly reflects the confidence inspired by the progress of reform since President Putin came to office. Still, the oil price focus highlights the fact that Russia's key task remains diversifying its economy and that the emphasis should be on pursuing the reform agenda. As Andrei Illarionov, the President's economic adviser, has remarked:

> Whether there will be a crisis or whether industrial growth will continue in Russia depends primarily on the economic policies pursued, and not on oil prices.

In fact, lower oil prices could actually provide the necessary encouragement to the Russian government to persist and work on more reforms to boost domestic and foreign investment and to diversify away from oil dependence. The Russian authorities have a track record of rising to the challenge posed by external stimuli and constraints, such as the pressure from the IFIs to improve the availability and quality of economic information, or pressure from creditors to service debt in full. In this regard, the decision of Paris Club creditors since 2000 to apply orthodox criteria to Russia (no financing gap, no relief) seems to have played an ambiguous role: on the one hand, servicing the Soviet-era debt reduced the budgetary resources available to support crucial long-term structural reforms, such as the reform of the public administration; but on the other hand, the debt burden seems to have concentrated the Russian authorities' minds on the reform task in hand; and the growth performance which reforms help promote improves debt service capacity and reduces the need for debt rescheduling.

The oil price could play a similar role to the 1998 debt crisis in highlighting the long-term challenges which Russia faces and the need to complete the reform agenda. Just as the policy of full external debt service (including Soviet-era debt) has proved to be a factor in stability, reducing exposure to external risks, the Russian economy should continue to grow irrespective of the oil price. Recent Russian economic history seems to show that in policy terms, Russia performs better under pressure than when cushioned with financial assistance; and as things stand, there are definite signs of progress towards financial stability.

NOTES

1. This chapter draws on material from the report 'International Financial Architecture: Case Study Russia' which I wrote for the project 'Reform of the International Financial Architecture: View, Priorities and Concerns of Government and the Private Sector in the Western Hemisphere and Eastern Europe', commissioned by DFID and directed by Professor Stephany Griffith Jones from the Institute of Development studies (IDS) at the University of Sussex.
2. Stephany Griffith-Jones has published extensively on Financial Architecture and a full list of her works can be found on the Institute of Development Studies web site.
3. IMF (December 1998), p. 28.
4. Russia has also joined the Paris Club as a creditor country. This may help her to recover at least a fraction of her massive claims (about $130 billion) on developing countries (India, Iraq, Libya, Vietnam, Yemen, Cuba, and many others).
5. OECD (2000), p. 66: part of this increase is also explained by a buildup of $23.6 billion in debt during 1998. This consisted of commercial borrowing, eurobond issues and payment arrears on the former Soviet debt.
6. The new eurobonds will have a 30-year maturity with a seven-year grace period and over one-third lower face value than the original maturities (as opposed to 15–20 years remaining maturity of the previous bonds; interest arrears will be rescheduled on less favourable terms). The debt service will be reduced by about $1.5 billion in the first five years and by close to $2 billion in the following five years.
7. Russia owed $48.6 billion to the Paris Club of sovereign creditors and wanted to restructure and partially write off the ex-USSR part of this debt, which totalled $38.7 billion. Some 40 per cent of the total debts are owed to Germany, which has demanded Russia pay, citing the strength of Russia's currency reserves. The idea of debt for equity has been discussed, but the German position was that such swaps would only be applicable to Russia's Soviet-era debt to the former GDR. Also owed to Germany is some 6.4 billion of transferable rubles in debts to the GDR and talks on the issue appeared to have stalled recently, with Russia claiming that the former GDR benefited economically under the Soviet-era trade deals.
8. Preliminary estimates from the Ministry of Economic Development and Trade suggest that GDP growth accelerated from 4.9 per cent year-on-year in the first quarter of 2001

to 5.9 per cent year-on-year in the second quarter of 2001 and estimates that economic growth in 2001 should be above 5 per cent and around 4 per cent in 2002.

9. Description of data dissemination practices are available on http://www.gks.ru/eng/ssrd/default.asp. Ministry of Finance data are available on http://www.minfin.ru/macroeng/sdds.htm.
10. See especially http://www.cbr.ru/eng/dp/statistics.html.
11. See William Tompson, in this volume.
12. Ruble/US dollar exchange rate in 2001: 31.
13. Suppel and Ovanessian (February 2001).
14. Notably in an interview in *Vedomosti* (5 November 2001).
15. Statement by the IMF's official spokesman, Tom Dawson, at a regular news briefing, 6 December 2001.

REFERENCES

Ferguson, Niall and Brigitte Granville (2000), 'Weimar on the Volga: Causes and Consequences of Inflation in 1990s Russia Compared with 1920s Germany', *Journal of Economic History*, 60, No. 4 (December 2000), Berkeley, USA, pp. 1061–1087.

Granville, B. (1995), *The Success of Russian Economic Reforms*, published by RIIA, distributed by Brookings.

Granville, B. (2001), 'The Problem of Monetary Stabilisation', in B. Granville and P. Oppenheimer (eds), *Russia's Post-Communist Economy*, Oxford: Oxford University Press, pp. 93–130.

International Monetary Fund (IMF) (1998), *World Economic Outlook and International Capital Markets, Interim Assessment*, December.

Organisation for Economic Co-operation and Development (2000), *Economic Surveys, Russian Federation* (March).

Suppel, Ralph and Julia Ovanessian (2001), 'Understanding Russia's Fiscal Strategy', *Economic Research*, Global Data Watch, JP Morgan (4 May).

Tompson, William (2001), 'Russian Banks after the August Crisis: From Omnipotence to Irrelevance?', April, mimeo.

Index